EARLY
VICTORIAN
ILLUSTRATED
BOOKS

FABLES
DE LA FONTAINE

IMPRIMERIE DE FOURNIER
RUE DE SEINE N. 14

EARLY VICTORIAN ILLUSTRATED BOOKS

Britain, France and Germany

1820–1860

BY

JOHN BUCHANAN-BROWN

THE BRITISH LIBRARY

AND

OAK KNOLL PRESS

2005

IN MEMORY OF MY WIFE

(*Frontispiece*) François Louis Français's design for Furne's
1839 edition of La Fontaine's *Fables* gives the engravers
far larger billing than the artist Grandville. Among them
is the craftsman who cut this block, the émigré English
engraver M.U. Sears [BL 12304 g 14]

First published 2005 by
The British Library, 96 Euston Road
London NW1 2DB
and Oak Knoll Press, 310 Delaware Street,
New Castle DE 19720

Text copyright © John Buchanan-Brown 2005
Illustrations copyright © The British Library Board 2005

British Library Cataloguing-in-Publication Data
A catalogue record for this book is available from
The British Library

Library of Congress Cataloguing-in-Publication Data
Buchanan-Brown, John
   Early Victorian illustrated books: Britain, France, and
   Germany, 1820–1860/by John Buchanan-Brown.
      p. cm.
   Includes bibliographical references and index.
   ISBN 1-58456-169-6
   1. Illustration of books—Europe—19th century.
   2. Illustration of books, Victorian—Europe. I. Title.

NC977.B827 2005
741.6'4'09034–dc22

                                    2005051287

ISBN 0 7123 4794 1 (British Library)

ISBN 1-58456-169-6 (Oak Knoll)

Designed and typeset in Monotype Garamond
by James Shurmer

Printed in England by Cromwell Press
Trowbridge, Wiltshire

CONTENTS

PREFACE

This book originates from a very long-standing interest in French typography and in books illustrated by woodcut and wood-engraving. Study of the French *livre romantique* showed the close interrelation between the British technique of end-grain wood-engraving and the art of the French book in the 1830s and 1840s and prompted a study of contemporary British book-illustration. This bore fruit in the introductions to selections reproduced from the book-illustrations of George Cruikshank and of Hablot Knight Browne and published in 1980 and 1978 respectively.

Both were artists in the traditional British style, but it soon became apparent that, if British innovation in wood-engraving could revitalize the craft in France, so innovation in German draughtsmanship had an equally stimulating effect upon British book-illustration. Indeed, the whole period proved to be one of immensely fruitful cross-fertilization, both technological and artistic, between the publishing trades of the three major languages of northern Europe.

In this respect, however, anyone who looks at the Bibliography will notice that I am not so well qualified to deal with Germany as I am with France. Accordingly, since German language sources have been closed to me, I have relied upon William Vaughan's *German Romanticism and English Art* (1979) for the broad outline and on the detail to be obtained from Arthur Rümann's *Die illustrierten deutschen Bücher des XIX Jahrhunderts* (1930) to point me in the right direction. My judgement of German illustrated books thus depends upon the selection which I have been able to examine and upon what my own eyes have told me.

In so far as the technical aspects of the media for graphic reproduction available in Britain are concerned, Michael Twyman's *Lithography 1800–50* (1970) and Basil Hunnisett's *Steel-engraved Book Illustration in England* (1980) cover these important methods in such detail as to absolve me from more than a cursory description here, while Ruari McLean's *Victorian Book Design* (1972) does the same for colour-printing processes in general. British wood-engravers and wood-engraving have, however, suffered some neglect by comparison with the later period of the 1860s. Accordingly, in Appendix 1 I have tried to redress the balance and also to say something about the significant contribution of women to the craft.

This Appendix was printed in the *Journal of the Printing Historical Society* in 1984 (no. 17 for 1982/3, 31–61) and included a checklist of those wood-engravers whose signatures I had noted in the books which I had examined. It is reprinted here with some slight amendments, but Rodney K. Engen's *Dictionary of Victorian Wood Engravers* (1985) has made the checklist redundant. I have therefore only retained a list of those engravers whose names do not appear in the *Dictionary*.

A feature of the period is the migration to the Continent of British craftsmen: Appendix II is intended to offer preliminary material for any future survey of migrant steel-engravers.

My Bibliography is confined to books (journal sources are mentioned in the text with references in the footnotes) and comprises those works consulted in preparing the text with selected titles which have appeared subsequent to 1982 when the book was completed. Students are therefore advised to consult journals for such specific information as James Burns's children's list (Brian Alderson in the *Bulletin of the John Rylands University Library of Manchester*, vol. 76, no. 3, Autumn 1994), Noel Humphreys's work in general and his connections with Paul Gerrard in particular (Howard Leathlean in *The Book Collector*, vol. 38, no. 2, Summer 1989, and vol. 40, no. 2, Summer 1991) or the relationship between the publisher John Van Voorst and the Duke of Bedford's librarian, John Martin (Paul Goldman in *The Book Collector*, vol. 47, no. 2, Summer 1998).

However, the most important source for a detailed study of end-grain wood-engraving from its original in early eighteenth-century Constantinople and in England (where it flourished by the end of the century) and its spread to France and throughout Continental Europe is contained in Remi Blachon's *La gravure sur bois au XIXe siècle*, published in 2001. This replaces Pierre Gusman's *La gravure sur bois en France au XIXe siècle*, the standard work since 1929. I am fortunate at the eleventh hour to have had, and gladly acknowledge, the benefit of his researches.

In so far as British book-illustrators are concerned, full biographical details may be found in Simon Houfe's *Dictionary of British Book Illustrators and Caricaturists 1800–1914* (1978). I have, however, provided brief notes of French and German artists in Appendix IV. Appendix V provides a short glossary of technical terms.

The Title Index of books mentioned in the text represents a proportion only of those which I have examined and does not in any sense pretend to offer a checklist, however desirable this might be for British illustrated books. (The Germans have Arthur Rümann and of a number of French bibliographies I have found Léopold Carteret's *Le trésor du bibliophile* the most useful.)

JOHN BUCHANAN-BROWN

ACKNOWLEDGEMENTS

I should like to express my thanks to the following copyright holders for permission to quote or to print: British Museum (Department of Prints & Drawings), extracts from Percy Roberts's notes; Dr Basil Hunnisett and the Scolar Press Ltd, quotations from *Steel-engraved Book Illustration in England*; the Longman Group Ltd, extracts from the Longman Archive in the University of Reading Library; John Murray (Publishers) Ltd, correspondence from Owen Jones; William Vaughan and the Yale University Press, quotations from *German Romanticism and English Art*; the Victoria and Albert Museum, part of a letter from John Thompson to [Sir] Henry Cole.

I am also grateful to the following institutions for access to materials in their possession: the British Library; the British Museum (Department of Prints & Drawings); the Saint Bride's Printing Library; the Tate Gallery; the University of Reading Library; the Victoria and Albert Museum. Thanks, too, are due to the staffs of these libraries, with particular appreciation of the kindness of the staff of the North Library and North Library Gallery of the British Library.

Finally, I should like to thank the following individuals who have helped in various ways in the preparation of this book: Mrs Elizabeth Bonython, with information on the connections between Sir Henry Cole and the family of John Thompson; Mrs Joan Butler, with information about wood-engravers in general and the Byfield family in particular; Dr Basil Hunnisett, with information on British steel-engravers; Mr Philip Kirby, with valuable comments and criticisms; Brigid Peppin, with access to her unpublished notes on Victorian book illustrators; and Mr Ernest Pearce who has been kind enough to allow me to include his observations on British wood-engravers; Remi Blachon for his notes on my Appendix I and specifically for his observations on French women engravers; and Michael Scott for his technical assistance in preparing the Select Bibliography.

J. B.-B.

PROLOGUE

'Early Victorian' is a convenient time-frame for the British books in this study: 'Romantic' might, perhaps, be more descriptive. Although it translates literally a specific term of French bibliography, *le livre romantique*, it can be applied to a much broader geographical field and to a wider time-span than the period of the Romantic movement in French literature with which it is associated. France may date her Romantic period in literature from 1830 to 1843, from the triumph of Victor Hugo's *Hernani* to the disaster of his *Les Burgraves*, but Romanticism had been the dominant literary current in England and Germany since the end of the previous century. In British books the Romantic landscapes and the realistic vignettes of rural life in Turner's designs for steel-engraving and in the wood-engravings of Bewick and his successors are the graphic expressions of Wordsworth's and Byron's responses to nature. The chromolithographic books of Noel Humphreys and Owen Jones reflect the Gothic revivalist and Oriental elements in Romanticism, while in Germany the same revivalist spirit may be epitomised in the great and influential 1840 edition of the *Nibelungenlied*. Thus the term 'Romantic Book' is a valid classification of a European phenomenon which embraces the immensely influential and specific *livre romantique*.

To use the words 'embellished' and 'embellishment' for 'illustrated' and 'illustration' may seem pedantic, but I use these words deliberately and they better define the scope of my book. I am not concerned with illustrations in the strict sense of pictorial aids to the understanding of a text: my concern is with wood- and steel-engraving and with lithography as the decorative rather than the explanatory adjuncts of letterpress. Both words are good period words – the publisher Charles Tilt described his editions of the English poets as 'Tilt's Embellished Classics' – and they describe exactly the function of these illustrations. It was to create a beautiful object which would attract both the sophisticated book-buyer and, far more importantly, members of the new mass-market for books in the newly-created urban lower-middle and upper-working classes.

Despite the fact that publishers were more than ready to meet the needs of this market and that, in consequence, illustrated books were issued in ever-increasing numbers, it is still true to say today what Percy Muir said some fifty years ago, that 'the immediate post-Bewick period, on which so little has been written as yet' has been 'unduly neglected',[1] at least in any general survey of Victorian book-illustration. Perhaps the reason is that we think of the 'Sixties Book' as the 'Victorian Book' *par excellence*, when in truth it is only the mid-Victorian book. Yet even were we to conceive of an early-Victorian book, we should find that it could not be confined strictly to the early-Victorian period, from 1837 to the Great Exhibition of 1851, but would really belong to the preceding reigns of George IV and William IV as well. (In fact the years 1820–51 form a transitional period between what can loosely be described as Regency books and those generally conceived as books of the Victorian age.) Although this has not affected the investigation of specific technical processes – and here one thinks of Michael Twyman's *Lithography* (1970), or Basil Hunnisett's *Steel-engraved Book Illustration in England* (1980), or Geoffrey Wakeman's studies of colour-printing – if one can find fault with such excellent general surveys as Ruari McLean's *Victorian Book Design* (1972) or Eric de Maré's *The Victorian Woodblock Illustrators* (1980), it is that they are perhaps too meticulous in applying the term Victorian.

As a result, while there is no neglect of the highest achievements of the Romantic period in British book-illustration, the full range of that achievement has yet to be registered and, in particular, the achievement of the facsimile wood-engravers. Because contemporary critics[2] disparaged their work as mere mechanical copying – which assuredly it was not – and because, unlike their successors in the 1860s, the Dalziel Brothers and Edmund Evans, they left no reminiscences or records apart from their engravings, serious misconceptions tend to creep into what are in all other respects admirable books.

For example, William Vaughan, in a study which is indispensable to any appreciation of the all-important German influence upon the younger illustrators of the period,[3] can assert that 'It was in fact on the Continent, that wood engraving first began to become respectable'. While Basil Hunnisset, so sure a guide to the steel-engraving of the period can state the half-truth that, 'After the death of Thomas Bewick in 1828 and of Robert Branston in 1827, wood-engraving lost the impetus obtained in the previous forty or fifty years and went into decline.... The real problem was lack of designers ... not solved until the 1860s, when designers and cutters like the Dalziel brothers came together to breathe new life into the medium.'[4]

Had Vaughan used the word 'respected' of the craftsmen, the cutters, he would have been quite correct, for sadly Britain never gave them the respect in which, as we shall see, the Thompson brothers were held in France and Germany. Yet it was precisely because wood-engraving had become eminently respectable by the end of the Napoleonic Wars in an England which, in so many fields, dominated the Continent, that continentals, and initially the French, adopted the craft with such enthusiasm. Nor, and without in any way wishing to minimize the achievements either of the Dalziels or of the Sixties illustrators whose work they engraved, is it fair to characterize the craft of the Thompson or Williams families – among so many master-engravers – as one sinking into a decline, or the era of William Mulready, Daniel Maclise and John Tenniel, or of George Cruikshank, Phiz (Hablot Knight Browne) or Richard Doyle as one which lacked designers.

Yet to pretend that to correct these misconceptions is the sole *raison d'être* of this study would be disingenuous: I write about Romantic books because their British, French and German examples can be a source of real aesthetic pleasure. More than this, the period and the people who produced them are both interesting and engaging. Spanning the age of the stage-coach and that of the railroad, it retains something of the grace of the old world and yet is instinct with the driving energy which, through the power of steam and of machinery, created the new. It has a surface glitter. Men's dress is not yet drab and women have yet to reach that degree of bustled embattlement which caused the artist Gavarni to write to his friend Louis Leroy that 'when the Englishwoman is dressed, she is no longer a woman, but a cathedral – it would be less a matter of seduction than of demolition'.[5]

The reverse side of the age was the cruel exploitation of the industrial worker and the rural poverty which aroused a radical reaction in the liberal-minded younger generation. For if, on the one hand, Romanticism attempted to enshrine aristocratic privilege in a Gothic revival, it also espoused a revolt against that same absolutism (re-imposed upon Europe by the Holy Alliance after the fall of Napoleon) and supported decolonization, when national liberation movements freed Greece from the Ottoman and Latin America from the Spanish and Portuguese empires. Bourgeois liberalism and working-class radicalism combined in movements which reached their climax in the revolutions of 1848. The excitement of the Romantic age is of young men attacking political and social abuses. In this perspective one sees why the early novels of Charles Dickens were regarded as being so 'vulgar' and appreciates Thackeray's radicalism, not to say republicanism. Thus his attacks on the monarchy in *The Four Georges* (1860), which contemporaries regarded as cheap pandering to the American audience for which these lectures were originally prepared, were in fact the expression of long-held views on the House of Hanover.

To see these Victorian giants not as portly, bearded, middle-aged and successful, but as young men with all the passions and idealism of youth, is one of the attractions of the Romantic period. Romanticism, with its emphasis upon the individual and the individual's emotions, is the perfect medium through which to express the egocentricity of youth. The idealization of mediaeval chivalry or the superluxuriance of Oriental imagery sometimes have those slightly ridiculous airs of youth taking itself just a little too seriously. At times, too, as in some of Phiz's illustrations, youthful high spirits degenerate into mere horseplay, but the saving grace is the irreverence and lack of pomposity evident in so much of the graphic work of the period.

Yet what is at times a saving grace is symptomatic of the most serious defect in much of the run-of-the-mill illustration, and especially the British illustration of the period. When contrasted with contemporary Continental designs, the work of far too many British illustrators betrays an amateurism absent from that of even the least inspired French or German artist. Nor is the reason far to seek: too many British illustrators were self-taught at a time when organized art-teaching on the Continent ensured a far higher and more professional standard of draughtsmanship.[6]

Given, then, the initiation in the 1840s of a system of art-education based upon German models, it is hardly surprising that some of its first-fruits, the graphic work of the Sixties book-illustrators, should demonstrate far higher standards of average competence in these areas than that of the Romantics. Thus, while the Romantic period is recognized in Germany and, more especially, in France as an important epoch in book-illustration, it has been unfairly neglected in Britain. This, as I have said, must largely be because so much of the work of British Romantic illustrators is patently inferior as specimens of draughtsman-ship and composition to that of their successors in the 1860s. Book-illustrations, however, are not autonomous works of art: they cannot exist independently of the texts they illustrate and of the pages which they decorate. They are not there to distract attention, but to concentrate it. Thus, paradoxically, what may be inferior as an independent work of art may, in its typographic setting, be superior as a book-illustration.

It is, therefore, as illustrated books rather than simply as book-illustrations that the work of the Romantic period can stand comparison with the justly celebrated products of the 1860s. It can do so because typographically the age is the heir of a great age of British printing, the Regency, just as the younger Charles Whittingham was his uncle's heir at the Chiswick Press. There might be no other real rivals to Bulmer or Bensley, but their salutory influence was still felt, and there was plenty of fine printing by Vizetelly, for example, or by Robson, Levey & Franklyn. Moreover, while the machine tended to call the tune in the 1860s, the printers of this earlier period were still able to impose the standards of the hand-press upon the new machines.

The crucial factor in the period is the mechanization of newspaper, magazine and book production to meet the vastly expanded market for print. It sees the adoption of the mass-production of paper by the Roberts/Foudrinier continuous belt method, of successful experiments in mechanical type-casting and the first steps towards mechanical composition. Above all, efforts were concentrated upon gaining higher and ever higher impression rates from the printing press.

The initial objective, to harness steam power to the printing press, was first achieved by two German inventors, A.F. Bauer and F. Koenig, with the backing of the principal London master-printers. Their first attempt, to adapt the traditional platen press, was unsuccessful, although such a press was used to print some 3,000 sheets of *The Annual Register* in 1811. They then adopted the principle of the flat-bed press with impression cylinder and inking rollers, patenting a single-cylinder machine in 1811 and first successfully printing from a two-cylinder machine for *The Times* in 1814 [fig. 1]. This machine could produce 1,100 impressions per hour, compared with 250 per hour from the best hand-press, the iron Stanhope [fig. 2]. But it could only print one side of the sheet. Two years later Bauer and Koenig introduced their first perfecting machine – that is, a press which could print both sides of the sheet in one continuous operation – and the partners continued to improve upon their basic design until Koenig returned to his native Bavaria. There he became engaged in the design of paper-making machines until his death in 1833.

1 A model of Koenig's and Bauer's printing machine built for *The Times* in 1814 and the first press driven by steam (from the 150th anniversary number of *The Times*, reprinted in Withers *et al.*, *A Newspaper History 1785–1935*, London, 1935) [BL 011851 k 37]

2 The iron printing press designed by Earl Stanhope in 1800 and in use throughout the 1820s: note the pressman's refreshments in the background (Johnson, *Typographia*, London, 1824) [BL 125 k 1, 2]

While the initiative for presses with ever-increasing impression rates came most strongly from the newspaper industry – it was to culminate mid-century in the introduction of the rotary press – mechanical power was of equal interest to book-printers. Applegath and Cowper's Royal perfecting machine (1818) [fig. 3] was the earliest reliable steam-press for both book and magazine work, succeeded in 1824 by the Nay-Peer [fig. 4]. Despite its lower impression rate, this press gave extremely accurate register and was widely employed for high-quality book work. Finally, in 1858, came the Wharfedale, a press which continued to serve, with improvements, for almost as long as hot-metal printing lasted.

The age of the machine was also the age of the image – of illustrations in newspapers, magazines and books. Although there were many experiments in methods of graphic reproduction and widespread use of both steel-engraving and of lithography, it was ultimately the high impression rate of the new steam presses and the need to print illustrations in relief and in conjunction with the letterpress which dictated the most economic method – and this was to be wood-engraving. While, therefore, due attention will be paid to the planographic and the intaglio processes of lithography and of steel-engraving and -etching, wood-engraving and the techniques which it developed to meet the requirements of the machine will tend to dominate this study of Early Victorian illustrated books.

NOTES

1 *Victorian Illustrated Books*, 26, 36.
2 For an example *see* Appendix 1, p. 287a.
3 *German Romanticism and English Art*, 157.
4 *Steel-engraved Book Illustration in England*, 207.

5 F. and J. de Goncourt, *Gavarni* (1879), 208.
6 Cf. W.M. Thackeray, 'On the French School of Painting' in *The Paris Sketch Book* (1840), 1, 76ff.

3 Applegath's and Cowper's perfecting machine (1816): white paper (A) is fed to the first impression cylinder (B) and passed to the second impression cylinder (D) which prints the other side of the sheet (Edward Cowper, lecture delivered to the Royal Institution, 22 February 1828, on 'Recent Improvements in Printing') [BL 619 k 26]

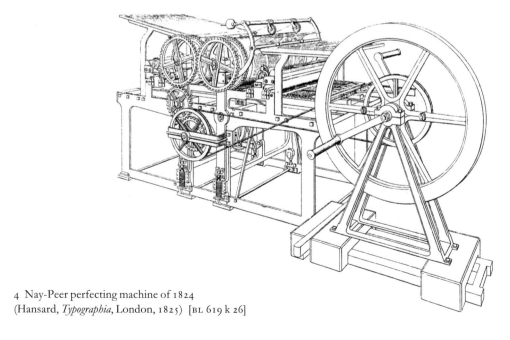

4 Nay-Peer perfecting machine of 1824
(Hansard, *Typographia*, London, 1825) [BL 619 k 26]

5 Serial publication: cover for the 19th instalment of Bernardin de St-Pierre's *Paul et Virginie*, published in volume form by Léon Curmer in 1838 [author's collection]

PLATE 1   Chromolithographic title-page from Curmer's edition of Bossuet's *Discours sur l'histoire universelle* (1842) [BL 1305 l 1]

PÉRÉGRINATIONS D'UNE COMÈTE.

HAFIZ

AMONGST all the poets of Persia, he whose *name*, if not his works, is most familiar to the English reader is Mohammed Schems-ed-din Hafiz, the prince of Persian lyric poets, of whom Shirâz may boast, that to that charming city a greater

(*Above*)

PLATE 5   British mediaevalism:
H. Noel Humphreys's chromolithographic
page decorations (*Maxims and Precepts of
Our Saviour*, 1848)   [BL C30 b 41]

(*Left*)

PLATE 6   'Evening Prayer',
chromolithograph by Owen Jones
(*The Book of Common Prayer*, 1845)
[BL C30 l 2]

(*Right*)

PLATE 7   Page from a French translation
of *De imitatione Christi* surrounded by the
chromolithographic copy of a Renaissance
illumination chosen by Count Bastard
(à Kempis, *Livres de l'imitation de Jésus Christ*,
reprinted 1856–58)   [BL C30 m 3, 4]

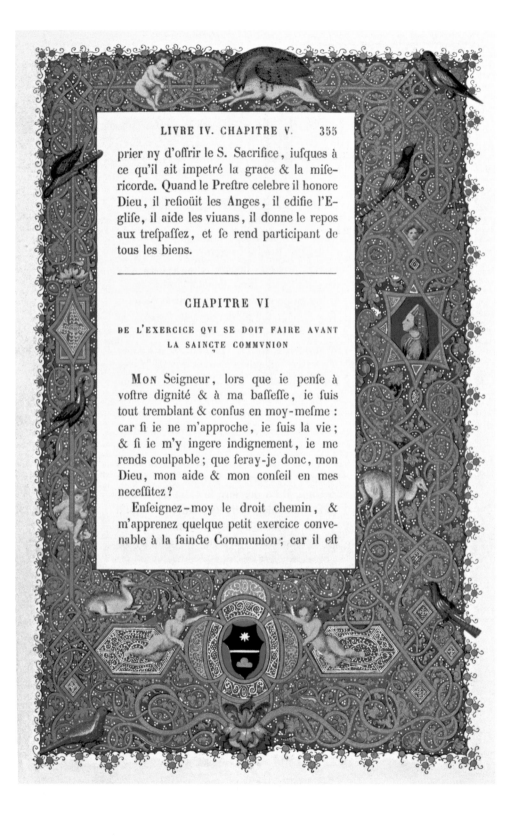

prier ny d'offrir le S. Sacrifice, iufques à
ce qu'il ait impetré la grace & la mife-
ricorde. Quand le Preftre celebre il honore
Dieu, il refioüit les Anges, il edifie l'E-
glife, il aide les viuans, il donne le repos
aux trefpaffez, et fe rend participant de
tous les biens.

CHAPITRE VI

DE L'EXERCICE QVI SE DOIT FAIRE AVANT LA SAINCTE COMMVNION

Mon Seigneur, lors que ie penfe à
voftre dignité & à ma baffeffe, ie fuis
tout tremblant & confus en moy-mefme :
car fi ie ne m'approche, ie fuis la vie ;
& fi ie m'y ingere indignement, ie me
rends coulpable ; que feray-je donc, mon
Dieu, mon aide & mon confeil en mes
neceffitez ?

Enfeignez-moy le droit chemin, &
m'apprenez quelque petit exercice conve-
nable à la faincte Communion ; car il eft

QUINTI

HORATII FLACCI

CARMINUM

LIBER PRIMUS

Sailors on a Cruise

PLATE 10 'Le Chicard', hand-coloured wood-engraving after Gavarni (*Les français peints par eux-mêmes*, II, 1840) [BL 1457 k 9]

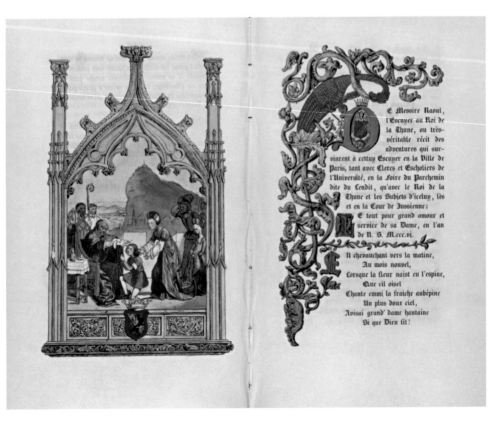

I

THE FRENCH CONNECTION

The Revival of Wood-engraving

In 1835 the Parisian publishers Paulin, Dubochet and Hetzel issued in 40 parts, at 40 centimes each, an illustrated edition of René Lesage's picaresque classic, *Gil Blas*. It was in the true sense an epoch-making book, for, as Robert Brun has written:

> The publisher Paulin set in train a revolution which was to transform the trade in books – sale by instalment [fig. 5] in high print-runs and at low prices. With the full weight of publicity behind it and its publication spread over a long period, a book could now reach social strata hitherto indifferent to fine printing.[1]

This epitomizes the aims and methods of publishers of the Romantic period – fine books which the bourgeoisie and working-classes could afford – aims which satisfied both the sound commercial instinct to exploit a new mass market and the idealistic streak of liberals and republicans determined that books for the people should be worthy of the people.

Furthermore, the book itself epitomizes the design features of the French style of the *livre romantique* – lavish illustration, comprising over 850 vignette illustrations designed by Jean Gigoux, decorated initials and head-pieces, all used in a quite revolutionary way. Here was no half-hearted introduction of the vignette by way of head- or tail-piece and occasional integrated embellishment, but an almost continuous combination of text and image. Equally revolutionary was the abandonment of the *hors-texte* plate, a full-page illustration, separately printed on one side of the leaf, with the reverse blank, and bound in to the body of the book. *Gil Blas* sets the pattern for illustration becoming integral by enclosing vignette and letterpress within a rule border to make a picture-frame around each page [fig. 6].

Although the Romantic period is notable for the variety of new media available for graphic reproduction – lithography, steel-engraving and steel-etching – it is in the revival of end-grain wood-engraving and its employment for the first time on a large scale which gives it an especial flavour. In Britain, these newer media tended to draw attention away from wood-engraving, a well-established craft by 1835; but Romantic books are a European phenomenon and it is in the context of Europe that we must consider wood-engraving.

The relief woodcut had been the earliest method of illustrating the printed book and was in general use from the fifteenth until the end of the sixteenth centuries in western Europe. Thereafter it was gradually ousted by the copper-engraving until, by the end of the eighteenth century, the craft had virtually died out in France, while in Britain it was confined to chapbooks and similar cheap ephemeral publications. However, London, unlike Paris, did not act as the vampire of talent. Britain was blessed by a lively provincial culture and just as Birmingham had in John Baskerville the first British printer with a European reputation, so Tyneside produced Thomas Bewick to revive the craft of wood-engraving.

quinze ans que j'habite impunément celle-ci. Je m'appelle le capitaine
Rolando, je suis chef de la compagnie, et l'homme que tu as vu avec
moi est un de mes cavaliers. »

6 *Captain Rolando*: wood-engraving after Jean Gigoux (Lesage, *Gil Blas*, 1835) [BL G18301]

The second book to publish his engravings – they had been awarded a premium by the Society for the Encouragement of Arts – was a volume of *Select Fables*. It was published in Newcastle-upon-Tyne by T. Saint in 1776 and it is instructive to compare Bewick's engravings with the woodcuts illustrating an edition of *Les fables d'Ésope mises en François* published in Lyons 'Aux dépens des [libraires] Associés' in the previous year. Now although Bewick's designs are derivative, being based upon those used to illustrate Revd Samuel Croxall's edition of Aesop in 1722 and they, in turn, were inspired by Francis Barlow's seventeenth-century copper-engravings, at least they represent a living tradition [fig. 7]. The Lyons set, by contrast, clearly demonstrates the moribund state of wood-engraving in France. The cuts are not adaptations, but clumsy replicas – perhaps executed towards the end of the seventeenth century – of the set designed by the Renaissance master Bernard Salamon for an edition of Gilles Corrozet's translation of Aesop printed at Lyons by Jean de Tournes in 1547 [fig. 8].

As a designer Bewick followed a tradition; as a craftsman he was to prove an innovator. Fifteenth- and sixteenth-century woodcuts were carved with a knife *on the plank*. Bewick, apprenticed to the metal engraver Ralph Beilby, used the metal-engraver's tool, the burin, to cut the design *on the end-grain* of the block which, as Remi Blachon points out, was common practice in England by the mid-eighteenth century.[2] Nor were the English the 'inventors' of end-grain wood-engraving, first employed towards the end of the seventeenth century and the first quarter of the eighteenth by Armenian presses in Constantinople. However, in Bewick's day the English were its sole European practitioners. Indeed the great eighteenth-century wood-cutter J.B.M. Papillon regarded end-grain engraving as impossible for fine work, noting that only a Lyonnais publisher of coarsely-printed playing-cards named Foy (or Foix) employed the technique.[3]

Bewick's skill now raised the status of the end-grain wood-engraving from the lower end of the market, where it dominated, to some of the most finely printed books of the last quarter of the eighteenth century, that first great age of British typography.

7 *The Thief and the Dog*: wood-engraving by Thomas Bewick (*Select Fables*, Newcastle, 1776). Compare with the stilted woodcut (fig. 8); for John Tenniel's interpretation see fig. 133 [BL 12305 bbb 29]

8 *The Thief and the Dog*: woodcut copy of a 16th-century design (*Les Fables d'Ésope mises en François*, Lyons, 1775) [author's collection]

Bewick used the white-line method to achieve engravings of great strength and delicacy to match the brilliancy of the modern faces used in fine printing at the end of the eighteenth century. For while the Newcastle editions of the *Fables* (1776ff.), of *The General History of Quadrupeds* (1790ff.) and of *British Birds* (1797ff.) established Bewick's fame as an artist and an engraver, it is the editions of *Poems of Goldsmith and Parnell* and of William Somerville's didactic poem *The Chace*, in which his brother John was associated, which were to have the greater influence upon the future of wood-engraved book-embellishment.

These books came from the press of William Bulmer in 1795 and 1796 respectively. Bulmer, Tynesider and fellow-apprentice of Bewick, enjoyed a European reputation comparable with that of Giambattista Bodoni in Italy or of Pierre Didot in France and few, therefore, were better qualified than he to show the beauty of the end-grain engraved vignette when carefully printed in conjunction with good typography. It must, then, be due in large measure to Bulmer's support that the wood-engraving had by the beginning of the nineteenth century become the fashionable medium of book-embellishment in Britain and a serious rival to the traditional copper-engraving.

A striking instance of this change in fashionable taste is provided by the successive illustrated editions of the poems of Samuel Rogers. Littérateur and banker, Rogers had the wealth to commission the best illustrator of the day, Thomas Stothard, and to employ a printer of almost equal standing with Bulmer, Thomas Bensley. The first illustrated edition of Rogers's *The Pleasures of Memory* appeared in 1794 with Stothard's designs engraved on

9 *Her senses had fled!*: copper-engraving after Stothard (Rogers, *The Pleasures of Memory*, 1794) [BL 11641 aaa 46]

10 Wood-engraved head-piece after Stothard (Rogers, *The Pleasures of Memory*, 1810) [BL 11645 bbb 32]

copper by James Heath (1756–1834) [fig. 9], one of the most skilled of London engravers. These intaglio engravings illustrate the enlarged reprint of 1796, yet when a new edition was called for in 1810, Rogers commissioned a fresh series of designs from Stothard to be printed as vignettes from the wood-engravings of one of Bewick's ablest pupils, the unfortunate Luke Clennel [fig. 10].[4] W.J. Linton, himself a master engraver, wrote that although in these black-line engravings 'Clennel forsook his own manner [i.e. the white-line technique] to perfectly render these daintinesses of Stothard ... we do not see an engraver's translation; we have pure Stothard'.[5]

Wood-engraving, then, could rival copper in quality of reproduction and it should have been cheaper, not so much because of the relative costs of the materials, although this must have been a factor, but because the wood-engraving could be printed with the type-matter at one pull of the press, whereas copper-engravings had either to be printed separately as *hors-texte* plates, or else the printed sheets had to be passed through the engraving press to receive the copper-plate vignettes. The pressure of the rollers impressed the edges of the copper plate into the paper, and these plate-marks had then to be removed by passing the sheets through a hot press to obtain a smooth finish. Thus the copper vignette required three workings by comparison with the single working of the wood-engraving.

In practice, however, the best wood-engraved illustrations were still confined to the embellishment of up-market books because, while in theory they should have been able to reduce the cost of embellishment, they failed to do so because of the complications inherent in obtaining 'colour' from a wood-engraving. To achieve this variation in the intensity of the black a system of overlays was perfected by Charles Whittingham the elder at the Chiswick Press. Thus the need for such time-consuming make-ready, as well as constant adjustments during the run, largely negated the economic advantages inherent in a process of printing, in relief, text and illustration at one pull of the press.

By the end of the eighteenth century, Britain had established an industrial and techno-logical lead over the rest of Europe and it was inevitable that developments in graphic reproduction should arouse considerable interest abroad. In 1813, therefore, the French printer Firmin Didot and his son, Ambroise, visited Charles Whittingham the elder at Chiswick.[6] It was a visit with important consequences, for the Didot family occupied a key position in the French publishing trade, not simply as printers and booksellers, but as typographers, paper manufacturers and technologists as well.[7]

Yet perhaps the most important development in the context of this visit was that of stereotyping which the family, as government printers, had successfully applied in 1790 to the production of *assignats*, the paper promissory notes of the First Republic. They went on to apply the process to producing plates from the type of standard works, thus furthering good, cheap reprint publishing. It was impossible economically to keep type standing, and stereotyping eliminated the cost of resetting books for which there was a regular demand. Additionally stereotyping offered a means of duplicating vignettes and printer's ornaments from a matrix and, while Firmin Didot was undoubtedly interested to observe Whittingham's technique for printing illustrations, it may, perhaps, have been this more mundane consideration which motivated his visit.

Indeed, he had already looked outside France for possible sources for the supply of wood-engraved matrices. In 1810, when Napoleon was able to enforce a Continental blockade of British manufactures, Didot had turned to Berlin, where the engraver Wilhelm Gubitz was almost unique in the practice of the craft of the woodcut in Continental Europe,[8] and from him had purchased a number of vignettes and ornaments.

By 1813, Napoleon's power was on the wane and Firman Didot's son Ambroise could investigate the British market for himself. That he did so was due to two factors – the manifest superiority of the British over the Berlin engraver and because, with the possible exception of the elder Godard of Alençon, whose son Pierre François (1797–1864) was to become one of the leading engravers of the Romantic period, there was no competent French engraver at the time. Firmin Didot's solution was simple – to import not the engravings but the engravers.

Accordingly, once peace was restored, he invited Charles Thompson, younger brother of the great engraver John Thompson and pupil of Robert Branston the elder, to come to Paris and to set up his studio there. In 1816 Thompson duly arrived and, until his death in 1843 at Bourg-la-Reine, he engraved vignettes and ornaments for the type-founders and vignette illustrations for some notable books but, whatever may have been Didot's intention, failed to establish a school of engraving. With the exceptions of Jules Fagnion (1813–66) and possibly Adolphe Best (1808–60), Charles Thompson's sole pupils appear to have been Louis Bougon (1786–1838) and his wife Marie. (Bougon was the first Frenchman independently to produce an end-grain engraving in 1808.) Having first established himself with Bougon, Thompson set up a separate establishment when he made Bougon's wife his mistress: he married her in 1839 after her husband's death.[9]

Blachon suggests[10] that perhaps Thompson attempted to keep to himself the secret of end-grain engraving to preserve the lucrative trade for the London engravers: consequently the numbers of French engravers was initially restricted and Thompson's dominance resented. Blachon quotes Balzac[11] hailing the advent of the French engraver Godard the younger to rival the Englishman, while Godard's friend Langlois vaunted him as the young man to give Thompson a boot up the backside.[12] Ultimately it was the volume of work demanded by the expansion of illustrated book- and periodical-publishing which drew increasing numbers of British engravers to Paris. There they passed their skills to their French counterparts, but as the numbers of French engravers grew, some of the British returned to London, others remained, still others migrated to Germany (see p. 73) and one of their number, Henry Brown became a respected teacher of wood-engraving in the art-schools of Belgium and Holland.[13]

This, however, is to anticipate developments in the 1830s and 1840s; the immediate results of importing the craft were several books embellished with wood-engravings. In France Bourbon Restoration style followed the classic English pattern in which the engravings were used as head- and tail-pieces, and during this period Charles Thompson was the principal and virtually the sole engraver. A book with which he was associated was the charming little edition of Rabelais published by Thomas Desoer in 1820 in three volumes, of which the first two are embellished by fourteen full-page designs by Alexandre Joseph Desenne and Victor Adam [fig. 11]. It is very much a *livre de bibliophile*, being printed on white, mauve, blue, orange, yellow and pink paper.

More typical is the series of books in which the engraver was associated with the first of the great French Romantic illustrators, Achille Devéria. These included editions of La Fontaine and Molière (both 1825–6) and of the *Chansons* of Jean Pierre de Béranger (1827). However, perhaps the most interesting from the historical, if not from the artistic, viewpoint is the ninth edition of Casimir Delavigne's *Messéniennes* (1824), since it combines wood-engraved vignettes with small squared *hors-texte* engravings on copper. The text is finely printed by Pinard, who had himself been involved in the introduction of wood-engraving with his edition of Montesquieu's *Le temple de Gnide* (1820).

Messéniennes was published by Ladvocat, whose imprint sets him firmly in the Romantic camp with his announcement that he is the publisher, too, of the complete works of three foreign authors who strongly influenced the movement – Shakespeare, Schiller and Byron. In his preface, Ladvocat makes it plain that this is a book for the connoisseur when he speaks of the difficulties of printing a book 'worthy of the finest [artistic] talent of the day and able to satisfy the collector whose taste has become so hypercritical with the introduction of luxurious typography'. He remarks that Achille Devéria's designs 'rival in vigour and grace those of Britain's Westalls and Smirkes'; seven are reproduced in copper-engraving and twenty on wood by Charles Thompson 'who had hitherto been unable to find a printer capable of doing full justice to the originality of his talents, by reproducing his engravings on wood with all the charm of copper-engravings.'

Note, in passing, this assumption that the aims of both wood- and copper-engraving were identical. However, the most surprising reference in Ladvocat's preface is that to Richard Westall (1765–1836) and Robert Smirke (1752–1845). However high their reputation as book-illustrators may have been in their day, it has not survived and it comes as a shock to find them emulated by French artists. Yet, as with wood-engraving, this is evidence of the prestige which Britain enjoyed on the Continent in the years following Waterloo. Thus without in any way overemphasising the influence of Westall and Smirke, their importance in the development of the French 'pre-Romantic' book-illustration is indisputable and can assuredly be seen in the work of the most important – Achille Devéria.

11 *Gargantua pays his toll on arrival in Paris – and drowns 26,418 men plus women and children*: wood-engraving by Charles Thompson in Desoer's edition of Rabelais (1, 1820) [BL C29 a 10]

Both Achille (1800–57) and his brother Eugène (1805–65) were painters. Eugène sprang to fame with his *Naissance d'Henry IV*, the sensation of the Salon of 1827, in which he totally eclipsed Delacroix. He was never able to sustain this premature elevation to the leadership of the Romantic school, but continued to turn out history paintings in the *style troubadour* with increasing lack of success. He was a very occasional illustrator, unlike his elder brother who, late in life, also turned to history painting.

However, Achille's fame was that of a portrait painter – most of the leading artistic and literary figures of the day sat for him – and as a lithographer. With the military painter Nicholas Toussaint Charlet (1792–1845) [fig. 12], he was one of the earliest to work extensively in the medium and one of the first to achieve real success in it: his contemporary, Jean Gigoux, paid tribute to the quality of his early work and to the extraordinary facility with which Devéria drew on the stone.[14] The quality brought him a flood of commissions and the facility enabled him to execute them at a rate which, according to Gigoux, brought him the very considerable sum of between two and three hundred francs a day. Gigoux also suggests that it was the need to support the extravagances of his mother and his sister which drove Devéria to the daily two or three designs, with the inevitable result that the quality itself suffered and the commissions fell away.

Although the bulk of his graphic work was in the form of lithographs for the print-sellers, Devéria has a respectable body of book-work to his credit. His designs for wood-engraving

12 *The Two Grenadiers*: copper-engraving after Nicholas Toussaint Charlet (Béranger, *Œuvres complètes*, III, 1834) [BL 011483 b7]

13 *The Bacchante*: copper-engraving after Achille Devéria (Béranger, *Œuvres complètes*, I, 1834) [BL 011483 b7]

are to some extent inhibited by the novelty of the medium. *Messéniennes* is, however, an early work and Devéria was able to achieve better effects as his experience grew and he was able to establish a closer rapport with his principal engraver, Charles Thompson. Nevertheless, his best work is still his designs for traditional copper-engraving contributed to a wide range of books, from Auguste de Chambure's *Napoléon et ses contemporains* (1824–7) to the complete works of Beaumarchais (1828) and Béranger (1834) [fig. 13] or to the very interesting translation of *Robinson Crusoe* made by the *poète lycanthrope*, Petrus Borel, and published by Francisque Borel and Alexandre Varenne in 1836.

Although these designs may be examples of Romantic art, the books in which they appear are not themselves examples of *le livre romantique* since their illustrations are reproduced conventionally as squared *hors-texte* copper-engravings. In terms of wood-engraving, too, Jules David's designs for La Fontaine's *Fables* (1836–7), despite the Romantic borders which surround the pages, are as much in the classic British tradition of the engraved head-piece as those of Devéria for the *Messéniennes* twelve years before. Thus Devéria the illustrator should be considered as a Romantic artist who gave the period flavour of Romanticism to conventionally conceived books, rather than as an illustrator of the *livre romantique*. We should also constantly bear in mind that this long-established convention of the illustration as a separate entity co-existed with and influenced books in which illustration was conceived as the fully integrated embellishment of the printed page.

That so much of Devéria's work – and indeed at this time that of the Romantic illustrator *par excellence*, Tony Johannot – should have been reproduced in metal rather than in wood, is indicative of the status of wood-engraving both in Britain and in France between 1820 and 1835. In both countries wood-engraving had been employed as the fashionable embellishment for books designed for the upper end of the market. At the same time – especially in Britain – it also performed its traditional function at the other extreme for the chapbook printers of the Seven Dials. Yet even here the salutary influence of Bewick could be felt in that, having made wood-engraving respectable, the demand for engravers ensured that there were men and women available to devote the same skill required to translate both the artistry of Thomas Stothard or of John Thurston and to capture the lurid designs for a broadside ballad or the account of a gruesome murder.

Nevertheless, Charles Knight, who did so much to bring books to the people, was perfectly correct to write in his memoirs that 'the legitimate purpose of wood-engraving was not then attained. It is essentially that branch of the art of design which is associated with cheap printing'[15] – yet the choice seemed to lie between cheap printing, which was often nasty into the bargain, and the costly if exquisite artistry of the *livre du bibliophile*. The essential was to find a means of cutting or of printing the block cheaply enough to satisfy the new and growing middle market for illustrated books. This was the readership to which the Society for the Diffusion of Useful Knowledge appealed in Britain and at which their publisher, Charles Knight, directed his *Penny Magazine*.

First published in 1832, and imitated in France when *Le magasin pittoresque* was founded in Paris in the following year, *The Penny Magazine* achieved so large a circulation that formes had to be printed simultaneously from stereo-plates by several steam-presses. The steam-press, with an impression-rate some sixteen times higher than anything possible with the hand-press, was a most potent force in lowering the costs of letterpress printing to the level of this new market. It was also the means of achieving the economy inherent in the ability of the relief block to print illustration simultaneously with text and, moreover, to give those relief blocks the same 'colour' as the hand-press had gained through the use of overlays, but without the heavy additional cost of making-ready those overlays. The reason, as given by Chatto, Jackson and Bohn, was that:

> It is absolutely necessary that wood-cuts intended to be printed by a steam-press should be lowered in such parts as are to appear light; for as the pressure on the cut proceeds from the even surface of a metal cylinder covered with a blanket, there is no means of *helping* a cut as is generally done when printed by a hand-press by means of overlays.[16]

This 'lowering' of the block is well described in the layman's language of Henry Cole: 'Instead of *unequal* pressure on an *even* surface [overlays], they use *equal* pressure on an *uneven* surface, by lowering the surface of the block according to the sort of tint required.'[17]

This was no new process: Thomas Bewick had employed the technique early in his career to take advantage of the customary soft-packed tympan and to prevent over-inking by the crude dogskin balls used in the eighteenth century. The advent of the iron press and of inking rollers in the early years of the new century and, more particularly, the need to obtain from the engravings a sharp, black impression to match the clarity of the new 'modern face' types, led him to abandon the practice in favour of overlays. Yet clearly the knowledge and probably the practice of the technique survived, to be resurrected in what Chatto, Jackson and Bohn describe as 'an epoch in the history of wood engraving'.[18] This was the part-publication in 1832 by the Society for the Diffusion of Useful Knowledge of W. Youatt's treatise, *Cattle: their Breeds, Management and Disease* in an edition of 12,000 copies. It was the first work illustrated by lowered blocks to come off the steam-press. Not only had the blocks themselves suffered no damage, but very considerable financial benefits had accrued to the

14 *Gil Blas and Captain Rolando*: wood-engraving after Jean Gigoux (Lesage, *Gil Blas*, 1835) [BL G18301]

publishers since, as Chatto/Bohn claims: 'Had such a work as the Treatise on Cattle been printed at a common press without the blocks having been lowered, the cost of printing would have been at least double the sum charged by Messrs Clowes.'[19]

In aesthetic terms, too, the publication in 1835 by Charles Knight of *One Hundred and Fifty Wood Cuts selected from The Penny Magazine* showed how effective the medium of the lowered block could be to reproduce paintings and to provide a very wide range of illustrative material. The constraints of cheaper paper and the need to produce stereotypes for printing militated against the use of close hatching in magazine work, but the blocks had colour and, when printing from the block on better paper, the greatest delicacy of line could be achieved.

The revival of wood-engraving is thus inextricably connected with the birth and develop-ment of illustrated journalism. The methods which Charles Knight employed to print *The Penny Magazine* were followed in France on *Le magasin pittoresque* and there is little difference in the practices described by each periodical.[20] The technique which had been so success-fully applied to mass-circulation illustrated journalism was now applied with equal success and even greater *éclat* to illustrated books intended for the same mass market. Thus the success of *Gil Blas* not only brought wood-engraving into this broad middle ground and made it the predominant method of illustrating French books, but its influence, and that of rival Parisian publications, reinforced the trend towards wood-engraving in Britain where the medium had originated, as against newer and more fashionable techniques of graphic reproduction.

Steel, Copper and Stone

Although wood-engraving was the most important method of reproducing artists' designs employed in the Early Victorian period, other methods produced work that was typically 'Romantic'. Above all, this is true of the steel-engraving, the most characteristically British medium although, in fact, it was an American, Jacob Perkins, who had invented the process. Having successfully conducted experiments in the United States, he came to London in 1818 hoping to have his invention adopted by the Bank of England for use in banknote printing.

In this enterprise Perkins had been associated with the copper-engravers James and Charles Heath and, although it proved unsuccessful in that their application was rejected by the Bank, the partners applied the new process to the production of prints. Nor were they alone in seeing the commercial possibilities of steel-engraving, and other men and other methods of producing the steel-block on which the engraver worked were as early in the field.[21] Despite the intractability of the material by comparison with copper, steel offered some substantial advantages. Aesthetically it produced a more brilliant image which, like the white-line wood-engraving, harmonized with the modern face better than the softer copper. Publishers, however, are less swayed by aesthetic than by economic arguments, and the enormous advantage of steel over copper lay in its durability. As Messrs Otley & Saunders, the publishers, wrote in their guide to the aspiring writer, *The Author's Printing and Publishing Assistant*:

> Engraving on Steel is a modern and highly important improvement. Previously, elaborate Engravings on Copper would lose their delicate tints after Printing a few hundred copies, but from Steel many thousand impressions may be taken without the slightest perceptible difference between the first and the last. To this is chiefly attributable the present very moderate price of beautifully Embellished Works, the use of Steel instead of Copper rendering it no longer necessary to incur the heavy expence of Re-Engraving the Plates.[22]

Thus steel-engraving was used as a substitute for copper in reproducing the conventional full-page *hors-texte* illustration, and as early as 1820 the illustrations in Thomas Campbell's *Pleasures of Hope* and in 1822 Thomas Unwin's designs for Milton's *Paradise Lost* were so reproduced. However, and this is of great importance in bringing reproductions of works of art within the reach of a far wider public, the principal and most economic use of the steel-engraving was less in the reproduction of genuine book-illustrations than in the production of prints.

These, it is true, might well be conceived as a series to be bound up with appropriate letterpress, or as illustrations in the true sense, yet their subject-matter was such that they could have a continuing sales-life independent of any bound volume, for, as Basil Hunnisett writes:

> The most popular kind of illustrated book by far was that containing views, mainly topographical works … Antiquities … formed an offshoot to this category … Such works frequently contained up to 120 plates each and the text was merely a description of the scenes, with no independent existence of its own … In addition to texts with specially designed engravings, publishers issued series of illustrations for binding into any contemporary edition … *The Byron Gallery* [Smith & Elder *c.*1844] … *Landscape and Portrait illustrations of the Waverley novels* [Charles Tilt 1832] … *Landscape, landscape-historical and architectural illustrations to the works of Shakespeare* [How & Parsons, 1841–2].[23]

To the books mentioned in the last category might be added George N. Wright's *Landscape-historical Illustrations of Scotland and the Waverley Novels*, first published by S. Fisher & Son in 1836. The captions – and they are far from unique in this – are printed in both English and French, a hint of the Continental sales such engravings enjoyed, but more interesting is the fact that they were reprinted in 1842–3. This would seem to have been in anticipation of a new lease of life for the set to be bound in to the plain text of Scott which his publisher Caddell was issuing as 'The People's Edition' of the Waverley novels. They were appearing in weekly parts at 2*d.* per part for which the publishers claimed a circulation of no less than 60,000 copies.

Finally Basil Hunnisett mentions a 'third category [which] comprised art books nearly all of which were constructed around paintings by old and modern masters and contained a minimum of text.'

They served the purpose of widening the circle of appreciation of painting and almost the same may be said of the Annuals. With their sentimental engravings and diversity of bindings, they are so redolent of the period that they might stand for the peculiarly British contribution to the Romantic age in which they flourished and died.[24]

In addition to the sales of the annual itself, the publisher could expect a continuing sale from the single prints which illustrated it and of which the actual engraving and the copyright fees had formed the major item in its production costs. Nor were such sales confined to Britain: most publishers had Continental outlets[25] and, as Thackeray wrote in disgust, 'these countries [i.e. France and Germany] are ... inundated with the productions of our market, in the shape of Byron Beauties, reprints from the Keepsakes, Books of Beauty and such trash.'[26]

Nor was this the end of the useful life of the expensive steel plate for, as Thackeray, again arraigning the Annuals, wrote in *Fraser's Magazine*, '... such a beautiful vapidity pervades the chief portion of the pictures submitted to the public that to remember them is sheer impossibility ... so that the very best plan is this of Messrs Fisher, to change, not the plates, but just the names underneath, and make Medora into Haidee, or Desdemona, or what you will.'[27]

If steel-engraving finds its major application in print-making and is generally employed in book-publishing as a substitute for copper, there was one artist whose work was habitually reproduced in this medium who left an enduring mark upon British book design. The artist in question is J.M.W. Turner and the seminal books are Samuel Rogers's *Italy* (1830) [fig. 15] and *Poems* (1834) and the complete works of Sir Walter Scott published in a cheap five-shilling edition by Caddell between 1829 and 1836 [fig. 16].

Rogers was, of course, particularly sensitive to bibliophilic fashion and it is indicative of the status of steel- *vis-à-vis* wood-engraving that by 1830 it should in his eyes have ousted the latter from its position as the modish medium of graphic reproduction. This is of some interest in the history of nineteenth-century taste, but far more important in the history of Romantic book design are Turner's contributions (with Samuel Prout and Thomas Stothard) to these two books by Rogers. While in neither case, and in *Italy* less than in the *Poems*, are text and image so closely integrated as in the fully developed Romantic design, Turner's vignettes mark a definite stage in, and point the future development of, the *livre romantique*.

15 *The Bridge of Sighs*: steel-engraved vignette after J.M.W. Turner (Rogers, *Italy*, 1830) [BL 11659 b 84]

With Scott's works, Turner makes an equally decisive contribution to nineteenth-century book design. For each volume Turner – sometimes with the assistance of other artists – provided a full-page frontispiece and a vignette title-page design, both engraved in steel. Now there is nothing new about an engraved title-page – it is one of the glories of the seventeenth-century Baroque book. Nor is there anything original in its combination with an engraved frontispiece – it is simpler to tip-in a pair of conjugates rather than a single leaf. Books so designed can be found throughout the period of copper-engraved book-illustration. What is remarkable about Turner is the sheer power of his landscape vignettes [fig. 17] and these induced other publishers, both British and Continental, to follow suit.

On the Continent, French publishers developed the Romantic vignette, of which Tony Johannet was so prolific a designer, to embellish the title-page as a wood-engraving. In

THE POETICAL WORKS

OF

SIR WALTER SCOTT, BARᵗ

COMPLETE.

Abbotsford

ROBERT CADELL, EDINBURGH.

1841.

16 *Abbotsford*: steel-engraved vignette title-page to Sir Walter Scott's poetical works (1841) after J.M.W. Turner. Popularised (figs 17, 131), the style was widely taken up for type and wood-engravings (fig. 226) [BL 11614 h 1]

Britain the imitation of Turner was slavish and instantaneous. There is, for example, John Murray's attractive collected edition of the poems of George Crabbe, published in 1834 with frontispiece and title-page vignettes designed by Clarkson Stanfield [fig. 131]. This is a very obvious imitation in what is, after all, a similar collected edition: more important is its use by Richard Bentley for his series of five-shilling reprints, Bentley's Standard Novels, a series begun in 1829 and eventually to run to some hundreds of volumes.

Nor was the style confined to reprinted fiction. Its most important development was into the design of new novels of which it became an established feature, starting a tendency to move from a plain to an illustrated format for original fiction. Here, however, there is an important difference in the way in which the designs were executed. Etching, not engraving, was the method employed for all novels issued in parts and for most of those with a

THE

POETICAL WORKS

OF

JOHN MILTON.

VOL. VI.

St Michaels Mount. Shipwreck of Lycidas.

LONDON. JOHN MACRONE, 3. St JAMES'S SQUARE, MDCCCXXXV.

17 *St Michael's Mount: Shipwreck of Lycidas*: steel-engraved vignette title-page after J.M.W. Turner to Milton's poetical works (VI, 1835) [BL 1066 f 13]

substantial number of illustrations.[28] Apart from the cost factor, the very tight deadlines for the part-publication of novels meant that the infinitely more rapid process of etching was preferred to the lengthy method of steel-engraving. Just how quickly a steel-etching could be finished is demonstrated by Hablot Knight Browne's 'time-sheet' for one of the part-issues of *Nicholas Nickleby*. It shows the artist preparing preliminary studies for the two 'subjects' supplied by Dickens, submitting them for the novelist's approval, preparing finished drawings, transferring them to the steel and then etching the plates *in duplicate* – and all within the space of a fortnight, from the evening of 11 January to 26 January 1839.[29]

Of course, even the preliminary etching of a steel-engraving would require far more time than this since the detail was finer and the print-area generally larger. It was, however, the next stage, when the plate was cleaned and then finished with the burin, a particularly time-consuming process, which would tend to push up the costs. So, although the publication of steel-engravings could be highly profitable, it was a business which required considerable capital investment.[30]

It was perhaps as much this need for heavy capital expenditure as the lack of local expertise in France and Germany which makes steel-engravings, until the 1850s at least, very much a British medium. On the other hand, its place was taken on the Continent, and especially as a means of reproducing works of art, by the German invention, lithography. Properly speaking, this should be termed 'chemical printing' since it was somewhat fortuitous that stone should have been used first in 1798 as the surface for this plano-graphic process by its inventor, Aloys Senefelder.

The exploitation of his invention is a story complicated by Senefelder's rather happy-go-lucky attitude to the patent laws,[31] but it suffices to say that the music publisher Johann Anton André of Offenbach immediately saw its potential in his trade. He helped to patent the invention in Germany and France, and in Great Britain during the lull in the Great War with France afforded by the Treaty of Amiens. Although a number of lithographs was published in London around 1803, the resumption of hostilities isolated Britain and stifled the new process at birth, thus lithography did not really become established in Britain until the 1820s. As a medium for the heavily-illustrated book it was never to achieve the popularity of the intaglio or relief processes until the invention of chromolithography made a notable contribution to the embellishment of books in the 1840s. Both in Britain, and to a degree in France, lithography is rather the medium of the caricaturist and of the topographical artist. In book-publishing its main use lay in the specialized fields of architectural and antiquarian studies and in providing conventional *hors-texte* plates far more cheaply than steel-engraving.

As might be expected, lithography was far more widely employed in Germany, where it early took the role which steel-engraving was to play in Britain as a method of reproducing copies of works of art. Here the importance of the new invention transcends the merely technical, for the subjects which early in the century the Munich publisher, Strixner, issued – Dürer's decorations for the prayer-book of the Emperor Maximilian (1808)[32] and reproductions of paintings from the Royal Bavarian collections and in those of the Brothers Boissière – were of the greatest cultural importance. The Dürer designs most directly inspired the artists of the German Romantic book: the dissemination of reproductions of mediaeval paintings was crucial to the whole German Revivalist movement, itself one of the mainsprings of Romanticism. Finally, and on a more prosaic level, one finds German publishers using lithography where British publishers would have used steel-engraving to provide conventional full-page illustrations.

The French occupation of Germany after the Prussian defeat at Jena in 1807 ensured that lithography was early introduced into France, where it enjoyed an enormous vogue throughout the Romantic period – but with print- rather than with book-publishers. As in Britain, there was a tendency to employ lithographs in the more specialized antiquarian, architectural and topographical books, of which Baron Taylor's *Voyage pittoresque dans l'ancienne France* (1820–78) is the prime example. In addition, French publishers, like their German counterparts, tend to employ the lithograph (and to some extent the wood-engraving) as a cheap means of providing the occasional full-page plate to illustrate a text, where British publishers would have used steel-engraving. However, the new medium enjoyed its widest popularity as the artist's lithograph – the Romantic fancies and portraits of Achille Devéria, the social commentary of Gavarni, the satire of Honoré Daumier, Henry Monnier and Grandville, and the military prints of Denis-Auguste-Marie Raffet, Nicolas-Toussaint Charlet and of Horace Vernet.

In Britain, by contrast, although Robert Seymour used lithography for his humorous caricatures, John Doyle (HB) for his political cartoons and Henry Alken for some of his sporting prints, largely through the influence of George Cruikshank, the copper- and steel-etching were still an accepted medium for caricature, while painting was more generally reproduced as a steel-engraving. Here the strongest motivation was economic for, as Thackeray points out,

> in France and Germany, where publishers are not so wealthy or enterprising as with us ... Lithography is more practised ... With ourselves, among whom money is plenty, enterprise so great, and everything matter of commercial speculation ... wood or steel engraving ... by the aid of great original capital and spread of sale, are able more than to compete with the art of drawing on stone.[33]

Books for the People

Publishing, like all consumer trades, is subject to fashion. If, at the beginning of the nine-teenth century, wood-engraving had briefly emerged as the fashionable embellishment for fine books in Britain, by the 1830s educated taste had veered towards steel, as that barometer of bibliophily, Samuel Rogers, has shown. Yet although the up-market book tended away from wood-engraving, some very fine examples in what may be termed the classic British style were still produced. They include the two series of James Northcote's *Fables*, the first published in 1828, the second posthumously in 1833. William Harvey transferred Northcote's designs to the wood as oval medallions within architectural cartouches for the first and as squared engravings for the second series and, in addition, supplied original designs for initial letters and vignette tail-pieces. Harvey, too, was the designer of the wood-engravings in the two volumes of E.T. Bennett's *The Gardens and Menagerie of the Zoological Society delineated* (1830–31), a fine book in the Bewick tradition. All four volumes were printed by Charles Whittingham the elder at the Chiswick Press.

The fame of Charles Whittingham the younger has tended to obscure that of his uncle and namesake, the founder of the Chiswick Press. More than this, the uncle's reputation as a printer of engravings had rubbed off on the nephew, who was as fine a letterpress printer. It is true that the younger Whittingham permanently engaged the services of the wood-engraver Mary Byfield, but her work was mainly upon the decorative head- and tail-pieces and initial letters. Imitated from the fifteenth- and sixteenth-century originals they were chosen as fit accompaniment to the old-face types which, under the inspiration of the publisher William Pickering, were so successfully revived at Whittingham's Took's Court press.

Charles Whittingham the elder, on the other hand, was a noted printer, through his system of overlays, of both relief and intaglio engravings. His triumph with the latter is perhaps the mezzotints for Milton's *Paradise Lost*, engraved by their designer, John Martin, and printed in 1827. This is one of the luxury editions with which he was associated, yet the most significant aspect of Whittingham's work is the way in which the same scrupulous craftsmanship was applied to a whole series of cheap reprints of the English classics in small formats.

The earliest were mainly for or in association with John Sharpe, beginning with the series of English poets edited by Thomas Park and printed at the Stanhope Press in Goswell Street, before the move to College House, Chiswick, in 1810. Illustration in this first series was confined at most to an engraved frontispiece and title-page, but was more generous in later editions of the British poets, many of the designs being supplied by Richard Westall. The whole scheme of publication seems to have been completed by the part-issue of 'Sharpe's Select Edition of the British Prose Writers' in fifty fortnightly parts in January 1827. Each part was 'beautifully printed in Royal 32mo, embellished with PORTRAITS and allegorical ENGRAVINGS', for Sharpe's editions are generally distinguished by intaglio rather than relief illustrations.

More relevant to the history of wood-engraving is the series – Whittingham's Cabinet Library – published in association with Thomas Tegg at prices running from 1s. to 3s. 6d. per volume and numbering over sixty volumes by 1827. Many were illustrated by wood-engraving, mostly anonymous, although William Harvey was very probably one of the artists involved and John Thompson was undoubtedly the principal engraver. Thompson, indeed, cut the thirty-two charming vignettes which embellish an edition of Oliver Goldsmith's *The Vicar of Wakefield* published in 1819; while Harvey designed the sixty illustrations for the famous ten-volume Shakespeare which Whittingham printed in 1826.

That a man of Whittingham's status should have been associated in the publication of these delightful little books with somebody like Thomas Tegg is most interesting. History has not been kind to the greatest remainder-dealer of his day and repeats the canard that in his reprint publishing he was prone to sacrifice the author's text to achieve an even working. What is, however, beyond dispute is that if Tegg liked his books to be cheap, he also liked them to be decently printed. As an example of this there is his one-volume edition of Shakespeare's *Plays*, printed by J.R. and C. Childs of Bungay in 1827, which stands comparison, as was doubtless Tegg's intention, with the 'wreath' edition published by

William Pickering the year before and printed in Corrall's celebrated miniature Diamond type.

This emphasizes a salient feature of the Romantic period that, with the aim to make standard authors available at prices which the mass of the population could afford, marches an equally laudable ambition of ensuring that the lowering of the price does not bring with it a debasement of the quality of the books themselves. Charles Whittingham and Thomas Tegg provide examples of this principle in operation in the 1820s and we can see it continuing into the 1830s in so unlikely an organization as the Religious Tract Society. For example, their 1831 reprint of a sound piece of eighteenth-century morality in dialogue form, *The Two Apprentices; or The Importance of Family Religion*, with its strong but crude wood-cut illustrations, belongs to an older tradition. In complete contrast, with its steel-engraved plates and vignettes engraved on wood, is *The Picture Testament for the Young* printed for the RTS by Whittingham in 1835. Around this date the RTS published *The Girl's Week-day Book* with delicate wood-engraved vignettes in the manner of William Harvey and employed in the classic British style as head-pieces. Both books express a new attitude towards 'improving literature', in its widest sense, and herald that shift of publishing policy which made the RTS one of the most important nineteenth-century publishers of children's books.

The early 1830s saw a spate of reprint and cheap publishing. In addition to Bentley's Standard Novels and Caddell's edition of Scott's works, John Murray launched his ill-fated Family Library in competition with Lardner's and the Edinburgh Cabinet Libraries. At five shillings per volume or thereabouts, all seem to be priced beyond the means of the new mass market for books which the social conditions of the early nineteenth century were creating. The population virtually doubled during the first half of the century, the bulk of it being congregated in the cities, and gas lighting was introduced so that those city-dwellers had the light to read by. Concurrently enormous efforts were made to combat illiteracy – through the Sunday Schools, through societies sponsored by the Established Church or by Dissenters, and by the Mechanics Institute movement which started in 1823. All these tended to create a new mass readership, but how far this readership was tapped by such comparatively expensive books is open to doubt. It would seem that they were too highly priced for the bulk of the newly-literate working classes and went instead to the equally fast-growing lower-middle and middle classes.

The needs of working-class readers were met by a vigorous and greatly expanded chapbook trade which at best was fed by such periodicals as John Limbird's *Mirror of Literature*, by his 8d. and 1s. 2d. 'British Classics' and 'British Poets' and by his reprints in the 1820s of novelists like Mrs Radclyffe who had been fashionable at the turn of the century. Similarly, the proprietors of *The London Stage* – a series of cheap reprints of the theatrical repertory of the day – issued in 1825 an edition of Shakespeare's *Complete Works*. This is a stout octavo of 886 pages illustrated with wood-engravings in the crude 'popular' style. It has a glossary and a wealth of introductory and explanatory matter of which the publishers justly boast, claiming to have placed 'within the reach of the humblest Reader, the cheapest and most complete Edition of the Works of Shakespeare that has ever yet been published.'

This is the better class of book coming from the Salisbury Square publishers, whose stock-in-trade was the penny dreadful, lurid crime or horror serials, or the mixture of crime, violence and sex to be found in Lloyd's *Police Gazette* and similar weekly papers, while from Seven Dials, Catnach and his rivals cashed in with topical news of every murder trial. The size of the market may be judged by the fact that in 1823 Catnach claimed to have sold 250,000 copies of his account of the murder of Mr Weare and half a million copies of his account of the murderer William Thurtell's trial and execution; the total from all the publishers concerned, in a case such as that of the murder of Isaac Jeremy by his son James Rush, could amount to two and a half million books, pamphlets and broadsides.[34]

The constant aim of the social reformers was to replace such entertaining literature with something improving and the Society for the Diffusion of Useful Knowledge had in their publisher, Charles Knight, a man who fully shared their views. His *Penny Magazine* (1832) and *Penny Cyclopaedia* (1833) were both designed to instruct as well as to entertain, and both were certainly successful in terms of circulation, although the *Cyclopaedia* was ultimately barely profitable. Knight also directed his energies into book-publishing and by 1842 had completed part-issues of the *Pictorial Bible* and *The Arabian Nights*, had planned *The Pictorial History of England* in seven volumes of which five had been published, and was running his *Pictorial Shakspere* [sic] in monthly parts at 2s. 6d. each and his *London* in weekly parts at 4d. each. Obviously Knight – and others like him – did penetrate to a genuinely working-class readership, but doubts must remain as to whether his most consistent subscribers were not a cut above those for whom the books were ostensibly designed.

Aside from their lavish illustration, the point which should be emphasized about Knight's books is their serial publication. Robert Brun, as we have seen, draws attention to the innovation in France of issuing books in cheap parts, but Knight was following a long-established custom of the British trade. 'Number' publishing was practised as early as 1692,[35] and in the eighteenth century became a staple of the book trade. In addition to bibles and standard works for home reference there was *The Monthly Amusement* (novels at a shilling a monthly part in the 1720s); John Bell's *Poets of Great Britain* (1776–92) and his *British Theatre* (1776–8); John Harrison's *Novelist's Magazine* reprinting standard fiction in the 1780s; and Cook's *Classics* sold in sixpenny parts at the turn of the century. Harrison, interestingly, embellished each of his fortnightly parts with at least one copper-engraving, most of the designs for which were provided by Thomas Stothard – a sustained feat of high-quality book-illustration which is perhaps little known and hence much undervalued.

This might be said to have established a precedent which was followed by the publishers of steel-engravings in the 1830s and 1840s[36] who served the upper end of the market with part-issues of primarily topographical and antiquarian books. Where, however, the British practice was to differ so completely from the French was in the part-publication of original fiction illustrated by steel-etchings.

That it did so was largely fortuitous and stemmed directly from the runaway success of Charles Dickens's *Posthumous Papers of the Pickwick Club* in 1836 which were to shape the pattern of fiction-publishing for two decades or more. Not only were novels generally published in parts but, since each monthly part was illustrated by at least two steel-etchings, literary magazines, in which fiction was serialized, had to follow suit. In consequence we find in the late 1830s and early 1840s that *Bentley's Miscellany* and *Ainsworth's Magazine* employed as a matter of policy the leading book-illustrator of the day, George Cruikshank, as their resident artist. Illustrated serialization in magazines was, indeed, to continue far beyond the Romantic period itself, *The Cornhill Magazine*, for example, being the canvas in the 1860s for J.E. Millais's splendid illustrations for Anthony Trollope.

In stressing this difference, equal emphasis should be placed upon the social and cultural pressures common to both countries. However, the liberal and radical ideology which motivated so much British publishing could not be freely expressed in France until the July Revolution of 1830 substituted the constitutional monarchy of Louis-Philippe for the absolutism of Charles X. The varied and deep-seated social and political discontents which led to the expulsion of the Bourbons were sparked into insurrection by the suppression of

18 *Don Alfonso on his sick-bed*: wood-engraved vignette after Jean Gigoux. Note the typical initial letter decorated in the Romantic style (Lesage, *Gil Blas*, 1835) [BL G 18301]

19 *The Rose-grower*: wood-engraved vignette after J. Gagniet
(*Les français peints par eux-mêmes*, I, 1840) [BL 1457 k 8]

the liberal newspapers and the revolt of the printing-
workers who were unemployed in consequence. Not
surprisingly, press freedom on the British pattern was
a major feature of the new constitution.

None used the new-won freedom of the press with
greater vigour or more virulence than the Republicans,
of whom Charles Philipon (1800–62) is perhaps the
best-known through his satiric political weekly,
La caricature. Philipon, himself a failure as a
lithographic artist, succeeded in attracting and in
fostering the very considerable artistic talents of
Honoré Daumier, Grandville, Henry Monnier and
Charles Joseph Traviès, among others, to work on this
and the less scathing and more social daily, *Le charivari*. The latter survived as a vehicle for
Gavarni's pictures of Parisian life and as a model for similar humorous magazines – *Punch*
was subtitled 'The London Charivari' – when Philipon was forced to discontinue *La
caricature* in 1835 on the re-imposition of press-censorship,[37] following the unsuccessful
insurrection in Lyons in 1834. Perhaps Philipon's greatest contribution to the art of the *livre
romantique* is that of discovering and encouraging so many of the artists who were to become
the historians and satirists of bourgeois society. Significantly, Philipon, through his brother-
in-law Aubert and their Galérie Véro-Dodat, is associated with the most characteristic and
successful essay in this field, the *Physiologies* of 1841–2.[38]

If the press laws of 1835 had the effect of closing *La caricature*, they also diverted the
energies of two other republican journalists from political agitation to publishing fine books
for the masses. Louis Paulin's *Le national* had provided the spark which had ignited the
Revolution of July 1830: under the July Monarchy Paulin brought Jacques Hetzel on to his

20 *The Book-collector*:
wood-engraved
head-piece after
Tony Johannot
(*Les français peints par
eux-mêmes*, III, 1841)
[BL 1457 k 10]

paper, and when, in 1835, they turned to book-publishing they linked with J.J. Dubochet. This was the trio which issued *Gil Blas*. Its success showed the existence of a large market for lavishly illustrated books published in cheap and regular part-issues and others were quick to follow their lead.

Their principal rival was probably Léon Curmer who, like both Paulin and Hetzel, had a strong streak of idealism to balance the profit-motive. Yet, whereas both Hetzel and Paulin belonged to the radical tradition of French Republicanism, Curmer seems to have been closer to the liberal attitudes of Charles Knight in seeking to diffuse unadulterated culture and knowledge beyond the confines of the aristocracy and the upper middle classes. His aim being to make fine books available to all, his publishing programme included editions of *Les quatre évangiles* and Thomas à Kempis's *De l'imitation de Jésus Christ* in 1836 – both of which drew rival editions from Paulin in the following year – his celebrated edition of Bernardin de Saint Pierre's *Paul et Virginie* and J.B. Bossuet's *Discours de l'histoire universelle* in 1839 [pl. 1], the eight volumes of gentle social satire of *Les français peints par eux-mêmes* (1840–42) [figs 19, 20], and a splendid natural history, *Le jardin des plantes* (1842), with text by

21 *The Law-student*: full-page wood-engraving after Gavarni (*Pictures of the French*, 1841: a selection in English translation from *Les français peints par eux-mêmes*) [BL 838 i 18]

22 *The Attorney*: full-page wood-engraving after Henry Monnier (*Pictures of the French*, 1841: a selection in English translation from *Les français peints par eux-mêmes*) [BL 838 i 18]

ous nous hâtions d'avancer sans dire un mot, et sans oser nous communiquer nos inquiétudes. Vers minuit, nous arrivâmes tout en nage sur le bord de la mer, au quartier de la Poudre-d'Or. Les flots s'y brisaient avec un bruit épouvantable: ils en couvraient les rochers et les grèves d'écume d'un blanc éblouissant et d'étincelles de feu. Malgré les ténèbres, nous distinguâmes, à ces lueurs phosphoriques, les pirogues des pêcheurs, qu'on avait tirées bien avant sur le sable.

quelque distance de là, nous vimes, à l'entrée du bois, un feu autour duquel plusieurs habitans s'étaient rassemblés. Nous fûmes nous y reposer en attendant le jour. Pendant que nous étions assis auprès de ce feu, un des habitants nous raconta que, dans l'après-midi, il avait vu un vaisseau en pleine mer, porté sur l'île par les courans; que la nuit l'avait dérobé à sa vue; que, deux heures après le coucher du soleil, il l'avait entendu tirer du canon pour appeler du secours; mais que la mer était si mauvaise, qu'on n'avait pu mettre aucun bateau dehors pour aller à lui; que

23 *Shore beaten by the Surf, Canoes drawn up on the Beach* and *Islanders around the Fire*: squared wood-engravings after J.L.E. Meissonier (Bernardin de St-Pierre, *Paul et Virginie*, 1838) [BL 1458 k 9]

P. Bernard, L. Couailhac and G. and M. Lenanont, answered immediately by M. Boitard's book of the same title from Dubochet.

Unlike his rivals, Curmer tended to use a varied means of reproduction within the same book and to combine the *hors-texte* full-page illustrations with integrated vignettes. Thus, in the *Gospels*, the à Kempis and the Bossuet, the text is set within wide historiated borders and the embellishments are in the form of *hors-texte* steel-engravings designed, in the *Gospels* and the *Imitation*, by Tony Johannot. Hand colouring is used to embellish the title-pages of these books, while the Bossuet is given an imposing series of chromolithographic half-titles. The *Gospels*, a handsome piece of book-production, has wood-engraved head-pieces and rather skimpy historiated initials. Both *Les français* [figs 21, 22] and *Paul et Virginie* [fig. 23] are embellished with wood-engravings exclusively and exhibit a feature common to books at the start of the Romantic period, namely the pulling of full-page wood-engraved illustrations on India paper, mounted on a *hors-texte* leaf, and frequently provided with a guard. In addition, *Paul et Virginie* contains four similar steel-engravings omitted from the English edition.

None of Curmer's books, the Molière (1836) and Cervantes (1837) illustrated by Tony Johannot, or Laurent de l'Ardèche's *Histoire de l'empereur Napoléon* (1839) illustrated by Horace Vernet, follows the pattern of *Gil Blas* in relying exclusively upon wood-engraved vignettes integrated with a text and enclosed within double rule borders. In this the Dubochet/Paulin/Hetzel editions excel and they are, in fact, less successful when they attempt to compete directly with Curmer's style, as, for example, in their 1837 edition of the *Gospels*. The hand-coloured engraved title-page of Curmer's volume is inadequately matched by a rather thin piece of chromolithography in pallid blue and silver, and although the wood-engraved chapter openings and initial letters designed by Théophile Fragonard are superior in detail to Curmer's, the ensemble is spoiled by the page-borders. The book tries too hard to outdo Curmer and the strain is very apparent.

In the vogue for illustrated books of the Romantic period, traditional styles of book design co-existed with the new Romantic style and the same artists were commissioned to embellish each type of book. J.P. Béranger's publishers, Perrotin, for example, issued a four-volume edition of the poet's works in 1834 with 104 vignette engravings by various artists printed in the traditional fashion as *hors-texte* illustrations [figs 12, 13, 24, 28, 31]. In 1837 they re-issued the work in three volumes and in association with another noted publisher of illustrated books, Fournier. The military artist Raffet provided seventeen designs on specifically Napoleonic themes [fig. 25], the remainder being in the hands of that great Romantic book-illustrator Grandville [fig. 26]. Although the designs are wood-engraved vignettes, once again they are printed in traditional style as *hors-texte* plates. In the following year Grandville designed the illustrations [fig. 27] for a translation of *Gulliver's Travels* for Fournier and his partner in the enterprise, Furne. These, it is true, are printed as integrated vignettes, for the acceptance of the new style was not immediate. Thus when Fournier and Furne first issued Grandville's designs for their edition of La Fontaine's *Fables* in 1838–40 the wood-engraved vignettes were printed as *hors-textes* [fig. 28]. Only with the reprint of 1847 – and subsequently – are the designs integrated as head-pieces for pages enclosed by rule borders, an effect achieved by enlarging the format from demy to large royal octavo.

A similar instance of gradual acceptance, or perhaps of the conservative influence of Curmer co-existing with the more revolutionary style of Dubochet, is provided by two books from the publisher Ernest Bourdin. His edition of the Abbé Prévost's *Manon Lescaut* (1839) is a sober

24 *Fair Round Belly*: copper-engraving after Eugène Lami (Béranger, *Œuvres complètes*, II, 1834) [BL 011483 b 7]

25 *The Song of the Cossack*:
wood-engraving after
D.A.M. Raffet (Béranger,
Œuvres complètes, II, 1837)
[BL 1163 c 12]

26 *Oran-outangs*:
wood-engraving after
Grandville (Béranger,
Œuvres complètes, III,
1837)

piece of printing, embellished by integrated vignettes and by about seventeen full-page illustrations, engraved on wood, pulled on India paper and, as in the case of *Paul et Virginie*, mounted as *hors-textes*. René Lesage's *Diable boiteux* (1840), on the other hand, is completely Romantic in idiom, with fully integrated vignettes and pages enclosed within rule borders [fig. 217].

Both books are illustrated by Tony Johannot (1803–52) who is *the* artist of the French *livre romantique*. His career, and that of his brother Alfred (1800–37), typify one very important facet of the explosion of print and particularly of illustrated print in the Romantic period – the birth of the professional book-illustrator. Both brothers trained as copper-engravers under their elder brother, Charles (d. 1824): neither received any formal artistic training. As Jean Gigoux notes, 'the Johannot brothers were a pair of young engravers who, so to speak,

VOYAGE CHEZ LES HOUYHNHNMS. 221

soit par l'orifice d'en bas,

selon leur fantaisie; et cette médecine, qui relâche les entrailles, entraîne avec elle tout ce qu'elles contiennent,

27 *The Clyster*: vignette wood-engravings after Grandville (Swift, *Voyages de Gulliver*, II, 1838) [BL 838 f 24]

et prend le nom de purgation ou de clystère. La nature, disent-ils fort ingénieusement, nous a donné l'orifice supérieur et visible pour l'introduction des aliments, et l'orifice inférieur pour la déjection de leur superflu :

43

28 *The Taper*:
wood-engraving
after Grandville
(La Fontaine,
Fables, 1839)
[BL 12304 g 14]

29 Wood-engraved
vignette after Tony
Johannot (Lesage, *Le diable
boiteux*, 1840) [BL 12511 i 7]

jumped straight from the burin to the pencil without any preliminary training. They had not even seen an old master painting …'.[39] Both seem to have been completely dedicated professionals and, in an age which encouraged wholesale egoism and exhibitionism, to have retained the modest confidence of true craftsmen, as Gigoux himself witnessed.

> The two brothers both avoided rowdy self-advertisement, leading a peaceful and ever modest existence in their studio. They really put into practise Pascal's phrase 'Le moi est haïssable.' They never even talked about themselves.[40]

Notwithstanding, Tony Johannot is estimated to have designed in a career of some twenty years over 3,000 vignettes for more than 150 different books.

Johannot was associated from the first with the Romantic movement, some of his earliest published designs being for Charles Nodier's *L'histoire du roi de Bohème et ses sept châteaux* (1830). Since the author is one of the seminal influences upon the literary movement and since Johannot's embellishments comprise integrated wood-engravings, the book is often hailed as the first *livre romantique*. Robert Brun is, however, right in categorising it as a *livre à vignettes* [fig. 30].[41] Although the wood-engravings are integrated in a style to match the fantastic nature of Nodier's text, the embellishments are a development of the conventional book with wood-engravings and prefigure rather than take precedence over the revolutionary use of the medium in *Gil Blas*.

As if to confirm this, we should also note that *Le roi de Bohème* had no immediate successor and that the appropriately Romantic decoration for a book from the Romantic movement in literature was the simple – and might one say Turner-influenced – title-page vignette and frontispiece. Johannot was much sought after for this sort of embellishment and Lamartine, Hugo, Dumas and de Musset, as well as many minor figures, had their books decorated with such appropriate wood-engraved vignettes in the years immediately following 1830. In addition Johannot received many commissions before 1840 for designs for metal-engraving and, although the bulk of such work was executed by other engravers, in a few instances both he and his brother Alfred put their

30 Wood-engraved vignette after Tony Johannot (Nodier, *L'histoire du roi de Bohème et ses sept châteaux*, 1830) [BL 837 f 11]

31 *Winter*, designed and engraved on copper by Alfred Johannot (Béranger, *Œuvres complètes*, 1, 1834) [BL 011483 b 7]

own drawings on copper [fig. 31]. Although, too, the books in which they appeared, the Béranger of 1834 or a La Fontaine *Fables* of 1840, for example, are conventional in design, these illustrations are important in demonstrating the basis of Johannot's far larger *œuvre* for wood-engraving.

Their ancestor is undoubtedly the British school of Smirke and Westall, but shaped by the developments which Devéria and other exponents of the *style troubadour* had introduced. As a copper-engraver and one who worked in watercolours when designing for copper-engraving,[42] Johannot was thoroughly conversant with the tonal quality of that medium, yet when he comes to designing for wood-engraving he is not obsessed, as were William Harvey and his followers in England, with tints to the detriment of line. Johannot, in fact, seems to have as strong an understanding of the properties of the wood-block and his line is always apparent, in strength, delicacy and smooth flow, in the countless designs which he made in this medium after 1830.

We have already noted in passing some of the commissions which were entrusted to him by J.J. Dubochet or by his associates Paulin and Hetzel, as well as by Léon Curmer. These are among the earliest of the very many publishers who clamoured for his work and hence it is very difficult to single out for especial mention any one book, when the numbers which he illustrated are so great and their range so wide – from children's books, such as Charles Nodier's *Le trésor des fèves* (1845), topography with Jules Janin's *La Bretagne* (1844), literary classics, contemporary novels, poetry, or memoirs, such as Silvio Pellico's *Mes prisons* (1843)

32 *Shepherds*: wood-engraved vignette after Tony Johannot (Janin, *L'âne mort*, 1842) [BL 12512 i 5]

– but of all these books Jules Janin's *L'âne mort* (1842) stands out for me through the strength and beauty of its draughtsmanship, combined with a wholly appropriate and chilling sense of the macabre [figs 32, 33].

Tony Johannot's great and well-deserved reputation spread across the Channel and ordinary British book-buyers were able to sample his art in English translations of the books which he had illustrated, thanks to the trade in polytypes and electros. In consequence, the artist was on at least two occasions commissioned to illustrate English books. In 1846 he provided designs for *Anne of Geierstein* [fig. 34] in the Abbotsford edition of Sir Walter Scott's Waverley novels – the only foreign artist so honoured – and one can only hope that this compensated for the disappointment of his earlier involvement with the novelist William Harrison Ainsworth.

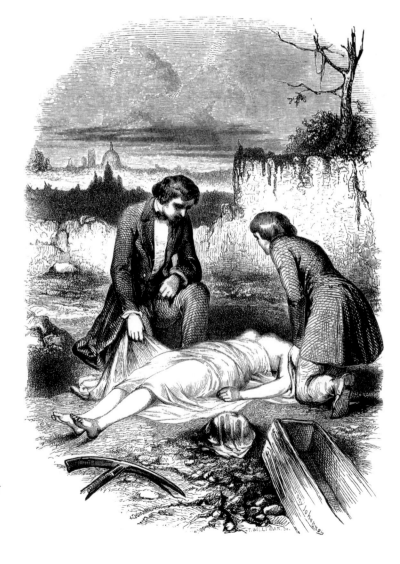

33 *The Interment*: full-page wood-engraving after Tony Johannot (Janin, *L'âne mort*, 1842) [BL 12512 i 5]

Ainsworth, who had succeeded Charles Dickens as editor of *Bentley's Miscellany*, decided in 1840 to set up a periodical of his own. George Cruikshank, his regular illustrator, was tied by contract to Richard Bentley and, in any case, Ainsworth was disenchanted with Cruikshank. In his efforts to break free by securing his dismissal by Bentley, the artist had been deliberately submitting inferior work – and that included the etchings for Ainsworth's own novel *Guy Fawkes*. The novelist describes his solution to the problem in a letter of 17 December 1840 to his lifelong friend, James Crossley:

> I have made all arrangements to start my magazine at Christmas next, and have engaged Tony Johannot (the artist), who is now at work for me. I went over to Paris for that purpose ... Windsor Castle, of course formed the main feature of the design.[43]

Chapter the Third.

Cursed be the gold and silver, which persuade
Weak man to follow far fatiguing trade.
The lily, peace, outshines the silver store,
And life is dearer than the golden ore.
Yet money tempts us o'er the desert brown,
To every distant mart and wealthy town.
                HASSAN, OR THE CAMEL-DRIVER.

34 Wood-engraved chapter-heading after Tony Johannot (Scott, *Anne of Geierstein*, 1846) [BL 1458 i 11]

Unfortunately, instead of appearing in December 1841, the first issue of *Ainsworth's Magazine* was not published until February 1842, by which time Ainsworth and Cruikshank had become reconciled, Cruikshank had become the new magazine's resident artist, and the venture had been launched with the serialization of Ainsworth's next novel, *The Miser's Daughter*, illustrated by Cruikshank. *Windsor Castle* was postponed and poor Johannot rather summarily superseded by Cruikshank after completing just four soft-ground etchings and a cover-design engraved on wood by John Thompson. Small though this contribution is, it is notable as an example of Johannot's skill both as an artist and as an etcher. Although they cannot compare with the set of etchings for Charles Nodier's *Contes* (1846), the *Windsor Castle* series enable a comparison to be made between the very different styles and techniques of the leading French and British illustrators of the day.

246   PAUL

des frégates, des coupeurs d'eau, et d'une multitude d'oiseaux de marine, qui, malgré l'obscurité de l'atmosphère, venaient de tous les points de l'horizon, chercher des retraites dans l'île.

Vers les neuf heures du matin, on entendit du côté de la mer des bruits épouvantables, comme si des torrents d'eau, mêlés à des tonnerres, eussent roulé du haut des montagnes. Tout le monde s'écria : « Voilà l'ouragan ! » et dans l'instant, un tourbillon affreux de vent enleva la

35 *The 'St-Geran' labouring in the Hurricane*: wood-engraving after J.L.E. Meissonier (Bernardin de St-Pierre, *Paul et Virginie*, 1838) [BL 1458 k 9]

deux relais de vigoureux coulis, ou porteurs, de quatre hommes chacun; deux portefaix; un

porteur d'eau; un porteur de gargoulette, pour le

rafraîchir; un porteur de pipe; un porteur d'om-

chi, ou porte-flambeau, pour la nuit; un fendeur

de bois; deux cuisiniers; deux chameaux, et leurs

conducteurs, pour porter ses provisions et ses ba-gages; deux pions, ou coureurs, pour l'annoncer;

quatre cipayes ou reispoutes, montés sur des che-vaux persans, pour l'escorter; et un porte-étendard,

brelle, pour le couvrir du soleil le jour; un masal-

The larger number of etchings and the subjects themselves give Cruikshank far greater opportunity to express himself at his best, particularly in his dramatic chiaroscuros, and he tends to dominate the book. Yet Johannot's quieter style is by no means negligible and in so far as historical verisimilitude is concerned, there is little to choose between the Tudor England of the French artist or of the inimitable George.

Other artists, too, at times achieve the right period atmosphere, notably Edmond de Beaumont in Jacques Cazotte's *Le diable amoureux* (1842) and Célestin Nanteuil in the 1836 translation of *Robinson Crusoe* by Petrus Borel. Yet perhaps the French illustrator with the best historical sense, at least so far as the eighteenth century is concerned, was Jean Louis Ernest Meissonier (1815–91).

His career demonstrates strikingly the way in which the demand for illustration eased the lot of the young painter. Obviously there was now a large and hungry market to be supplied in the main publishing centres of Europe and regular commissions from publishers for illustrations provided a financial security so vital to a painter with a name to make. Indeed, an artist such as the German Romantic painter and illustrator Ludwig Richter regarded these commissions as so supportive and so important to his career 'that he made [his illustrative work] virtually the sole topic of the last chapter of his reminiscences, the chapter that dealt with his life during the decade following his return to Dresden in 1836.'[44] In the case of his

36 (*left*) The integrated
illustrations of 'the learned
doctor' on his travels (after
J.L.E. Meissonier) take on the
characteristics of a comic strip
but show the differences
between black- and white-line
wood-engraving (Bernardin de
St-Pierre, *La chaumière indienne*
included in the 1838 edition
of his *Paul et Virginie*)
[BL 1458 k 9]

37 Wood-engraved vignette after J.L.E. Meissonier
(*Lazarille de Tormès*, 1846) [BL 12518 v 2]

38 Wood-engraved head-piece after
J.L.E. Meissonier to *The Preacher*
(Chevigné, *Contes rémois*, 1858)
[BL 11482 f 13]

fellow-countryman, Adolf Menzel, a single book – Kugler's *Geschichte Friedrichs des Grossen* (1840) – brought him such fame internationally that his fortune as an easel painter was made[45] and thereafter he had no need to work as an illustrator.

Meissonier's career almost exactly matches Menzel's. His first designs probably appeared in 1835 in *Le magasin universel,* one of the illustrated rivals of *Le magasin pittoresque,* but his real opportunity came when Léon Curmer commissioned work from him for *Paul et Virginie* in 1838 [figs 23, 35]. Although he was paid at the derisory rate of between 10 and 40 francs a drawing, his designs for *Paul et Virginie,* and more especially for Bernardin de Saint-Pierre's *La chaumière indienne* [fig. 36] which Curmer appended to the longer novel, became the foundation of his success as a painter. So highly were they regarded that, from about 1841, Meissonier could live exclusively from his painting. In consequence his book-illustrations thereafter are somewhat sparse, but include a dozen vignettes for *Lazarille de Tormès* [fig. 37], a genuine picaresque novel which prefaces the 1846 reprint of the Gigoux-illustrated *Gil Blas.* However, his undoubted masterpieces are his designs for the Comte de Chevigné's *Contes rémois* in 1858 [fig. 38], when Meissonier was established as the military painter to Napoleon III. The designs are printed as head-pieces in a book which is very much in the classic British tradition of some forty years before and they have not simply a delicacy, but a genuine feeling for the eighteenth century in which they are set and which they depict with such accuracy.

Another French designer whose work became well known to contemporary British readers was Grandville. His illustrations to the translation of *Gulliver's Travels* published by Fournier and Furne in 1838 were used for an English reprint of Jonathan Swift's classic in 1840. They had been preceded by a collection of his work issued as *Illustrated Fables* by Charles Tilt. By the 1850s he was so well known as to have his designs copied and abused in such humorous publications as *Comical People met with at the Great Exhibition* (1851) or *Merry Pictures* (with Phiz and John Leech, 1857). These, however, trivialize what is an extraordinary talent.

39 *Waiter! Waiter!*: wood-engraved vignette after Grandville from his *Petites misères de la vie humaine* (1843) [BL 1459 k 2]

Grandville, whose real name was Jean Ignace Isidore Gérard, was born in 1803, trained in his father's art of miniature painting both with his father and with Mansion in Paris and, after a notable lack of success in this genre, turned to lithography. A violent Republican who had taken an active part in the Revolution of July 1830, it was only natural that his loathing for Louis-Philippe should draw him into Charles Philipon's stable, and the slight exaggeration of the caricaturist marks all his more conventional work. Nevertheless, he avoids the grotesque of the British 'comic' artist and the bias is only noticeable when he can be contrasted with a 'straight' draughtsman.

This is possible if one studies the illustrated editions of two of Louis Reybaud's novels. In 1846 Grandville illustrated *Jérôme Paturot à la recherche d'une position sociale*; in 1849 Tony Johannot was the artist chosen for its sequel, *Jérôme Paturot à la recherche de la meillieure des Républiques*. Perhaps because the format for which Johannot is asked to design is impossibly large, perhaps because the novels are themselves satires, Grandville the caricaturist seems to give his illustrations a bite which the more realistic figures lack.

This astringent quality is, however, best seen in his *Petites misères de la vie humaine* (1843)

40 *Seeing the proof of what she called 'my intemperance'*: full-page wood-engraving after Grandville (*Scènes de la vie privée et publique des animaux*, 1, 1842) [BL 1457 k 1]

41 *A well-dressed insect and a lovely dancer*: full-page wood-engraving after Grandville (*Scènes de la vie privée et publique des animaux*, 1, 1842) [BL 1457 k 1]

[fig. 39] and *Cent proverbes* (1845) and it illuminates his two more classic sets, the designs for Swift's *Les voyages de Gulliver* (1838) and J.P. Béranger's *Œuvres complètes* (1837) [figs 26, 27], and it is its absence from the full-page designs – the vignettes are better – which makes the 1840 Boileau so disappointing. I would, nonetheless, stress the quality of his figure drawing because his reputation both among contemporaries and subsequently has been based so very firmly upon his work as a fantasist of powerful and extraordinary imagination.

Contemporaries, I suspect from the designs most copied by British publishers, saw in him the supreme master of the animal-into-human-being metamorphosis. Even C.H. Bennett and the Swiss artist Ernest Griset, both so popular with the mid-Victorians, fall short of Grandville, his only rival being Thomas Landseer with his extraordinary series of engravings, *Monkey-ana* (1828). Grandville's earliest essay in this vein dates from the same year, 1828, and comprises a series of 73 lithographic prints, which were reproduced as

158   LES GRANDS ET LES PETITS.

s'étaient donné rendez-vous dans cette promenade ne pouvaient être que les grands du pays.

La présence de Puff sembla causer un certain éton-
nement parmi les promeneurs. Les uns le toisaient dédai-
gneusement, les autres se baissaient pour le considérer

42 *Les Grands*: wood-engraving after Granville (*Un autre monde*, 1844) [BL 1458 k 10]

coloured wood-engravings and re-issued in 1854 as *Les metamorphoses du jour* with a text by Taxile Delord and others. Greater mastery is evident in his designs for La Fontaine's *Fables* (1838–40), but his masterpiece in this genre is undoubtedly contained in the two series of *Scènes de la vie privée et publique des animaux* (1840–42) [figs 40, 41] to texts by his publisher, Hetzel, by Balzac, Georges Sand, Charles Nodier, Jules Janin and others.

However, Grandville's continued fame into the twentieth century, when he influenced the Surrealists, has depended very largely upon his even more imaginative flights and his even more violent metamorphoses. Taxile Delord's *Les fleurs animées* (1847), despite its reputation with collectors, is perhaps surpassed by *Un autre monde* (1844) [figs 42, 43; pl. 2], which contains both the best and worst of Grandville's draughtsmanship. Perhaps its most disturbing element, the manifestation of what was to become an unbalanced mind (he was to die in 1847 in an asylum) are its haunting essays in perspective [fig. 44].

LES GRANDS ET LES PETITS.   159

d'un air de pitié insolente. Puff entra dans la ville sans comprendre les motifs d'un tel accueil.

Ce fut bien autre chose quand il eut mis le pied dans la première rue : ouvriers, porteurs d'eau, gens du peuple le regardaient avec des yeux effrontément railleurs, et poussaient des éclats de rire. Voilà une hilarité bien extraordinaire, se dit Puff ; il me semble que ce serait bien plutôt à moi de me moquer de ces avortons si

rapprochés du sol. Singulier pays, où l'on ne voit que hauteur et abaissement ! Les grands sont orgueilleux et les petits impolis : c'est donc ici comme partout !

En continuant sa course, Puff fut constamment accueilli de la même manière et frappé du même spectacle. Tous les gens qui ne faisaient rien étaient très-hauts, et

43 *Les Petits*: wood-engraving after Grandville (*Un autre monde*, 1844) [BL 1458 k 10]

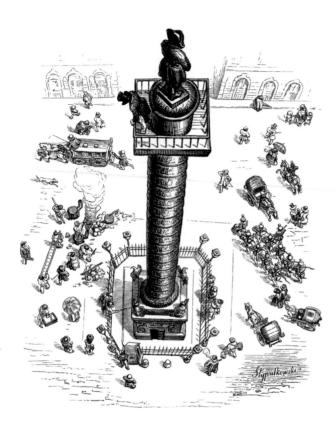

44 A vertiginous view of the column of the Place Vendôme. Napoleon's statue was hurled down by the Comunards in 1871 and replaced by the statue of Liberty in 1874. Wood-engraving after Grandville (*Un autre monde*, 1844) [BL 1458 k 10]

British Engravers and Publishers

Mention of both Johannot's and Grandville's designs in books printed and published in London has been slightly to anticipate this brief survey of the way in which French Romantic book design exerted its influence in Britain. This influence was, indeed, pervasive, since the London trade was kept constantly in touch – at least during the decade from 1835 – with every new development in French book-illustration through the individual craftsmen and the wood-engraving firms who undertook such a substantial number of commissions for Parisian publishers.

From the very start, and although most of the blocks for *Gil Blas* [fig. 45] were cut by French engravers or by such English craftsmen as Beneworth or Elwall as had migrated to Paris, a proportion was engraved in London by John Jackson, Samuel Slader, John and Eliza Thompson and the firm of Wright and Folkard. Indeed, it will have become apparent from the relatively small sample of the French books already mentioned that the sheer quantity of wood-engraving required for their embellishment was such as to be beyond the unaided power of the nascent French craft to supply. Accordingly recourse was had to London, and British engravers helped their Parisian rivals to produce the blocks from which the illustrations of so many of the books were printed.

Of course such French books were readily available through specialist booksellers, whose customers formed part of the far more cosmopolitan society of this period. There was a substantial resident British community in Paris and a constant and ever-increasing flow of visitors and tourists. But above all, the intellectual climate of the age was cosmopolitan by contrast with the insularity of outlook which became increasingly evident after 1848. Dr Kathleen Tillotson remarks this intellectual openness to outside influence in pointing to the way in which French novelists – whose work was regularly reviewed in such magazines as *Blackwood's* and *Fraser's* – influenced British writers.[46] The publishing trade, knowing in advance their Parisian confrères' activities, were able to take advantage of this cosmopolitanism to produce English versions of the French texts and to illustrate them with the designs of French artists which had appeared in the Paris editions.

At the lowest level this involved straightforward piracy by small houses such as Strange which, in 1840, issued an English translation of Laurent de l'Ardèche's *Histoire de l'empereur Napoléon* illustrated by coarse copies of Horace Vernet's designs for the French edition of 1839. Similar crude copies of Jean Gigoux's celebrated illustrations for *Gil Blas* appear in a re-issue of Smollett's translation by Willoughby in 1841. Such piratical copies debased the original designs and a far more potent force was co-publication using copies of the original blocks from which the illustrations of the French edition had been printed. Since this ability to make faithful copies in metal of relief wood-blocks is one of the most important technical developments of the period, it is well worth examining, if only briefly.

As we have seen, both *The Penny Magazine* and *Le magasin pittoresque* printed text and illustrations together from stereotypes. For single blocks and for vignettes especially and for ornaments, dabs or polytypes were generally produced. Both methods needed

45 *The Death of the Hermit*: wood-engraved tail-piece after Jean Gigoux (Lesage, *Gil Blas*, 1835) [BL G 18301]

very considerable skill to reproduce the delicate detail of the black-line wood-engravings used in book work, however effective they might be for the coarser magazine blocks or printer's ornaments. What was required was the means of reproducing in metal an exact replica of the engraved surface and this was achieved in 1839 by the invention of electrotyping.

While the importance of the process in relation to illustrated journalism has been appreciated, its early adoption by the nineteenth-century printing trade for book-illustrations tends to be overlooked. Pre-1839 duplicates of engraved blocks were printed from stereo- or polytypes, and in 1841 the printer and wood-engraver Henry Vizetelly was still employing polytypage to duplicate decorated page-borders.[47] Yet, within a year, when in 1842 Longman published an edition of James Thomson's *The Seasons* illustrated by members of the Etching Club [figs 169, 170], Bolton Corney, the editor of the volume, was writing in his 'Advertisement':

> It may be interesting to the scientific reader to know that the illustrations are printed from copper blocks formed by the electrotype process. This method has been found to be attended with several advantages in printing, besides the means it affords of preserving the original blocks, and of renewing the electrotypes, thus forming a perpetual security against inferior impressions of the designs.

It would thus appear that, while the process itself was recent enough to retain a novelty-interest, it had in a matter of two or three years come into wide, if not general, use at least in Britain. Nevertheless, the older and far cheaper methods persisted and, when in 1845 Longman published an English translation of Leopold von Orlich's *Travels in India*, they purchased for £40 from the Leipzig engravers J.G. Flegel, a set of casts or stereotypes of the rather coarse German illustrations.[48]

From this it might be inferred that the new process was adopted only gradually on the Continent, yet there may be grounds for thinking that French engravers – and especially the printing firm of Lacrampe which specialized in producing wood-engraved *hors-textes* – had acquired electrotyping facilities by 1842 as well.[49] Nevertheless, British readers had, since Charles Tilt issued *Gil Blas* with Gigoux's embellishments in 1836, been able to appreciate the work of French Romantic illustrators in books printed in English whether by poly-, stereo- or electrotypes.

There were, nonetheless, pitfalls, and these are perhaps best demonstrated by considering the edition of *Gulliver's Travels* published *c.*1840 by Hayward & Moore. This they illustrated with the designs made by Grandville for Fournier and Furne's edition of 1838. Unfortunately the British publishers printed them in a royal octavo instead of the crown for which they were drawn. As a result, the integrated vignettes are lost in the larger type-areas of the English edition, and only the full-page vignettes demonstrate their power, although in a way never intended by the artist.

Whereas Charles Tilt could introduce the French *livre romantique* as part of the stock of a bookseller who specialized in French lithographs and in English engravings and illustrated books in general,[50] the vogue for the embellished book and the opportunities for acquiring foreign, and particularly French, illustrations cheaply by purchase from the originating publisher of polytypes or the more faithful electrotypes of the original wood-blocks, provided a wide if speculative market for the smaller publisher. The opportunities and inherent dangers of this trade are typified by the career of Joseph Thomas, who seems to have based the greater part of his list upon it. From Paulin and Dubochet he acquired the set of illustrations designed by Tony Johannot for their 1837 edition of *Don Quichotte* and Horace Vernet's for their 1839 *Vie de l'empereur Napoléon*, wisely substituting in the latter a new life by George Moir Bussy for Laurent de l'Ardèche's exercise in chauvinism. Thomas published both books in 1840 and in the following year took from Ernest Bourdin Johannot's illustrations for Lesage's *Le diable boiteux*. From Paulin again he took the illustrations by a group of French artists, which included Gigoux, Grandville, Monnier and Traviès, for the six-volume *Le livre des enfants* (1836–8), translating Elise Voiart's and Amable Tastu's text as *The Child's Fairy Library* in six volumes.

Nor was his trade one-way: in 1841 Bourdin issued a French translation of Laurence Sterne's *A Sentimental Journey*, taking from Thomas the illustrations designed as integrated vignettes by Joseph Fussell and Charles Jacque [fig. 46], the French artist, and adding full-page vignettes by Tony Johannot. In fact, the book had not originated with Thomas, but had been acquired by him from John Nicholls, who had first published it in London in 1839.

---

18 A SENTIMENTAL JOURNEY	THROUGH FRANCE AND ITALY. 19

certain turn of mind take, Monsieur Dessein, in their own sensations. I'm persuaded, to a man who feels for others as well as for himself, every rainy night, disguise it as you will, must cast a damp upon your spirits. You suffer, Monsieur Dessein, as much as the machine."—

" *C'est bien vrai*," said he. " But in this case, I should only exchange one disquietude for another, and with loss : figure to yourself, my dear sir, that in giving you a chaise which would fall to pieces before you had got half-way to Paris ;—figure to yourself, how much I should suffer in giving an ill impression of myself to a man of honour, and lying at the mercy, as I must do, *d'un homme d'esprit*."

The dose was made up exactly after my own prescription : so I could not help taking it ; and returning Monsieur Dessein his bow, without more casuistry we walked towards his *remise*, to take a view of his magazine of chaises.

I have always observed, when there is as much *sour* as *sweet* in a compliment, that an Englishman is eternally at a loss within himself whether to take it or let it alone : a Frenchman never is.—Monsieur Dessein made me a bow.

46 Wood-engravings after C.E. Jacque, typical of the '*livre à vignettes*' (Sterne, *A Sentimental Journey*, 1839)
[BL 012643 pp 70]

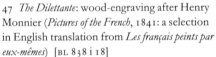

47 *The Dilettante*: wood-engraving after Henry Monnier (*Pictures of the French*, 1841: a selection in English translation from *Les français peints par eux-mêmes*) [BL 838 i 18]

48 *The Speculator*: wood-engraving after Gavarni (*Pictures of the French*, 1841: a selection in English translation from *Les français peints par eux-mêmes*) [BL 838 i 18]

This is where Thomas's weakness lay: the bulk of his books originated in France and very few, even of his English books, were original. As with the Sterne, he tended to take over titles and illustrations from other publishers, 'Thomas's Burlesque Drama', for example, being a re-issue of seven plays illustrated by George and Isaac Robert Cruikshank and first published in the 1820s. Not surprisingly the publishing enterprise went under and Thomas's imprint is only to be found in the few years around 1840–42.

That Thomas's career as a publisher was so short-lived was due to the very simple fact that, despite the cosmopolitanism of the 1840s, a viable list cannot be built on what were essentially second-hand books. How foreign illustrations could be used more wisely within a soundly-based publishing programme is typified by William Orr, who would seem to have been engaged in concerted co-publication schemes with the Parisian publisher Léon Curmer. This involved Orr in publishing in 1839 a translation of *Paul et Virginie* with the illustrations of Curmer's edition of 1838 – but omitting *La chaumière indienne* – and in issuing in the following year in English translation a selection from Curmer's *Les Français peints par eux-mêmes* as *Pictures of the French* [figs 47, 48]. Curmer, for his part, published in 1841 a French translation of Christopher Wordsworth's *Greece*, which Orr had issued in 1839.

Paul et Virginie and *Greece*, moreover, are not simply examples of Anglo-French co-publishing, but of an almost unique Anglo-French style of book-illustration. Set side by side, the influence of the one upon the other is readily apparent. The French element predominates in the section-openings of Wordsworth's book, for which the bulk of the designs were provided by the little-known English artist G.F. Sargent. True the French artists Charles François Daubigny, François Louis Français, Huet, Jacque and Meissonier also contributed, but, whatever the nationality of the artist, these openings are essentially French in their elaboration. Equally British in both books is the style of the small, squared wood-engravings which revert to the Bewick tradition of the white-line rather than to the more fashionable black-line style which superseded it. In this respect both books stand somewhat in isolation. Finally, it should be noted that while *Paul et Virginie* demonstrates the somewhat conservative approach of Curmer in its lavish use of *hors-texte* embellishments, these embellishments are in the French taste for wood-engraved vignettes printed on India paper, mounted and guarded: *Greece* is as typically British with its *hors-texte*, squared, steel-engraved landscapes.

This promising collaboration, however, seems to have been nipped in the bud by the apparent failure of *Pictures of the French*. Although this is as handsome and well-printed a book as any on Orr's list, with spirited contributions from Gavarni and Henry Monnier, the

49 *The Army*: wood-engraved head-piece after C.E. Jacque (*Les français peints par eux-mêmes*, V, 1842) [BL 1457 k 12]

full-page vignettes again pulled on India paper, mounted and guarded, it does not appear to have enjoyed the success of *Paul et Virginie*. While *Les français* was to run to eight volumes between 1840–42 [fig. 49], the only other *Pictures of the French* to appear in England was the rather shoddy volume issued under the imprint of the great remainder merchant and cheap edition publisher Thomas Tegg in 1841. Curmer for his part issued *Les Anglais peints par eux-mêmes*, a translation of Orr's *Heads of the People* published in two volumes (1840–41) with full-page plates by Kenny Meadows.

Orr also provides an instance of the way in which intelligent use of foreign material could add variety to a publisher's list in his children's series, 'Comic Nursery Tales'. These were initiated by a printer, Henry Vizetelly, who had purchased in Paris a set of *clichés* of illustrations by the French caricaturist Cham.[51] These Orr was to use for an English text, but when the series was published in 1843 to meet the current vogue for children's books, it included titles illustrated in the same spirit by the English caricaturists John Leech and Alfred Crowquill.

Orr followed a similar policy when he added to this set of children's books illustrated by monochrome and tinted wood-engravings others in a larger format illustrated in colour. Although John Absolon is credited with the designs in at least eight of the books published in 1844, in four of these instances he is merely the copyist. He certainly executed those for Charles Cowden Clark's *Perseverance* and his *Princess Narina*, and for Mrs S.C. Hall's *Little Chatterbox* and her *Number One*. However, the illustrations for George Gaspey's *Glory* are copies of French engravings designed by Lorentz, Horace Vernet and others. Similarly, those for J.D. Haas's *The Savoyard Boy* are copied from the French, while those for Mary Howitt's *The Picture of the Virgin* and her *The Curate's Favourite Pupil* – adapted from the German of Christoph Schmid and Karl Stober respectively – are copies of Julius Nisle's and, apparently, of Ludwig Richter's originals.

Yet it is not so much in these direct borrowings as in the influence exerted upon the design and layout of books which he himself originated that William Orr's list is of interest. By 1847 it included fiction in the early novels of Charles Lever; poetry, 'Orr & Co's Cabinet Editions' of the standard poets; children's and school books; humour; and, among the illustrated books, Byron's *Poems and Tales*, with steel-engravings after Henry Warren was in 1848 to join the edition of Shakespeare with designs by Kenny Meadows first published in 1843. However, its basis was the series of practical books, mainly botany, horticulture and farming, which included such miscellaneous items as *Walker's Manly Exercises*. The eighth edition revised by 'Craven' shows how, even in this apparently unpromising category, French influence could affect the design of a practical handbook.

The illustration – and it is genuine elucidation of the text – comprises sixty-four *hors-texte*, copper-engraved plates which by the eighth edition were showing very obvious signs of wear. What gives the book its unmistakably Romantic feeling is, however, the way in which it is further embellished. Frontispiece and vignette title-page are supplied in a tinted wood-engraving, there are vignette head- and tail-pieces also engraved on wood while the pages – and this is so typically French – are surrounded by a double rule border. Similarly, Orr shows his sympathy for the French in the treatment he gave to the only one of Charles Lever's novels for the publication of which he was solely responsible.

The conventional way of illustrating novels, and especially those published in parts, was with the *hors-texte* steel-etching. Only one major novelist, Thackeray, consistently supplemented these with integrated wood-engraved vignettes and wood-engraved initials, and only once does Dickens, in his *Old Curiosity Shop* [fig. 159] and *Barnaby Rudge*, abandon steel altogether in favour of the integrated wood-engraving — but then they appear in *Master Humphrey's Clock*, planned as a magazine and retaining magazine format and embellishment. In *The Tower of London* (1840) Harrison Ainsworth has integrated architectural subjects engraved on wood and follows the same practice in *Windsor Castle*, which also contains a number of openings in the French Romantic style designed by W.A. Delamotte. In this it is, perhaps, unique, for the standard embellishment of the English novel in the Romantic period is simply the steel-etched *hors-texte* illustration. Nor are Charles Lever's now-forgotten best-selling novels an exception to this general rule and only in *Jack Hinton the Guardsman*, which forms the first volume of *Our Mess* (1843), are some half-a-dozen small wood-engravings integrated into the text.

An Irish doctor, Lever's early novels were published between 1839 and 1845 by William Curry of Dublin for whom William Orr acted as London agent. In 1844 Lever changed publishers, first to Henry Colburn with *Arthur O'Leary*, and then to Chapman & Hall who were to remain his publishers for the next twenty years or more. In 1849, however, Lever published *The Confessions of Con Cregan* with William Orr. The essentials of the illustrations, provided by Phiz, his regular illustrator, are the series of steel-etched *hors-textes* which are *de rigueur* for the English novel of the period. Where Orr made his influence felt was in the format, which he reduced from the standard demy to crown octavo, and in commissioning from Phiz a series of designs for wood-engraved chapter openings, combining a headpiece in a modified form of the French style with an initial letter [fig. 50]. It is the interesting aberrant from the publisher of illustrated books who was not a regular publisher of new fiction.

50 Wood-engraved chapter-opening after Phiz (Hablot Knight Browne) (Lever, *The Confessions of Con Cregan*, 1849) [BL 12620 C 18]

CHAPTER ·XXVII·

"GUAJAQUALLA."

HERE are few things in this world gold cannot buy; but one among their number assuredly is—"a happy dream." Now, although I went

Finally, mention must be made of what was probably Orr's most successful book, the collection of parodies by W.E. Aytoun and Theodore Martin, *Bon Gualtier's Book of Ballads* [fig. 51]. First published in 1845 with some of the best work of the caricaturist Alfred Crowquill to illustrate it, the later augmented editions are augmented in their turn by the designs of John Leech and Richard Doyle. Crowquill's embellishments are engraved on wood and fully integrated with the text within the picture frame of rule borders. It is a most attractive example of the French style adapted to a British book and, significantly, was printed for Orr by Henry Vizetelly, himself a most important figure both in the context of French influence and of British book design in general.

Henry Vizetelly (1820–94) was the third generation of printers in a family of Italian origin which had been settled in London since the late seventeenth century. He was apprenticed to the wood-engraver George Bonner, himself the nephew of Robert Branston the elder,

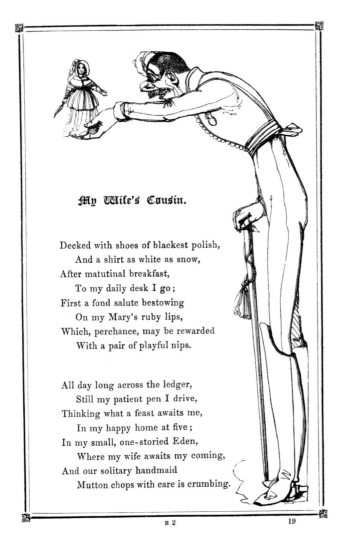

My Wife's Cousin.

Decked with shoes of blackest polish,
    And a shirt as white as snow,
After matutinal breakfast,
    To my daily desk I go;
First a fond salute bestowing
    On my Mary's ruby lips,
Which, perchance, may be rewarded
    With a pair of playful nips.

All day long across the ledger,
    Still my patient pen I drive,
Thinking what a feast awaits me,
    In my happy home at five;
In my small, one-storied Eden,
    Where my wife awaits my coming,
And our solitary handmaid
    Mutton chops with care is crumbing.

B 2   19

51 *My Wife's Cousin*: wood-engraving after Crowquill (*Bon Gualtier's Book of Ballads*, 1845) [BL 1466 b 15]

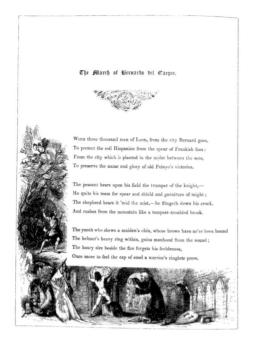

52 *The March of Bernardino del Carpio*: wood-engravings after Henry Warren (Lockhart, *Ancient Spanish Ballads*, 1840) [BL 640 k 22]

founder of the London – as opposed to Bewick's Newcastle – school of wood-engraving, through the partnership between his father and Branston's son, Robert.

Bonner was one of the most skilled practitioners of his craft. From him the young Henry Vizetelly was to gain a thorough grounding in the art of wood-engraving. However, in 1836, before Vizetelly could complete his indentures, Bonner died and his apprentice served out the remainder of his time with an equally fine engraver, John Orrin Smith.

It was here that Vizetelly first encountered the work of the French Romantic illustrators, for Orrin Smith's shop was one of the most active of those accepting commissions from Parisian publishers.[52] Among the books to which reference has already been made, his work is to be found in the Molière of 1835–6, the Cervantes of 1837, *Les saints évangiles* (1836), *L'histoire de … Napoléon* (1839) and *Les français peints par eux-mêmes* (1840–42), and it continues to be found up to his death in 1843. He was, moreover, closely concerned in engraving blocks for Léon Curmer's edition of *Paul et Virginie*. Among the designs for the book those by the then unknown French artist Meissonier so deeply impressed the entire work-room by their microscopic detail that Smith's apprentice was to recall their effect half a century and more later in his memoirs.[53] It is not fanciful, therefore, to suggest that very early in his working life Henry Vizetelly came to appreciate the virtues of Parisian book design.

When he came to join the family firm of Vizetelly & Branston, Printers, Henry was the skilled engraver who was subsequently proud to record that the artist Frederick Tayler had congratulated him upon engraving his designs for the 1842 Etching Club edition of

James Thomson's *The Seasons* with the remark that the work was 'cut with much feeling and expression' [fig. 170].[54] Yet he could not find satisfaction in the exercise of his art alone and, after his father's death following the unfortunate speculations which brought down the firm, he determined to salvage something from the wreck. With his elder brother he established the new firm of Vizetelly Brothers, Printers, and with this he retrieved the family fortunes.

While one would not claim for their productions the typographical distinction achieved by Charles Whittingham the younger, Vizetelly's own skill as a wood-engraver enabled him to succeed the elder Whittingham as one of the best printers of wood-engravings of his day. He was, indeed, fortunate to be able to demonstrate this skill very early in his printing career when, in 1840–41, John Murray entrusted the fledgling firm and its 21-year-old master with

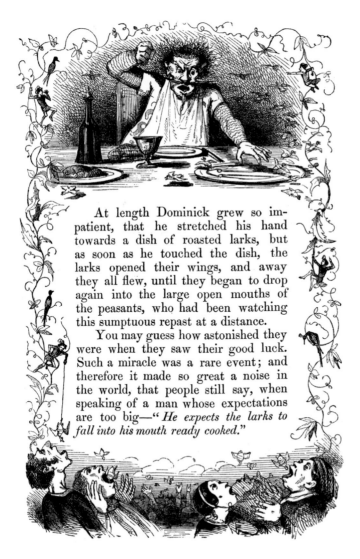

At length Dominick grew so impatient, that he stretched his hand towards a dish of roasted larks, but as soon as he touched the dish, the larks opened their wings, and away they all flew, until they began to drop again into the large open mouths of the peasants, who had been watching this sumptuous repast at a distance.

You may guess how astonished they were when they saw their good luck. Such a miracle was a rare event; and therefore it made so great a noise in the world, that people still say, when speaking of a man whose expectations are too big—"*He expects the larks to fall into his mouth ready cooked.*"

53 Wood-engraved page-decorations after Bertall (Dumas, *Good Lady Bertha's Honey Broth*, 1846) [BL 012807 df 50]

the very heavy responsibility of producing a superbly embellished edition of J.G. Lockhart's *Ancient Spanish Ballads* [fig. 52].

This was the first of three books produced for Murray by the joint efforts of Vizetelly and Owen Jones, Jones being responsible for the overall design of the books – including the bindings and, where appropriate, the end-papers – and, of course, for designing and printing chromolithographic title and half-title pages for all three.[55] However, the engraving and printing of the decorative borders and initial letters from Jones's designs were Vizetelly's responsibility and result in a *tour de force* of two- and three-colour pages. In addition to Owen Jones's designs, other artists contributed numerous vignette and full-page illustrations cut by Vizetelly and demonstrating, in the full-page engravings, a technique in which he excelled – that of the tinted wood-engraving.

This is a device borrowed from the lithographer by which a tint – generally yellow but sometimes grey – is used to heighten the black of the design. Nor need it be a flat tint, but can be broken to allow the white of the paper to help to achieve the desired effect. An obvious example of this occurs in landscape designs – both in lithography and in wood-engraving – where the tint can be broken to suggest cloud, but the technique can be just as effectively employed to highlight any detail in a given design.

So much for the artistic effects. No less important to the printer was the use of the yellow tint when printing in gold – one of Vizetelly's specialities. Until comparatively recently no gold ink has been available which will print directly on to paper. In Vizetelly's time, gold required to be printed on a base of yellow ink, hence the combination of gold with the tinted wood-engraving was both artistically effective and economical into the bargain.

Obviously Vizetelly was not the only engraver to employ this technique, nor was he the first. The edition of *Manon Lescaut* published by Ernest Bourdin in 1839, for example, has a frontispiece portrait of the author after Wattier, reproduced as a tinted wood-engraving.[56] It was a technique which could be employed for all classes of work, from luxurious books produced for John Murray to cheap ephemera. It is used for the 'plain' copies of Thackeray's *Christmas Books* and, to my taste at least, such copies of *Mrs Perkin's Ball* (1846 for 1847) or *Our Street* (1847 for 1848), challenge the 'coloured' copies. Yet what Vizetelly would probably have regarded as the culmination of his work as a printer is *Christmas with the Poets*, published by David Bogue (1850 for 1851). With its tinted wood-engravings from designs by Birket Foster and its lavish use of gold in initial letters, their marginal extensions and the rule borders which surround the whole, it may appear somewhat extravagant to modern taste, but it more than satisfied contemporaries. At the time of the Great Exhibition of 1851 and when the organizers had failed to provide a class for printed books, the authorities at the British Museum put a copy of *Christmas with the Poets* on show as an example of contemporary British fine printing.

Contemporaries thus paid tribute to Vizetelly both as an engraver and as a printer both of letterpress and of wood-engravings, yet his legacy could be assessed as a designer of books and as a prime channel of French influence. The recent phenomenon of the publisher's typographic designer should not blind us to the vital part played by the printer in the design of books up to the mid-twentieth century. Naturally the printer always worked in close association with the publisher – a classic example of this is the collaboration between

William Pickering and Charles Whittingham the younger – but the printer was often able to introduce his own ideas. In Vizetelly's case these ideas were inspired by the French Romantic book and were realized in his work for a number of different publishers.

Two very good examples may be seen in books printed for Longman. The first, a collection of sketches by the north-country journalist 'Martingale', *Sporting Scenes and Country Characters* (1840), could hardly be more British in theme or illustration – the designs are by Henry Alken and Sir Edwin Landseer, among others. Nevertheless, the enclosing of the text with its integrated wood-engravings within rule borders and, in particular, the decorative style of head-pieces and initial letters at the chapter-openings make this one of the British books of the period most strongly influenced by French Romantic design. Somewhat similar in style is another book printed for Longman by Vizetelly, Richard Lane's *Life at a*

CHAPTER X.

Namur – The Blancq' Klocq' – View on the Sambre – The Stilt-Fighters – The Melans and the Avresses – The Field of Battle – The Canon of St. Aubain – Poem on Stilt-Fighting – Rules of the Combat – The Brigades – Edicts against the Stilters – Revival of the Games – The last Fight – Renewed Prohibition – Attempts at Revival – The Bleus and Nankinets – The last Exhibition.

THE situation of Namur, at the confluence of the Meuse and Sambre, is very fine; but the city itself does not contain much that is attractive,—at least for those who visit Belgium in the expectation of meeting everywhere with fine pictures and quaint architecture. It once boasted a

54 Chapter-opening to Dudley Costello's *Tour through the Valley of the Meuse* (1846): wood-engravings from the author's sketches [BL 1430 f 11]

Water Cure (1846). Lane, who describes himself as 'Lithographer to Her Majesty and HRH the Prince Albert', provided a lithographic frontispiece and one plate and a number of rather mediocre designs for wood-engraving, most attractively presented, with text and image integrated within the frame of rule-borders. This preference for a similarly integrated page can be seen in such diverse books produced by Vizetelly as the revised and enlarged edition of *The Boy's Own Book* (David Bogue, 1846) or the charming first edition of *Bon Gualtier's Book of Ballads* (Orr, 1845).

As we have seen, in 1843 Vizetelly had printed for Orr the series of 'Comic Nursery Tales', with *clichés* purchased in Paris. Subsequently he acquired electros of the engravings which Hetzel had used to illustrate his series *Le nouveau magasin des enfants*, for a group of children's books which he printed for Chapman & Hall in 1846. 'Picture Story Books by

PROCESSIONS. 223

the Third conferring on St. Rombant his mission to the Low Countries, and surrounded by a group of cardinals, no doubt very much astonished to find themselves in the presence of a pope who flourished several centuries before the first creation of cardinals. With these came a crowd of saints, allegorical personages, heralds, huntsmen, pages, chamberlains, the great officers of the Crown, the court and royal family; a vessel with three masts, *steered by St. Catherine;* a family of giants, Fortune and her wheel, Venus and Cupid on horseback, and, finally, the famous courser, Bayard. The *Ommeganck*, or " Procession of Giants," at Brussels, would also have been incomplete without him.

55 Wood-engraving after the author's sketch (Costello, *Tour through the Valley of the Meuse*, 1846) [BL 1430 f 11]

THE ROCHE A BAYARD.

Great Authors and Great Painters' were published at 8*d*. per volume and in this laudable attempt to reduce the price, printer and publisher economized on the quality of the paper. As a result, the engravings are not shown to the advantage of the original French edition [fig. 53].

Such activities are consonant with Vizetelly's intimate and varied connections with the Parisian publishing trade. He was on close terms with Fillineau, who acted as agent for French publishers sending blocks to London for engraving, and when Fillineau was looking for a way of running a smuggled cargo of English binder's cloth across the Channel it was Vizetelly, with his intimate knowledge of the Whitstable smuggling fraternity, who acted as contact man in this abortive scheme.[57] On a more legitimate basis, he continued Orrin Smith's practice of engraving for the Parisian trade, and his signature is to be found, for example, on engravings in *Le jardin des plantes* (Curmer, 1842) and *Les beautés de l'opéra* (1845). But these are really peripheral activities, for, like Ebenezer Landells who backed *Punch*, Vizetelly immediately saw the lucrative market which illustrated journalism offered a wood-engraver with the capital, facilities and journeymen available. Thus he was one of Herbert Ingram's close associates in the foundation of *The Illustrated London News* in 1842, parting company with him to establish two successive and rival periodicals, the short-lived *Pictorial Times* and *The Illustrated Times* which Ingram subsequently purchased from Vizetelly and suppressed.

Superficially, Vizetelly can be dismissed as an opportunist, an entrepreneur who used every available means to make a profit – engraving, printing, illustrated journalism, trade in electrotypes, speculation in book-publishing. What distinguishes him are his skill as a printer and his high standards as a designer, and among his triumphs in the second role must surely be included Dudley Costello's *A Tour through the Valley of the Meuse* (1846) [figs 54, 55]. Here the wood-engraved vignettes from the author's sketches are imaginatively integrated with the text, the arrangement of the chapter-openings being particularly happy. In addition, his letterpress is always unobtrusively good and his printing of tinted and coloured wood-engraving excellent, so that a very high proportion of the finest illustrated British books of the Romantic period will be found to have emanated from Vizetelly Brothers, Printers.

NOTES

1 *Le livre français*, 122.

2 *La gravure sur bois au XIXe siècle*, 14a.

3 Ibid., 19a–20a.

4 He became insane in 1817.

5 *The Masters of Wood-engraving*, 166.

6 Didot, *Essai sur la gravure sur bois*, 281.

7 François Ambroise Didot had invented the point system for classifying type sizes *c.*1775; his son Pierre l'Aîné produced, among other fine books, the celebrated *éditions du Louvre* of the French classical authors in 1797; Leger Didot built the first paper-making machine in France in 1810,

and Henri was to invent a type-casting machine in 1823.

8 See pp. 72–3.

9 Blachon, *La gravure sur bois* ..., 50b–52a, 202b–203a.

10 Ibid., 72.

11 Ibid.

12 Ibid., 73.

13 Ibid., 118ff., 204–5.

14 *Causeries*, 181ff.

15 *Passages of a Working Life*, II, 114–15.

16 *A Treatise on Wood Engraving* (1861), 619ff.

17 *The London and Westminster Review*, XXXI, ii, 272.

18 *A Treatise on Wood Engraving* (1861), 624.

19 Ibid., 625.

20 *The Penny Magazine*, supplements for Oct./Nov. and Dec. 1833; *Le magasin pittoresque*, 1834, 408ff.

21 Basil Hunnisett, *Steel-engraved Book Illustration in England*, 10–31.

22 6th edn (1842), 47.

23 Hunnisett, *Steel-engraved Book Illustration in England*, 135–6.

24 Frederick W. Faxon (*Literary Annuals and Gift Books*) has traced the vogue from Rudolph Ackermann's solitary *Forget-me-not*, inspired by the German *Taschenbuch*, in 1823, to a peak of no less than 63 annuals in 1832. They declined to 20 by 1845 and closed with just three in 1853. In their heyday they could make considerable profits. For instance, Alaric Watts, who edited the long-running *Literary Souvenir*, records that the 1827 edition cost £2,620 to produce in an edition of 10,169 copies on ordinary and 750 copies on large paper. Receipts from sales between November 1826 and April 1827 amounted to £3,283, excluding the price received for the 700 copies sold to an American publisher and the 1,400-odd ordinary paper and the 222 large-paper copies in stock in April, but believed by Watts to have been sold at full price (A.A. Watts, *Alaric Watts*, 1, 250).

25 Hunnisett, *Steel-engraved Book Illustration in England*, 161.

26 *The Paris Sketch Book* (1840), II, 4.

27 'Our Annual Execution', Jan. 1839, 63.

28 There are exceptions, but I believe them to have been rare, having myself encountered only three novels illustrated by steel-engravings: Captain Marryat's *The Pirate and The Three Cutters* (1836), illustrated by Clarkson Stanfield, Sarah Stickney's *Family Secrets* (1843), illustrated by Edward Corbould and her *Social Distinctions* (1848–9), illustrated by Henry Warren.

29 Buchanan-Brown, *Phiz!*, 21.

30 Hunnisett, *Steel-engraved Book Illustration in England*, 64–9.

31 F.H. Man, *Artists' Lithographs*, 1–14.

32 '… it was extremely influential. The first important publication of Ackermann's [lithographic] press in London, *Albert Durer's designs of the Prayer Book* … 1817 … was a version of it … Another edition was produced by Stuntz in 1820 … Further editions were published by Stöger in 1839 and 1845' (Twyman, *Early Lithographed Books*, 204).

33 'Caricature and Lithography in Paris', *The Paris Sketch Book* (1840), II, 4, 3.

34 Figures from Altick, *The English Common Reader*, 382.

35 Ibid., 54ff., 264.

36 Hunnisett, *Steel-engraved Book Illustration in England*, 153ff.

37 *See* Bechtel, *Freedom of the Press, passim*.

38 *See* p. 229.

39 *Causeries*, 176.

40 Ibid., 180.

41 *Le livre français*, 121.

42 Marie, *Alfred et Tony Johannot*, 18.

43 Ellis, *William Harrison Ainsworth and his Friends*, 1, 430 (misdated 1841).

44 Vaughan, *German Romantic Painting*, 208.

45 Ibid., 22.

46 *Novels of the Eighteen-forties*, 7–9.

47 See p. 151.

48 These the London engraver Robert Branston the younger mounted on wood, charging £3 for this and for the provision of two sets of proofs (Longman Archive, Impression Book X, 240).

49 See p. 157.

50 For a survey of his activities see pp. 157ff.

51 'Philipon … published in 1842 in one of his periodicals a series of humorous illustrations to "Bluebeard" designed by Cham, and followed these up with other illustrations to Perrault's popular "Contes" treated in a similar grotesque fashion' (Henry Vizetelly, *Glances Back*, 1, 210–11).

52 There is a medallion portrait of Orrin Smith in the vignette following the list of illustrations in his *Paul et Virginie* (1838).

53 Henry Vizetelly, *Glances Back*, 1, 145.

54 Ibid., II, 202.

55 For Jones's part see pp. 150ff.

56 By contrast, however, with the technical perfection of the plates for *Spanish Ballads*, not all impressions of the portrait produced a perfect image: of the two copies in the British Library in one (838 k 10) the colours are clean, but in the other (1456 k 10) they are blurred.

57 Henry Vizetelly, *Glances Back*, 1, 192.

II

GERMAN INFLUENCES

Techniques of Graphic Reproduction

While developments in the production and design of British and French illustrated books run easily and chronologically in parallel, German book-illustration in the period does not fall into this comfortable pattern. The reasons for this are manifold – geographical, economic and cultural – but the overall effect is for the German book to stand somewhat apart. So German critics might see the Romantic period as coming at the end of a century of development,[1] whereas British and French critics would regard it as a part, and indeed as the beginning, of the wider pattern of nineteenth-century typography and literature. Again, the economic developments – industrialization and urbanization – which created the market for cheap mass-circulation periodicals and books, occur somewhat later in Germany, so that eighteenth-century conditions survive when in Britain and France publishing had moved fully into the industrial age of the nineteenth century. Finally, although the War of Liberation (1813–14) had aroused the national consciousness and set in motion a drive towards German reunification, it would be wrong to think of German book art as a national manifestation. Rather it is the expression of the individual artist's affiliation to a strong regional culture, as Hamburg, Dresden and Berlin in the cases of Speckter, Richter and Hosemann respectively.

Yet it would be totally wrong to consider Germany in any way a backwater. On the contrary, German Romantic and Revivalist schools of painting were the leaders of early nineteenth-century European art and were profoundly to influence British painting and thus inevitably British book-illustration. They were, however, but one manifestation of that confident upsurge in all departments of German life, in commerce and industry as much as in scholarship and the arts, which was the inevitable consequence of the victorious War of Liberation. This not simply led to the downfall of Napoleon, but to the casting-off of a French cultural dominance as old as the seventeenth century and to the revival of a new and immensely energizing national consciousness. If, then, socio-economic factors caused the retention of copper-engraving, the older method of reproducing illustrations, up to about 1840 in German books, thereafter the new techniques of wood- and steel-engraving came rapidly into their own.

In so far as wood-engraving was concerned, geography dictated that the British revival of the end-grain technique should be transmitted as much via Paris as directly through British engravers working in Germany – and this despite the fact that in Germany alone of Continental countries wood-cutting had survived to the end of the eighteenth century. Yet although the main practitioner in the early nineteenth century, Wilhelm Gubitz (1786–1870) of Berlin, was neither an artist nor a craftsman of the first rank, the tradition was there, to be applied now to end-grain engraving. Expansion thereafter was rapid after an initial period during which the German publishing trade had to rely upon foreign craftsmen.

Prominent among these was the Parisian firm of Andrew, Best and Leloir, but at least one commission went to London, where British craftsmen engraved all but one of Eugen Neureuther's designs for J.G. von Herder's *Der Cid* (1838). However, German craftsmen gained their most useful insights into the techniques of end-grain engraving and of 'lowering' the block from foreigners who emigrated to German publishing centres. Among them was a Frenchman, Peupin, but the most important would clearly have been the English group which included John Allanson, William Nicholls and M.U. Sears. (The latter had moved from London to Paris in the 1830s, to Leipzig in the 1840s, only to return to London in the 1850s.)

Economic factors must clearly have motivated these emigrant craftsmen, but cash was not the sole consideration. In London the status of the facsimile engraver was simply that of the skilled craftsman: in Germany he enjoyed considerably more respect. There, as part of the reorganized teaching of the applied arts, wood-engraving had become a recognized subject, and its teachers, such as the great Hugo Bürkner of the Akademischen Atelier für Holtzschnitte in Dresden, were given professorial status. This same respect for the craftsman may also be observed in such a seeming triviality as his signature on the wood-block which he had engraved. In London it was the accepted custom of the trade that even if the journeyman had cut the block it would be signed, not by the journeyman, but by his master. In Germany, however, both the assistant who actually engraved the block and his master's firm have their names below or on the design.

Among this new generation of German engravers Hugo Bürkner is outstanding as teacher, engraver and designer for wood-engraving, a good example of his work in two of these roles being the vignettes for Rosalie Koch's book of children's religious verse, *Stilleben* (1856) [fig. 56]. Nor should individuals such as F. Unzelmann, E. Kretzschmar, A. Vogel, or

56 Hugo Bürkner as
artist and engraver
(Koch, *Stilleben*, 1856)
[BL 1362 k 17]

W. Georgy, to mention but a few, nor such firms as J.G. Flegel of Leipzig, or Braun und Dessauer and Braun und Schneider be forgotten. From them developed an industry more than capable of cutting unaided the ever-increasing amount of wood-engraving commissioned by the periodical and book publishers of the 1850s and 1860s.

Very much the same pattern may be seen in steel-engraving in Germany at this time. Here, however, British influence was far stronger. The technique was wholly new and wholly British, and London publishers exploited the situation to engage in a large and lucrative export sale of British engravings to the Continent. London engravers, too, found a market for their skill in engraving steels for Continental publishers. In this respect France and Germany were on more or less an equal footing. In 1836, for example, Finden engraved the plates for the publisher Eugène Renduel's illustrated edition of Victor Hugo's *Notre Dame de Paris* [fig. 230] and similarly in 1843 Eugène Lami's designs for Jules Janin's *L'été à Paris* [fig. 228] were sent to London for engraving on steel.[2] The same practice was followed in Germany where, for example, the Stuttgart publisher Cotta sent the bulk of Wilhelm Kaulbach's designs for an illustrated edition of Goethe's works to London for engraving in 1845. In addition, individual steel-engravers took their skills abroad just as did wood-engravers. In France, for example, we find a T. Doherty working as a steel-engraver in the period, while James Outhwaite worked consistently for French publishers for a period of over twenty years *c*.1840–60, and became a French citizen.

Yet perhaps as useful an indicator as any of the state of steel-engraving in Germany at the end of the 1830s is provided by a major publishing project using the medium, *Das malerische und romantische Deutschland*. In these twelve volumes of German topography published between 1836 and 1842 there are about 450 steel-engravings.[3] Of this number, close on 80 per cent were engraved by thirty-three British engravers, either as individuals, as firms, or, in two instances, as partners of German engravers.[4] The remaining plates, slightly over 20 per cent of the total, were engraved by thirty-one different German craftsmen, hailing from Berlin, Darmstadt, Dresden, Leipzig, Munich, Nurnburg, Rudolstadt, Stuttgart and Vienna. A number of the plates were both engraved and printed in London, others may have been engraved there but printed in Leipzig, where at least three presses had been set up to print steel-engravings – F.A. Zehl, R.O.O. Binders's Kunst Verlag and the Englische Kunst Anstalt (perhaps also known as the Englische Druckerei) – while there were two presses at Darmstadt, C. Susemihl und Sohn and its successor E. Grünewald, the map-publishers G. Serz of Nurnburg and J.H. Leiderhecker of Stuttgart. Other plates again were engraved by Englishmen working in Germany and printed on one or other of the presses mentioned above. Henry Winkles, for example, seems to have been associated with Binders's Kunst Verlag until he formed his own firm in 1843, A.H. Payne had already founded the Englische Kunst Anstalt, while an engraver called Cooke worked as partner with or assistant to E. Grünewald.

While it is certainly possible positively to categorize certain British engravers as emigrants, the evidence so far available is too fragmentary to draw firm conclusions in every case.[5] I would therefore suggest that of the thirty-three individuals or firms engaged upon *Das malerische und romantische Deutschland*, about half may have emigrated either before the book was published, or in anticipation of its publication, or as a direct consequence of having received commissions to engrave for it, while there is no evidence that any of the others ever left London. Nevertheless, one can conclude that, as in the case of wood-engraving, the German trade was anxious to acquire knowledge of and experience in the new process; that unlike wood-engraving there was no pre-existing base on which to build; that German energy rapidly solved the problem of training their own copper-engravers and printers to handle the new medium, but that in order to do so they had far more need of British expertise than was the case of wood-engraving. Thus very many more steel-engravers than wood-engravers can be found to have worked in Germany – the converse is true in France – and their numbers do in some degree justify the author of an article in *The Art Union Journal* who, in 1839, sounded the alarm at this drain of British craftsmen.[6]

If the growth of the two new engraving media was therefore slower in Germany than in Britain and in France, by mid-century all three countries were upon an equal technical footing. In the interim, however, German publishers continued to employ copper-engraving and, as might be expected in the country of its origin, lithography as a general rather than a special medium of illustration.

Professional Illustrators

The explosion of illustrated books in Britain and France in the 1830s and, above all, the birth of illustrated journalism which accompanied it and its rapid growth in the 1840s, created the professional illustrator – the draughtsman or painter who drew his income not from the sale of his easel pictures but from the commissions which he received from book and periodical publishers – on a scale dwarfing such English precursors as Thomas Stothard, John Thurston or William Marshal Craig. The conditions for this revolution came later into operation in Germany and consequently the number of professional illustrators active at this time is distinctly limited. They are nonetheless individually of considerable interest and they belong to a strong tradition of book-illustration.

Whereas the French eighteenth-century masters Charles Nicolas Cochin (1715–90), Jean Honoré Fragonard (1732–1806), Pierre Clement Marillier (1740–1808), Jean Michel Moreau le Jeune (1741–1814) and Pierre Paul Prud'hon (1758–1823) represent the end of an era to which earlier representatives are Hubert François Gravelot (1699–1773) and Charles Eisen (1720–78), with only Alexandre Desenne (1785–1827) to carry on the tradition, the German illustrator of European reputation Nicholas Chodowiecki (1726–1801) seemed to herald an age of German artistic revival. Although their direct influence may best be seen in his immediate successors and such longer-lived contemporaries as John Heinrich Ramberg (1763–1840), whose illustrations to Goethe's *Faust* have a distinctly eighteenth-century flavour, his moral influence was perhaps even more important. This, coupled with the European eminence of German painting, meant that the three artists whom we shall be discussing could each develop his own very different style with a confidence which contemporary French illustrators might seem to have lacked.

Theodor Hosemann (1807–75) studied art at Dusseldorf *c.*1821–8 before returning to Berlin to practise as a genre painter in oils and watercolours. In fact, he was to build a much greater reputation as an illustrator and caricaturist and his lithographs of Berlin and the

Berliners won him the name of the German Gavarni. His output, though prolific, was not so extensive as that of the Parisian artist, Felix Man crediting him with 600 lithographs and Arthur Rümann with contributions to more than 340 books.[7]

In his book-work, generally reproduced as copper-engraving, frequently hand-coloured, he is happiest when commenting upon the Berlin social scene as in such serial publications as A. Brennglas's *Berlin wie es ist* (1837–46) [pl. 3]. The same delicacy and humour are to be found in his designs for W. Bornemann's *Gedichte in plattdeutscher Mundart* (1843). All are reproduced by copper-engraving as are the competent but uninspired set for the complete works of E.T.A. Hoffmann (1844–5). Indeed, Hosemann's genius lay in recording the contemporary scene and as a result he is not at his best in the eighteenth century of F.W. Zacarie's *Der Renommist* (1840), nor in his illustrations to *Munchausen Reisen* (1849). The latter have considerable delicacy and charm, but miss completely the grotesque elements of burlesque which are the essence of the text and were so well caught by the vigour of Gustave Doré.

Hosemann was also a leading illustrator of children's books and his earlier designs had all the delicate irony of his adult work. Unfortunately as time went by a certain coarseness crept in, seen perhaps at its worst in his designs for the coloured wood-engravings of A. Glassbenner's *Die Insel Marzipan* (1851). It is possible that by this time Hosemann's style was becoming old-fashioned and that his attempts to satisfy a new generation of readers failed because they demanded something alien to his artistic nature. At all events he would appear to have come to grief with Gerstäker, his illustrations for the first volume of *Nach Amerika* (1855) being deemed insufficiently full-blooded for the Wild West adventures of the German R.M. Ballantyne, and the illustration of the last four volumes was entrusted to C. Reinhardt.

If Hosemann was supreme among his fellow Berliners and in his favourite Berlin, so Hamburg was the city of Otto Speckter (1807–71). Far less prolific than Hosemann as a book-illustrator – Rümann lists a mere forty-four titles[8] – his work is nonetheless intrinsically interesting and he himself notable as one of the not always representative minority of German designers whose work was published contemporaneously in Britain. Here he made his debut in 1844 when Longman published *A Children's Picture and Verse Book, commonly called Otto Speckter's Fable Book.*

Although Speckter had designed the illustrations, the author of the fables was, in fact, Wilhelm Hey, and the English translation comprised the two collections *Fünfzig Fabeln* and *Noch Fünfzig Fabeln*, first published in 1833 and 1837 respectively. These early editions in themselves provide an interesting commentary upon the development of German techniques of graphic reproduction. The designs for the first edition of *Fünfzig Fabeln* appear to have been printed by lithography, those of the third edition of 1836 by copper-etching; it was not until the two series were issued in a combined volume in 1840 that Wilhelm Gubitz of Berlin was employed to engrave Speckter's designs on wood. Rümann notes that the Hamburg publisher Friedrich Perthes issued a simultaneous edition in French translation.[9] Unfortunately I have not had the opportunity of examining either of these 1840 editions and can therefore only suggest that the somewhat coarse wood-engravings in the English translation of 1844 may be printed from stereo- or electrotypes of the Gubitz set. The fables would seem to have found a welcome among English readers for in 1858 George Routledge issued a new edition as *One Hundred Picture Fables* in which the Dalziel Brothers, who engraved the blocks, claimed that: 'OTTO SPECKTER had drawn the pictures on the Wood. They have been engraved expressly for this edition.' They and the illustrations for all the separate editions mentioned above differ in detail – and sometimes considerably – the one from the other. The same is true of those which Speckter designed for wood-engraving in the English language versions, *Fifty Fables for Children* and *Other Fifty Fables*, published by F.A. Perthes at Gotha in 1867 and 1869 respectively.

Meanwhile in 1844 John Murray had published *Puss in Boots* and followed it in 1847 with *The Charmed Roe*, in both children's books reproducing by lithography designs which Speckter had made for German publishers. In 1847 more lithographic copies of Speckter's designs appeared, this time from Chapman & Hall in *The Shoes of Fortune*, a small collection of fairy stories by Hans Andersen. If Speckter's contribution to British children's book art seems slight in quantity it must have clearly had considerable impact in terms of popularity with the British public. This can perhaps be gauged by his being commissioned to contribute designs for the 1861 edition of Mrs Gatty's *Parables from Nature* in the illustrious company of Millais, Tenniel and Burne-Jones.

As might be expected of the illustrator of Wilhelm Hey, Speckter excels as an animal artist, delightful examples of his work being found in C.F. von Rumohr's *Kynalepokomachia* (1847) [fig. 57]. Although, too, Speckter was best known – perhaps even only known – to his British public as an illustrator of children's books, his range was very much wider. He chronicled events in his native Hamburg, providing, for example, six lithographic illustrations to go with B. Avé-Lallement's published account of the third North German

57 Otto Speckter:
copper-engraving
by the artist
(von Rumohr,
Kynalepokomachia,
1847) [BL 1462 e 21]

Music Festival held in the city in 1841, and some of his best work is to be found associated with regional literature. This, I would suggest, lies in the illustrations which he contributed to the poems of Klaus Groth published in Hamburg in 1855 and more especially to the same poet's *Quickborn* [figs 58, 59] for which Speckter made the designs for 138 wood-engravings in the edition of 1856. Both books are key texts in the nineteenth-century revival of Low German literature, and in the latter something of the full range of Speckter's fine talent for book-illustration may be seen.

Although it may be stretching a point to classify Otto Speckter as a professional illustrator, there can be no doubt that the painter Ludwig Richter (1803–84) falls into this category. Indeed, the 400 books[10] which he illustrated wholly or in part during his long working life make it hard to do justice to his achievements in such a general survey as this.

Nu hört ihr lieben Leute,
Gestern ist nicht heute,
Heut ist nicht morgen,
Dat Künfti is verborgen,
Verborgen is dat Künfti,
Denken is vernünfti,
Vernünfti is dat Denken,
En Keb hett er Lenken,

58 Full-page wood-engraved design after Otto Speckter (Groth, *Quickborn*, 1856) [BL 11526 h 2]

59 Vignette wood-
engraving after Otto
Speckter (Groth,
Quickborn, 1856)
[BL 11526 h 2]

60 *Nut-Cracker and Sugar-Dolly*:
Joseph Cundall's adaptation (1849)
of the wood-engraved half-title after
Ludwig Richter for Fechner's *Die
Schwarze Tante* (1848) [BL 12805 g 40]

79

Like Speckter, he was closely concerned with the illustration of children's books and, like Speckter, it was through this genre that he built up a large following in Britain, although it was not until the 1860s and 1870s that his designs were reprinted in England on a large scale.

His work was certainly well known during the Romantic period and in 1848–9 English versions had appeared of a small collection of Clara Fechner's children's stories, *Die schwartze Tante*. Simultaneously with the German edition of 1848 the Leipzig publisher Georg Wigand issued an English translation by Charles Dana, *The Black Aunt*, which Joseph Cundall reprinted in London in the following year as *Nut-Cracker and Sugar-Dolly* [fig. 60]. Cundall presumably had purchased from Wigand electrotypes of Richter's designs, which are some of his most typical and engaging.

Lustspiel.

1. Att.

Hier liggt en Appel un dar liggt en Ber,
Dar kumt Hans un Greten her.

2. Att.

De Greten wull kaken,   Neem Greten en Staken,
Keem Hans un wull slicken, Slog Hans oppen Rüggen.

3. Att.

Hulterdepulter de Trepp hindal:
Hans un Greten küsst sik mal.

61 *Comedy*: wood-engraved vignettes after Ludwig Richter (Groth, *Voer de Goern*, 1855) [BL 11525 h 5]

62 *The Brave Flautist*:
vignette wood-engraving
after Ludwig Richter
(Bechstein, *Märchenbuch*, 1853)
[BL 012403 ee 7]

63 Wood-engraving after
Ludwig Richter for Schiller's
Die Räuber (*Illustrationen zu …*
deutscher Classiker, 1853)
[BL 1264 b 7]

64 Wood-engraving after Ludwig Richter in a more typically sentimental style for Goethe's *Hermann und Dorothea* (*Illustrationen zu … deutscher Classiker*, 1853) [BL 1264 b 7]

65 *The Tailor's Trip to Hell*: wood-engraved head-piece after Ludwig Richter (*Deutsches Balladenbuch*, 1852) [BL 11521 g 1]

66   *The Midnight Muster*: wood-engraved head-piece after H.F. Pluddemann (*Deutsches Balladenbuch*, 1852) [BL 11521 g 1]

While it is true that he is inclined to sentimentality and that he can be dismissed as comfortable, bourgeois and Biedermayer, yet in the final analysis Richter may be said to represent the lost innocence of a gentle, cultured and comfortable pre-industrial Germany [fig. 61]. With his sentimentality there marches a kindliness, so that his grotesques avoid the deliberate ugliness of so much contemporary British comic art and transmute the earthy peasant humour of the mediaeval misericord sculptor. Richter, in his book illustration, is in fact very much more the conscious academic artist than either Hosemann or Speckter. Although his wood-engravings use those tonal effects to be expected from a landscape painter who had contributed work for copper-engraving in W.A. Lindau's *Vergissmeinnicht* (1824) and for steel-engraving in *Das malerische und romantische Deutschland* (1836), their linear strength is directly due to the influence of the German Romantic school and in particular to its outline engravers.

Richter well deserves the high position which he achieved among German nineteenth-century illustrators and it is an almost impossible task to single out from the mass of books to which he contributed particularly outstanding examples of an *œuvre* notable for its consistently high standard. Yet almost inevitably one must cite his designs for J.K.A. Musaeus's *Volksmärchen* (1842), and two particularly charming examples of his style, J.P. Hebel's *Alemannische Gedichte* (1851) and the first illustrated edition of L. Bechstein's *Märchenbuch* (1853) [fig. 62].

The bulk of Richter's designs were executed in wood-engraving and an engaging aspect of the artist is his feeling for the historic role of the craft. This is early demonstrated between 1838 and 1842 in the series of designs which he made for the *Volksbücher*, the reprints of German chapbook literature edited by Dr G.O. Marbach and published by Otto Wigand of Leipzig. Their quality is variable but frequently, although not consistently, they revive most appropriately the German sixteenth-century style in a manner which transcends mere pastiche. However, if one were to summarize Richter's talents one might best employ a literary analogy. Richter, I think, might be compared with the master of lyric verse, a genre needing all the skill and craftsmanship of the tragic or epic poet, yet one which will inevitably be classed as lightweight in any direct comparison with an epic or a tragedy. This is readily apparent in his contribution to the *Deutsches Balladenbuch* of 1852 [fig. 65]. Excellent specimens of his lyric style, they seem almost frivolous by contrast with the starkly monumental or macabre qualities of the designs of Adolf Erhardt or Hermann Pluddemann [fig. 66].

The Painters

If publishing conditions limited the number of those who may be termed professional illustrators in the sense which we should apply the title to their British and French contemporaries, we find, by contrast, that established painters in Germany were far more closely involved in the illustration of books. This may in part be due to the Revivalist interest in all things mediaeval – including the mediaeval manuscript – but far more largely through the fashion for artists to express in visual terms and through the medium of the outline engraving the emotions aroused by great works of literature. Hence the vogue for *Umrissen* inspired by Goethe, Shakespeare or Schiller, to mention three favourite authors, albums of outline engravings, a style consonant with the simplicity of the Nazarenes and of the history painters whose frescoes adorned King Ludwig's capital, Munich.

Not that the *Umrisse* was originally German, for in fact the father of the outline engraving was the English sculptor John Flaxman. By a happy accident his artistic pilgrimage to Italy occurred before the Great War with France closed the Continent to the British. In 1793, towards the end of a seven-year Grand Tour which had begun in 1787, he issued the first edition of his outline drawings to Homer [fig. 67]. That they were published in Rome, and hence available to a cosmopolitan society of art-lovers, ensured their wider aesthetic impact; the same is true of his designs for Dante, although they were issued for private circulation only and in the same year.

Consequently Flaxman, whose sculptures were unknown on the Continent, could be hailed by Goethe, in an article in *Propyläen* in 1799, as 'the idol of all the dilettanti' and, in the same year, A.W. von Schlegel could devote a long and laudatory review in *Athenäum* to Flaxman's outline engravings.[11] Those for Dante were then issued in a general edition in 1803 from the original copper plates, probably as the result of the pirated French edition of 1802, and an enlarged edition of Homer appeared in 1805. Both were printed in London. In the meantime Flaxman had published in London in 1805 designs from Aesychlus and finally, in 1817, designs from Hesiod.

67 *Iris with the Torch of Discord*: outline engraving by Thomas Piroli after John Flaxman (Homer, *Iliad* [1793], 1796) [BL 75 g 19]

Flaxman's influence is difficult to judge. Other British painters certainly adopted the outline style, and around 1808 John Bell reproduced in his periodical *La Belle Assemblée* paintings by old masters as Raphael and Carracci and such moderns as Reynolds, Barry and West by outline engraving. Flaxman's own designs, too, were frequently reprinted and there were, for example, no fewer than fourteen editions of his Aeschylus between 1795 and 1828. In 1829 there was an abortive scheme to establish the 'London School of Flaxman or Society for the Improvement of Historical Composition', but whatever Flaxman's influence upon painting and sculpture, his direct influence upon book-illustration in Britain would seem, at best, to have been peripheral.

By contrast, his indirect influence was enormous and this influence was exercised through Flaxman's German imitators. Earliest of these was the painter Asmus Jacob Carstens whose outline engravings to the Argonauts were published posthumously in Rome in 1799. Once the style had been approved by Goethe and Schelgel it was widely adopted by a number of artists and most notably by Bonaventura Genelli. Nor was it a matter of style alone, for Flaxman, who deliberately denied any intention to *illustrate* a text in the conventional sense, confessed in a letter to William Hayley: 'My intention is to show how a story may be represented in a series of compositions on the principles of the ancients.'[12] In other words, Flaxman was using literature as a direct source of artistic inspiration to

68   *Faust and Mephistopholes*: outline engraving after Peter von Cornelius (*Bilder zu Faust*, 1830)
[BL 1762 b 1]

arouse an emotional response to its themes through the image rather than the word. In the hands of his German imitators, then, the outline engraving was to become almost a new artistic genre. Although many of them were to follow Flaxman in issuing unadorned albums of engravings, there was a tendency, as time went on, for the artist to append such extracts from his chosen author as would enable the purchaser more fully to appreciate the artist's intentions.

This growing cult of the *Umrisse* may be seen in the publishing history of Peter von Cornelius's designs inspired by Goethe's *Faust*. First issued in 1816 as conventional tonal copper-engravings, subsequent reprints translated them into outline engravings [fig. 68], a genre which attracted a host of lesser figures. Prominent among these was Julius Nisle. He was especially productive of this genre between the years 1837 and 1841 during which he published his *Umrissen zu … Hebel* (1837); *Uhland*, and *Christopher Schmid* (1838); an undated *Schiller, Lenau* (1841), and his *Goethe Gallerie* (1840–41). Meanwhile Ludwig Sigismund Ruhl between 1827 and 1841 produced his outline engravings to a number of Shakespeare's plays [fig. 69], doubtless goaded by the success in the British market enjoyed by Moritz Retzsch. For, although German artists had ready access to British purchasers through the book- and print-sellers who specialized in German materials,[13] so far as the great British public was concerned, in outline engraving Retzsch reigned supreme.

At the start of his artistic career Retzsch had had the good fortune to win from Goethe approval for the outline drawings which he had made for *Faust* [fig. 70] and, having engraved them, made his European reputation. Apart from the many editions which he himself published, the designs were pirated in Paris and copied by Henry Mosses to illustrate an English translation of the poem published by Boosey & Son in 1820. So well known did they become that Alfred Crowquill was able to parody them to effect in his verse-travesty of *Faustus* (1834) [fig. 71]. Retzsch also issued outline engravings inspired by the poems of Schiller[14] and felt secure enough of his public to issue a single engraving, 'The Chess Players', and six plates of *Fantasien und Wahrheiten* in 1831, and the five engravings of

69 *Romeo and Juliet*: outline engraving after L.S. Ruhl (*Sketches for Shakespeare's Plays*, the English edition of *Skizzen zu Shakespeare*, 1838) [BL 841 m 3]

PL. 8

Engraved by Henry Moses.

Drawn & Engd by Alfd Crowquill.

72 (*above*) High Art: *Christian combats with Apllyon*: outline engraving after H.C. Selous for Bunyan's *The Pilgrim's Progress*, the Art Union's Premium Book for 1844 [BL 1871 c 22]

73 (*right*) Low Art: Fuseli's painting of Puck reproduced as an outline engraving for *A Midsummer Night's Dream* in a cheap edition of Shakespeare's plays (1825) [author's collection]

Facing page

70 (*top*) *Faust sees Margaret for the First Time*: outline engraving after Moritz Retzsch (*Faustus*, 1830) [BL C 57 h 2]

71 (*bottom*) Crowquill's parody of fig. 70 (*Faustus*, 1834) [BL 638 i 23]

Der Junggesell und der Mühlbach.
Gesell.

Wo willst du klares Bächlein hin,
So munter?
Du eilst, mit frohem, leichtem Sinn
Hinunter.
Was suchst du eilig in dem Thal?
So höre doch und sprich einmal!
Bach.

Ich war ein Bächlein, Junggesell;
Sie haben
Mich so gefaßt, damit ich schnell,
Im Graben,
Zur Mühle dort hinunter soll,
Und immer bin ich rasch und voll.
Gesell.

Du eilest mit gelass'nem Muth
Zur Mühle,
Und weißt nicht, was ich junges Blut
Hier fühle.
Es blickt die schöne Müllerin
Wohl freundlich manchmal nach dir hin?
Bach.

Sie öffnet früh, beim Morgenlicht,
Den Laden,
Und kommt, ihr liebes Angesicht
Zu baden.
Ihr Busen ist so voll und weiß;
Es wird mir gleich zum Dampfen heiß.
Gesell.

Kann sie im Wasser Liebesgluth
Entzünden;
Wie soll man Ruh' mit Fleisch und Blut
Wohl finden?
Wenn man sie ein Mal nur gesehn,
Ach! immer muß man nach ihr gehn.

74 *The Bachelor and the Millstream*: copper-engraving after Eugen Neureuther (Goethe, *Balladen und Romanzen*, 1829–30) [BL 747 f 17]

75 *Leonora*: lithograph
after Eugen Neureuther
(*Randzeichnungen um
Dichtungen der deutschen
Classiken*, 1832).
Burger's ballad
inspired such British
artists as Daniel Maclise
(fig. 129) and
H.C. Selous (fig. 115)
[BL 789 b 22]

Der Kampf des Lichtes mit der Finsterniss in 1845, all from designs of his own imagining and all
with explanatory texts in English, French and German. This pattern of publication in
London, Paris and Leipzig reflects the pattern of his fame which, so far as his British public
was concerned, was based less upon his designs from the German poets than upon his long
series of outline engravings to Shakespeare's plays. This began in 1828 with *Hamlet* and
ended in 1844 with *The Merry Wives of Windsor*; during these years Retzsch engraved 95 plates
to a total of seven plays, the other five being *Macbeth*, *King Lear*, *Romeo and Juliet*, *The Tempest*
and *Othello*.

Retzsch is manifestly inferior as an artist to Cornelius when we compare their two
versions of *Faust*, and shows no marked superiority to Ruhl in the Shakespeare engravings
or to Nisle as an illustrator of Schiller. Consequently he was held in no particular regard in

76 Robert Reineck's design (engraved on copper) for the title-page of the first volume of *Lieder und Bilder* (1838) [BL 838 m 14]

Germany where he led a somewhat morose and solitary life and where he taught at Dresden from 1824 to 1854. Yet in Britain, as William Vaughan writes,[15] his 'outlines were … the objects of study and inspiration for some of the most eminent writers and artists of the period: amongst others, Byron, Shelley, Flaxman, Maclise, Millais, and Rossetti'. In so far as the professional art critics were concerned, Retzsch provided a yardstick in outline engraving with which to belabour British practitioners of the genre for their real or imaginary shortcomings. Nor could there be any doubt as to his popularity with the public at large. In the 'Introduction' to *Macbeth*, the second Shakespeare play which inspired Retzsch's designs, his publishers could boast that:

> In England, where the Artist's performance had obtained high reputation by his Gallery to Göthe's Faust and to Schiller's Ballads, and where they had been multiplied by means of copies by Moses [*sic*] and other engravers, those fancy-pieces to Hamlet gained so favourable a reputation, that in pictures of the manners of the fashionable world, of the persons of distinction who frequent Almack's and pass

the most delightful season of the year in their town-mansions – in novels – the drawing-room table of no lady is described as being without Retzsch's designs.

Perhaps it was this faithful British public which encouraged Retzsch to persist for over thirty years in a style of outline engraving which gradually became as outmoded in Germany as the fashion for albums in which, as Schlegel had written in his essay on Flaxman in *Athenäum*, 'the imagination is incited to complete the picture and to continue to create independently according to the stimulation received.'

In his original outlines, Flaxman had been influenced by Greek vase painting[16] and his designs have a classical purity. He limits the number of figures and either avoids or is exceedingly sparing in the use of architectural or natural backgrounds. In the hands of his German disciples, the composition tends at times to become crowded by a multiplicity of

77 *The Dead Bride*: panel decorations engraved on copper after Julius Hübner
(*Lieder und Bilder*, 1, 1838) [BL 838 m 14]

figures and of just that sort of background detail which Flaxman was at pains to avoid. One means of emphasizing the key components of the design was to vary the depth of the engraving – and hence the density of the black line; another was to achieve extra emphasis by thickening certain outlines or portions of outlines. The latter may be found in British examples from the extremes of William Mulready's designs for wood-engraving in *The Vicar of Wakefield* (1843), a classic among British illustrated books, or G.E. Hicks's for outline engraving in Thomas Campbell's *Gertrude of Wyoming*, the Art Union's premium book for 1846. Ultimately the solution – particularly when used for genuine book-illustration – was what Flaxman himself would probably have regarded as retrograde – the use of light hatching to suggest three-dimensional shape and perspective, and to give the composition dramatic emphasis.

78 *The New Simson*: copper-engraving after Adolf Schrödter (*Lieder und Bilder*, 1, 1838) [BL 838 m 14]

79 Wood-engraved section-opening after Alfred Rethel (*Nibelungenlied*, 1840)
[BL 11501 i 2]

It is strange that the outline style, and even its final 'shaded-outline' manifestation, should have appealed to and been the vehicle for the Revivalism of the Nazarene School and of the history painters. Flaxman had, after all, derived it from the classical: they applied it to the Gothic. This development may, however, reflect the common sympathy of sculptor and painters for pre-Raphaelite art, since Flaxman was among the first to appreciate the virtues of the Italian primitives.[17]

Although the outline album was originally devoted to major works of literature – epic poetry and Greek and Elizabethan tragedy, for example – it was inevitable that artists should turn to the decoration of short individual poems, one of the first to do so being Eugen Neureuther. The result, Goethe's *Balladen und Romanzen* (1829–30), was not simply a work of seminal influence, but a masterpiece of Romantic art [fig. 74]. Text and embellishment,

80 Copper-engraving after J.B. Sonderland (*Lieder und Bilder*, II, 1846) [BL 838 n 15]

engraved on copper and printed in colour on the recto of the folio leaf, are integrated within a single rule border in a manner reminiscent rather of William Blake than of the French Romantic book designers whose work we have considered. William Vaughan, however, has demonstrated quite convincingly that, while Blake's work may possibly have been known in Germany, similarities are evidence of parallel development rather than of direct influence.[18] So far as British book design is concerned one would agree wholeheartedly with his view that 'Blake's framing book designs … remained an isolated phenomenon in English art'.[19] Ironically Blake, the Romantic artist and creator of the most perfectly integrated books, seems never to have influenced his own generation of book-illustrators or their immediate successors, while publishers and printers were equally impervious to his ideas. Instead, it is this parallel development in Germany which will be seen to have been of decisive influence in determining the course of British book-illustration during the

81 Lithograph after
Theodor von Oer
(Reineck, *Die
Wurzelprinzessin*, 1846)
[BL 12806 g 8]

nineteenth century, while Blake had to wait until the twentieth century for full recognition.

Neureuther, meanwhile, followed his *Balladen und Romanzen* with similar collections, *Baierische Gebirgslieder* (1831) and *Radzeichnungen ... der Deutschen Classiken* (1832) [fig. 75]. In neither does he match the delicacy of his original set and, in particular, the lithographic line of *Baierische Gebirgslieder* seems coarse beside the copper-engraving of the *Balladen*. As with the first, so Neureuther uses the rule border to integrate text and embellishment in the later books, but what results in all three is not an illustrated book in the true sense, but a set of artist's engravings and lithographs. Nevertheless, such sets of prints were to affect book design, and more particularly when the basic idea was developed into an anthology of poems by different authors used by a whole group of artists as the inspiration for their prints. A typical and highly influential example of this type of book is *Lieder und Bilder*, published at Düsseldorf in three successive volumes in 1838, 1843 and 1846 [fig. 76].

The set provides a conspectus of contemporary German art, reproducing in copper-engraving the work of painters who are not primarily concerned with book-illustration as such, but simply inspired by literature to produce these series of decorative prints. (Typically, and at least so far as the first volume was concerned, sets of the engraved designs were issued by the 'Kupferdruckerie Königl. Academie zu Dusseldorf' before the appropriate texts were added to them to provide an engraved state *avant la lettre*.) The volumes include work which is purely conventional – the squared landscape most notably – as well as outline and shaded-outline engravings in the Romantic style. These will be discussed in their place; at this point I should prefer to draw attention to two decorative features of the designs in general. These were features which were to become characteristic of German Romantic book design, the broad vertical panels of decoration in the margins [fig. 77], and the 'stick' border [fig. 78].

83 *The Old Actor*: wood-engraving after Theodor von Oer (*Deutsches Balladenbuch*, 1852) [BL 11521 g 1]

'Stick' is, I hope, a useful descriptive term for a shaded, irregular double rule which serves a twofold purpose. When the decorative motif is floral, it represents rustic trellising; when architectural, moulding. In both cases the 'stick' border blends admirably with the shaded outlines of the figures and representational designs and derives ultimately from the same Revivalism from which painters drew their inspiration. It would seem to go back to those writing branches which the designers of the so-called *Nuremberg Chronicle* used to delineate the family trees of the Hebrew kings and patriarchs and is typical of the way in which the late Gothic and early Renaissance woodcut sets its ancestral mark upon the designs which the German Romantics made for both copper and wood-engraving [fig. 79].

This is certainly understandable in the context of a revivalism which expressed a new-won national consciousness in terms of the last great age of German culture. Yet it is perhaps unfortunate that Germany was one of the few areas in which master-painters – and one thinks immediately of Albrecht Dürer and Hans Holbein – designed for the woodcut,

84 *Song of the Brave Man*: wood-engraved vignette head-piece after Theodor von Oer (*Deutsches Balladenbuch*, 1852). For John Tenniel's interpretation see fig. 106 [BL 11521 g 1]

85 *The Three Indians*: wood-engraved head-piece after Erhardt (*Deutsches Balladenbuch*, 1852) [BL 11521 g 1]

and could therefore provide models not simply for the Revivalist easel-painter but for the book-illustrator as well, since they were designing for craftsmen cutting with the knife on the plank, rather than engraving with the burin on the end-grain. Effectively this was to deny the engraver the full potential of his medium and to perpetuate the dominance of black-line engraving.

Of the artists, however, who contributed to *Lieder und Bilder*, mention should be made of J.B. Sonderland (1805–78) for his mastery of the grotesque [fig. 80], and for the imaginative qualities displayed by Adolf Schrödter, his exact contemporary [fig. 78]. Equally engaging are the designs of Robert Reineck (1805–52), who wrote a delightful book for children, *Die Wurzelprinzessin* (1846), which he and Theodor von Oer illustrated with seven full-page lithographs [figs 81, 82].[20] A collected edition of Reineck's writings for children was published in 1872.

Von Oer is, however, more memorable for his contribution to a much later publication, the *Deutsches Balladenbuch* of 1856 [figs 83, 84]. Together with Adolf Erhardt [figs 85, 86] and H.F. Pluddemann [figs 66, 87] he contributed designs of a monumental quality and with a chilling sense of the macabre to what must be one of the finest wood-engraved books produced in Germany at this time.

Both Erhardt and Pluddemann contributed to *Lieder und Bilder*, but British students will identify more readily with another member of the group, Alfred Rethel (1810–59), whose artistic promise ended in insanity in 1853. His *Auch ein Todtendanz* [fig. 88] – six wood-engravings accompanied by a text by Robert Reineck – was highly praised by John Ruskin, and its plate of Death on the revolutionary barricades of 1848 rouse the atavistic instincts of every progressive art critic. Yet, since they were deliberately conceived in the chapbook tradition, it is perhaps unfair to contrast the somewhat coarse wood-engravings and the flat yellow tint on which they are rather crudely printed with the subtleties of Vizetelly's tinted wood-engravings. Preferable are his outline lithographs for Adela von Stolterforth's

86 *The Nun*: wood-engraving after Erhardt (*Deutsches Balladenbuch*, 1852) [BL 11521 g 1]

Facing page

87 (*top*) *The Wild Huntsman*: wood-engraved head-piece after H.F. Pluddemann (*Deutsches Balladenbuch*, 1852) [BL 11521 g 1]

88 (*bottom*) *Death Stalks the Countryside*: wood-engraving after Alfred Rethel (Reineck, *Auch ein Todtentanz*, 1849) [BL 1755 a 24]

Zweites Blatt.

Der Morgen schaut vom Himmelszelt
So klar wie sonst auf Stadt und Feld;

Da trabt mit wilder Hast heran
Der Freund des Volks, der Sensenmann.
Zur Stadt lenkt seinen Gaul er hin,

Schon ahnt er reiche Ernte drin.
Die Hahnenfeder auf dem Hut
Glüht in der Sonne roth wie Blut.

Die Sense blitzt wie Wetterschein,
So stöhnt der Gaul, die Raben schrei'n!

Rheinischen Sagenkreis (1834) [fig. 89], although these are of variable quality, or the handful of designs of New Testament subjects in the monumental but, alas, rather dull German Bible [fig. 90] of 1850, for which Julius Schnorr von Carelsfeld, Alexander Strähuber and Gustav Jager provided the bulk of the designs for wood-engraving.

Undoubtedly, however, the most successful designs from a restricted opus of book-illustration are those Rethel made for the 1840 edition of the *Nibelungenlied* [figs 79, 91] published at Leipzig by Georg and Otto Wigand. This can well be claimed to be the finest German Romantic book and although Rethel was responsible for only nine of the thirty-eight section openings, all his contributions are of a high standard of design and at least half of them are outstanding on any count.

A minor contributor to the *Nibelungenlied* was the *Lieder und Bilder* artist Frau Hermine Stilke [fig. 92], but the bulk of the illustrations, which if they cannot match Rethel at his best,

91 Wood-engraved section-opening after Alfred Rethel (*Nibelungenlied*, 1840) [BL 11501 i 2]

Facing page

89 (*top*) *The Templar of Lahneck*: lithograph after Alfred Rethel (von Stolterfoth, *Rheinischen Sagenkreis*, 1834; English translation, *The Rhenish Minstrel*, 1835) [BL 638 g 28]

90 (*bottom*) *Christ drives the Money-changers from the Temple*: wood-engraving after Alfred Rethel (*Die Bibel*, 1850) [BL 3041 dd 8]

are, nonetheless, of a consistently high standard, were engraved from the designs of Julius Hubner (1806–62) [fig. 93] and of his brother-in-law, Eduard Bendemann [fig. 94]. It is appropriate that the epic of the German people, which was to inspire Wagner's great operatic cycle and which was no less an inspiration to the national consciousness released by the War of Liberation, should provide an epitome of all that is best in German Romantic book design. The strain of Revivalism finds echoes, particularly strong in Rethel but by no means muted in the work of the other artists, of the German sixteenth-century masters of the woodcut. It is an immensely satisfying piece of work, which seems to have solved the problem of balance between text, the purely decorative functions of the borders and those of the illustrative designs.

92 Wood-engraved section-opening after Hermine Stilke (*Nibelungenlied*, 1840) [BL 11501 i 2]

93 Wood-engraved section-opening by Hugo Bürkner after Julius Hubner (*Nibelungenlied*, 1840)
[BL 11501i2]

94 Wood-engraved
section-opening after
Eduard Bendemann
(*Nibelungenlied*, 1840)
[BL 11501 i 2]

Once again, Bendemann's and Hubner's names are to be found among the contributors to *Lieder und Bilder*, for it is no accident that painters who had here explored the decorative possibilities of the printed page should have played so substantial a role in some of the finest illustrated books of the period. Yet they were neither the first nor the only painters to do so, Eugen Neureuther's book-illustrations being in this respect well worth study. His delicious engravings for Goethe's *Balladen* were, after all, the forerunners and mark an epoch in the involvement of German painting with German printing, even if his designs for book-illustration proper must seem disappointing by comparison. For the 1838 edition of J.G. von Herder's *Der Cid*, where the text is enclosed in the French style within a double-rule frame, he provided a title-page and sixty-nine canto openings – the latter mostly with a vignette design in addition to the decorated initial letter. Whether drawn directly on to the wood by the artist or transferred to it by the engravers, the designs appear heavy by comparison with Neureuther's earlier copper-engravings. There is an elaboration and an addiction to tone which obscures their linear strength and seems wholly uncharacteristic.

One might ascribe this to the fact that all but one of the designs were actually cut in London by British engravers, who might be accused of misinterpreting the artist's designs were the same traits not equally apparent in the full-page engravings – cut by the German craftsmen Rehle and Kretzschmar – which Neureuther designed for the 1843 edition of *Der Nibelungen Noth* [fig. 95]. This he illustrated jointly with Julius Schnorr von Carelsfeld for the Stuttgart publisher Cotta who had commissioned the *Cid* illustrations and for whom he provided designs for the 1846 edition of Goethe's *Götz von Berlichingen*. In many ways the most satisfying book, at least in so far as Neureuther's designs for the wood-engraved

95 Wood-engraving after Eugen Neureuther (*Nibelungen Noth*, 1843) [BL 11501 h 16]

vignettes are concerned, it suffers from an overelaborate page layout where the text is not only given a vertical panel of decoration but the whole is framed within double rules.

It is, perhaps, dangerously misleading to write, in connection with German books, of rule borders being 'in the French style'. There had been such close parallel development of this device that one cannot point to this as evidence of French influence in the same way as the 'stick' border is indicative of German influence. The only German exception to this would, however, be Franz Kugler's *Geschichte Friedrichs des Grossen* (1840), designed quite deliberately in the style of Laurent de l'Ardèche's *Histoire de l'empereur Napoléon* to show that Germany had heroes to match French heroes and artists to match French artists.

The book is Adolf Menzel's major essay as an illustrator – he issued a number of albums of lithographs and designed many frontispieces, but he was primarily a painter who

96 Wood-engraved chapter-opening in the French Romantic style after Adolf Menzel (Kugler, *Geschichte Friedrichs des Grossen*, 1840) [BL 1449 k 11]

produced nothing else on this scale. It would be infantile to attempt to adjudicate in terms of artistic superiority between Menzel and Horace Vernet: one can only be grateful that national pride should have produced two such fine books. Menzel, indeed, fully satisfies German honour on the score of draughtsmanship and the vignettes are interesting, too, for the technique of wood-engraving employed.

Many of the designs in the beginning of the book were cut in Paris by the French engravers Andrew, Best and Leloir, and by Piaud. Later, the absence of that very necessary personal contact between artist and engraver rather than any inherent lack of sympathy between French engraving and German draughtsmanship – as William Vaughan, following the German critics, suggests[21] – turned Menzel exclusively to craftsmen resident in Germany. The engravers are, however, of less importance than the actual style of the

97 Wood-engraved vignettes after Adolf Menzel. Note how the outer rule-border maintains their integration although they extrude from the inner border (Kugler, *Geschichte Friedrichs des Grossen*, 1840) [BL 1449 k 11]

vignettes, for in many of them Menzel employs a solid black which anticipates the chiaroscuro effects achieved by Pannemaker's and Sotain's 'new' school of Parisian wood-engraving in the 1860s [figs 96, 97].

Except in France in the 1820s, imitation of the classic style of British design with wood-engraved vignette head- and tail-pieces is extremely rare. A notable exception is provided by J.L. Pyrker's *Bilder aus dem Heiligen* (Vienna, 1847), where Joseph von Fürich's miniatures for squared and vignette head-pieces are redolent of the British school. They are as exceptional in German book design as they are in von Fürich's *œuvre* which reflects his Nazarene style and his profound religious commitment, typical in their mediaevalism and Catholicism being the eight copper-engravings illustrating the Lord's Prayer published in Prague in 1826. In the following year von Fürich published seventy-five Old Testament subjects engraved

98 Wood-engraving after Eduard Steinle: opening to Book III of the German translation of Thomas à Kempis, *De imitatione Christi*, 1839 [BL IX Germ 105]

99 Title-page
to Goethe's
Reineke Fuchs, 1846
(copper entraving
after Wilhelm
Kaulbach)
[BL 11501 k 5]

on copper and in 1844 *Die Geistige Rose*, his paintings of the fifteen mysteries of the Holy Rosary reproduced by lithography to a text by Father J.E. Veith. Secular works included shaded outline engravings inspired by Tieck's *Genovefa* and by Goethe's *Hermann und Dorothea*: all are prints, however, rather than book-illustrations.

Another primarily religious artist was Eduard Steinle, who provided designs for the six copper-engravings used as frontispieces to the issue in six parts (1842–3) of Wilhelm Naketenus's *Himmlische Palmgarten*. They are excellent examples of his work and include a strange and disturbing representation of the crucified Christ as the mystic vine. Earlier, Steinle had designed for an edition of Thomas à Kempis's *De imitatione Christi*, published in German translation at St Polten in 1839, four book-openings of slightly larger than half-page size, miniatures for chapter-openings and, very probably, the historiated and decorated borders as well. The book-openings are typical of the German outline style, but the vast majority of the borders employ the *criblé* ground so common in the decoration of Parisian printed Books of Hours of the late fifteenth and early sixteenth centuries [fig. 98]. It is significant that the Germans, with their tradition of woodcut book-illustration, should, at least here, take their models from printed books, while the French themselves found inspiration in similar circumstances in manuscript decoration.

Finally, mention should be made of Wilhelm Kaulbach (1805–74), if only that he was a painter whose work was highly regarded by his British contemporaries. Perhaps because his full-page illustrations to Goethe's *Werke* (1845) were on steel and nearly all engraved for the edition by Finden in London, they impress as being in the tradition of the neo-classical illustrators. Something of the same formality even pervades the designs for the monumental quarto edition of Goethe's version of *Reineke Fuchs* published in the following year [figs 99, 100]. The text is enclosed within a double-rule frame with wood-engraved head-pieces and initial letters and there are thirty-six *hors-textes* engraved on copper. The edition was reprinted in 1857 with the designs transferred to wood and printed as half-page integrated illustrations. They were repeated in an English version published in 1859.

Wilhelm Kaulbach gez.   Adrian Schleich gest

100 *Reynard as a Friar*: copper-engraving after Wilhelm Kaulbach (Goethe, *Reineke Fuchs*, 1846) [BL 11501 k 5]

If the embellishments of *Reineke Fuchs* were reproduced by copper-engraving six years after *Der Nibelungenlied* had shown what wood-engraving could achieve, and the designs only transferred to wood thirteen years later, it would seem to lend weight to the contention that the pace of industrial and social change was chronologically slower in Germany. That the book concerned was illustrated by a recognized painter and that so many other painters obviously enjoyed the challenge of designing for the printed page, exemplifies the lead which artistic circles in Germany had over both Britain and France. Finding their artistic inspiration in works of literature and expressing it in albums of *Umrissen* seems to have led to an earlier recognition of book-illustration as a legitimate field of artistic endeavour and to have made German painters forerunners in a movement which did not find full expression in Britain until the 1860s. Thus German Romantic book design influenced British artists, publishers and critics not simply as a style, but as an attitude towards the genre as a whole.

German Influences upon British Book Design and Illustration

German influences upon British art – and hence upon book-illustration – in the Victorian Age are one aspect of the interaction between the two cultures which dates back to the middle of the eighteenth century at least. This interaction is at the heart of the Romantic Movement in literature, philosophy and art. Hints of the Anglo-German cross-fertilization can be seen in such diverse and scattered examples as the popularity in Germany of Shakespeare, Young and Macpherson (the 'author' of *Ossian*); of the influence of the Transcendental philosophers Kant, Hegel and Fichte in England; of the strongly German elements which became part of the Gothic novel; of the common interest in ballad literature which effected its revival in literary form by Burger, Coleridge, Goethe, Keats, Schiller, Scott and Uhland; and of the impetus towards the revival of Gothic architecture in both countries and, in Germany, of Gothic painting. In Germany there is a conscious and in Britain a subconscious espousal of a national Romanticism in reaction to a Classicism which in art and literature is perhaps the outward symbol of a French cultural dominance which goes back to the seventeenth century.

In German painting the immediate fruits of this Revivalism were to be seen in the work of the Nazarene school and it was members of this group who made an immediate impact upon British artists visiting Rome when the end of the Great War with France in 1815 opened the Continent once more to British travellers. This was no momentary flash of enthusiasm for artistic novelty in painters starved of contact with the development of European art during long years of war and blockade. The Nazarene reaction to Classicism provided the means by which a new generation of British painters could break with the past and it continued to inspire – as late as the mid-century and through Ford Madox Brown – that anti-Establishment group, the Pre-Raphaelite Brotherhood.[22]

Nor was this a simple matter of stylistic influence, since German Romantic painting is an expression of a wider political and cultural revival, closely interwoven with an equally strong religious resurgence. The Protestant painter Overbeck, for example, became a convert to Roman Catholicism, but it was a Catholicism without that Ultramontanism which so frightened good Anglicans. Tractarians who could emphasize the 'catholic' traditions within the Church of England had every sympathy with that liberal Catholicism exemplified by Professor Döllinger who broke with Rome in 1870 when the first Vatican Council pronounced the dogma of Papal Infallibility.

One can therefore readily appreciate how very attractive things German were to the younger generation of the 1830s and 1840s, since they satisfied their Revivalist and religious aspirations and offered a new and revolutionary style of painting. With the Queen's husband, Prince Albert, a representative of the best aspects of the new German culture, making art education and industrial design his especial concern, it was inevitable that this German influence should make itself felt. Given, too, the close involvement of German painters with the embellishment of books it was equally inevitable that such influence should be felt not least in book design. Here one can isolate from any general tendency towards Germanization two men whose influence was decisive: James Burns, the Tractarian publisher, and Samuel Carter Hall, editor of *The Art Journal* and perhaps the most vociferous proponent of Germanistic tendencies in the period.

Samuel Carter Hall was to pride himself, in his two complacent volumes of reminiscence *Retrospects of a long Life from 1815 to 1883*, on the good causes which he sponsored as editor of *The Art Journal* from its foundation in 1839 – as *The Art Union Journal* – until his retirement in 1883. Among them he claimed that, through his advocacy from 1843 onwards of the Department of Science and Art's Governmental Schools of Design, the three such schools which had existed in 1840 had by 1880 increased to 150, to the immeasurable benefit of British industrial art and design, whatever *fin-de-siècle* aesthetes might say. Nor had the *Journal* played a less important role in sponsoring native painters and in recommending them to the patronage of British connoisseurs, even if this meant persuading the newly-rich north-country industrialist that a nice, big bright picture by a living artist was a better investment than a dingy and dubious Old Master.

His was not, however, the manner to endear itself to his contemporaries, and Henry Vizetelly, who printed his *Book of British Ballads*, thus describes him:

> Although devoid of the slightest critical faculty, and possessing only commonplace taste in matters of art, without even the power of expressing himself logically, Carter Hall had, with Hibernian self-confidence, set himself up as the artistic oracle of the day…. Pushing young artists and ambitious art-manufacturers competed for words of praise from his pen. Those who made offerings of little studies in oil or water colour, or choice examples of ceramic ware, were pretty certain to be belauded.[23]

Certainly two of Hall's ventures in illustrated books confirm this habit of exploiting young artists eager for recognition, for, as he himself virtually admits in his memoirs, when he came to write about the genesis of *The Book of British Ballads*,

> They were brilliant evenings when so many young artists – all of rare promise – assembled at the Rosery, Old Brompton [the Halls's house], as aids to illustrate the 'Book of British Ballads'…. It was my custom to read the ballad I had determined on selecting, and allot it to one of the artists; supplying each with the wood blocks on which he was to draw the head and tail pieces and the side slips – these slips sometimes numbering eight or ten.[24]

Twenty-seven artists were involved in illustrating the fifty-five ballads which eventually comprised Hall's collection, and we can be morally certain that these 'aids' were supplied gratis by struggling artists like the Irishman, John Franklin, who was solely responsible for illustrating no less than sixteen of the ballads, and whom Hall condescingly describes as 'an artist of prodigious capability who never gave himself fair play, frittering away his marvellous talent in comparatively small things and avoiding the great works in which he would undoubtedly have excelled'.[25] Such gratuitous assistance is, indeed, admitted when Hall describes how his wife's novel, *Midsummer Eve*, came to be illustrated with Joseph Noel Paton cast in Franklin's role [figs 101, 176].[26]

> I cannot, in common gratitude, pass without notice the aid the artist rendered in 1843 to Mrs. Hall in illustrating her story (published in the *Art Journal*, and subsequently [in 1848] as a volume).... I think there is no book of the kind that contains so many exquisite gems of art. That was mainly the result of Noel Paton's generous labour to sustain me in my attempt to create a periodical devoted to art....
> For the illustrations to 'Midsummer Eve' I had also the aid of Stanfield, Creswick, Goodall, Maclise,

PART THE SECOND.

HE kitchen at 'Dovecote,' as Mrs. Raymond, in happier days, had named her cottage, was a long rambling room; dried hams and fish, intermingled with bunches of herbs, were suspended from the rafters; and in a division, 'hurdled' off for the purpose, the Nurse's favourite poultry, and, occasionally, a weakly lamb, or a brood of tender turkeys, while their red heads were progressing, found a well-warmed shelter. It was sufficiently confused and straggling to be styled 'picturesque,' and as uncomfortable as picturesque interiors generally are; there was a more than usual quantity of piggins and noggins, and very fine old chairs—some gaunt and high-backed, others grotesque

101 Wood-engraved vignette after Joseph Noel Paton in traditional tonal style (for an example of the outline style he later adopted see fig. 175): head-piece and initial after Kenny Meadows (Mrs Hall, *Midsummer Eve*, 1848) [BL 12620 C 29]

E

Elmore, Frost, Topham, Franklin, Hulme, and Kenny Meadows, the greater number working for no other reward than the gratification of aiding me in my undertaking. Yet, beautiful as the book is, it was by no means a pecuniary success. Two editions, published 'on my own account', have not been productive.[27]

Small wonder then that Vizetelly should claim that Charles Dickens modelled Mr Pecksniff in his *Martin Chuzzlewit* upon Samuel Carter Hall, for he clearly had the habit of appropriating the work of others for his gain if not his fame, and he shares the fatuous pomposity of Dickens's creature, as Vizetelly unkindly demonstrates by this quotation from his writing, presumably in *The Art Journal*:

Without at all inclining to exaggerate our responsibilities, we know them to be great. We know there are many individuals (and it cannot be presumptuous to allude to a fact we have borne constantly in mind as one that ought to make us cautious as well as rigidly upright) who take our opinions as guides to their own – who give to our integrity and judgment that confidence which they have not in their own knowledge and experience, and who consequently look to us for determining the course they are to pursue in reference to purchases.[28]

Or what could be more condescending than this anecdote of the young Daniel Maclise?

In the year 1820, I was living in Cork. Entering one day the hall of the Society of Arts, the few models in which had been recently augmented by the generosity of George IV, I noticed a handsome and intelligent-looking boy drawing from one of the casts. I entered into conversation with him, examined his copy, and remarked, 'My little friend, if you work hard and *think*, you will be a great man one of these days.'[29]

And, according to Vizetelly, 'Hall talked even more priggishly and foolishly than he wrote.'[30]

It is, therefore, very easy to underrate the achievement of a man of such character and to dismiss *The Art Journal* with the nickname which *Punch* gave it, 'The Pecksniffery'; but clearly Hall had considerable influence which must be considered overall as beneficial to British art. He may have exploited young artists and one may laugh at the methods which he used to persuade north-country tycoons into buying modern British paintings, but at least young artists were recognized and modern paintings were bought. In so far as book illustration is concerned, while he was an influence, he was by no means so influential as he probably imagined. Clearly *The Art Journal* had a powerful critical voice, but the influence was pervasive rather than direct. The same is true of the Art Union's premium books – sets of outline engravings inspired by works of literature, on the German model – published from 1842 onwards and including work by artists who were to make a name as illustrators such as John Tenniel and H.C. Selous with their *Griselda* (1842) and *Pilgrim's Progress* (1844) [fig. 72], or those, such as F.R. Pickersgill, with his *L'Allegro and Il Pensoroso* (1848), who had already begun to make a name for themselves in this field. They served to propagate the German style of outline engraving and, of course, to publicize the artists responsible, but their landscape folio format and the fact that they really were no more than albums of artists' prints, meant that they had little real influence upon book design as such.

Of the two books with the design of which Hall himself was closely concerned, *Midsummer Eve* can hardly be said to have had much influence upon the development of the illustrated book in Britain. It is on any account a handsome book, if not quite matching Hall's claim that 'no work so perfect has issued from the Press during the century'.[31] The layout is not in the least innovative. By the time the story appeared in book form in 1848, the integrated vignette and the single rule framing the page had been a commonplace of European book design for nearly fifteen years. The innovative style of individual artists, such as Noel Paton, of the shaded outline school which was to dominate the next decade or so is more than outweighed by the majority of the embellishments in the more traditional tonal style. Only in the isolated designs – Alfred Elmore's outline engraving within an arched frame line, or R. Huskisson's circular frontispiece – can we see foreshadowings of the retreat from the vignette which was to be the feature of the later 1850s.

By contrast, *The Book of British Ballads*, which had been published in parts between 1842 and 1844, had been much more influential in introducing German styles to British books. It was avowedly inspired by one of the finest of all German Romantic books, the 1840 *Nibelungenlied*, Hall himself claiming that 'The idea of the book was suggested to me by the publication in Germany of a very beautiful edition of the "Niebelungenlied". It was on that ground that I dedicated the book to Louis, King of Bavaria, who had done so much for Art at Munich, and whose reign is a glorious epoch in Art history.'[32]

The resultant volume is one of the outstanding British illustrated books of the Romantic period, the German influence being seen in the general layout of the page, in the use of 'stick' borders, in the wide strips of historiation and decoration in the fore-margin, and in closer integration of illustrative and decorative elements [fig. 102]. Although, then, the structure is German, the German influence upon the draughtsmanship is only apparent in a greater or lesser degree through the work of the individual illustrators. Richard Dadd (his sole book illustration) [fig. 103], J.S. Brine, F.R. Pickersgill, J.R. Herbert, and John Tenniel are all very much of the new movement; Franklin himself, H.C. Selous, T. Sibson, William Bell Scott and Joseph Noel Paton are clearly influenced by the outline school; but E.M. Ward, C.H. Weigall, Edward Corbould, John Gilbert, Thomas Creswick and Samuel Williams are still very much in the English tradition best exemplified by William Harvey. Nevertheless, *The Book of British Ballads* made more than a temporary impact since it was reprinted in 1853.

It was, however, a single book, and it should be recognized that there are limits to what one book can achieve, even when its editor is so vociferous a publicist as Samuel Carter Hall. Setting a trend depends far more upon a consistent publishing programme aimed to expose the public to a new style and, if the publisher has judged public taste correctly, by its success to stimulate imitators. Hall's publisher, Jeremiah How, issued a number of interesting illustrated books, but curiously enough they were all in the French style of the rule border, not the German. Yet almost simultaneously with the publication of *The Book of British Ballads* just such a programme was being launched by a publisher who, although mentioned in passing by most writers on Victorian books, has hitherto received little credit for the far-reaching effects of his publications.

James Burns was born at Montrose in Scotland in 1808, the son of a Presbyterian minister. Himself intended for the ministry, he abandoned his studies at Glasgow University to come south and to enter the book trade, joining that nursery of Victorian publishers and booksellers, Whitakers in Ave Maria Lane, London, in 1832. By 1834 he had set up on his own account as a bookseller, from which it was a short step into publishing. It seems very

FAIR ROSAMOND.

WHEN as King Henry rulde this land,
    The second of that name,
Besides the queene, he dearly lovde
    A faire and comely dame.

Most peerlesse was her beautye founde,
    Her favour, and her face;
A sweeter creature in this worlde
    Did never prince embrace.

Her crisped lockes like threads of golde
    Appeard to each mans sight;
Her sparkling eyes, like Orient pearles,
    Did cast a heavenlye light.

Franklin, del   T. Williams, sc.

102 *Fair Rosamond*: the wood-engraving after John Franklin owes less to the *Nibelungenlied* and more to *Lieder und Bilder* (*The Book of British Ballads*, 1842) [BL 2288 g 4]

likely that behind this move to London there had been a crisis in Burns's religious faith, since he did not simply abandon Presbyterianism, but became an ardent Tractarian into the bargain. Indeed, his early lists are those of a religious publisher who had become one of the mouthpieces of the Tractarian movement through such periodicals as *The Englishman's Magazine* and *The Christian Remembrancer*; such series as 'The Englishman's Library'; through Archdeacon Manning's *Sermons*; through devotional works such as *Eucharistica*, a volume of prayers and meditations for Holy Communion; and through masses and masses of religious tracts and catechetical works. There was little to distinguish him from the rest of the trade except, perhaps, a nice sense of typography such as he shows in *Eucharistica*. This is a pretty little book, its text set within a red single rule frame, and with its title-page and the initial letter on the opening page and its marginal extension printed by chromolithography.

103 *Robin Goodfellow*:
wood-engraving
after Richard Dadd
(*The Book of British
Ballads*, 1842)
[BL 2288 g 4]

ROBIN GOODFELLOW

FROM Oberon in fairye land,
  The king of ghosts and shadowes there,
Mad Robin I, at his command,
  Am sent to viewe the night-sports here.
    What revell rout
    Is kept about,
  In every corner where I go,
    I will o'ersee, and merry bee,
  And make good sport, with ho, ho, ho!

More swift than lightening can I flye
  About this aery welkin soone,
And, in a minutes space, descrye
  Each thing that's done belowe the moone,
    There's not a hag
    Or ghost shall wag,
  Or cry, ware Goblins! where I go;
    But Robin I their feates will spy,
  And send them home, with ho, ho, ho!

Dadd, del.   Green, sc.

Nevertheless, it was because he was a Tractarian publisher that Burns became publisher to William Dyce, painter, art educationist, Government adviser on the arts and musicologist, and because he was Dyce's publisher that he came to play so important a role in the development of the Romantic book in Britain. Dyce was, in fact, the editor of the *Book of Common Prayer* and of the *Psalter* which Burns published in two volumes in 1843–4. In them Dyce had restored the old *canto fermo*, and his edition is thus a milestone in the history of English church music. Furthermore, they are very handsome books, printed by Robson, Levey & Franklyn who did so much work for Burns, in a Gothic letter in red and black within *criblé* borders. As an example of its publisher's typographic taste the volumes stand comparison with Charles Whittingham the younger's better-known work for William Pickering, but their real importance to us is that they establish a link between Burns and

But from the Holy Land soon came
  Returning pilgrims there,
And heavy tidings brought with them
  For Margaret's anxious ear.

For Wenzel is a captive made
  In Paynim dungeon cold,
And there must lie till ransom paid
  A hundred coins of gold.

Alas for Margaret ! should she spin,
  And all her store be sold,
In one long year she scarce could win
  A single piece of gold.

Yet love can hope through good and ill,
  When other hope is gone ;
Shall she who loves so well be still,
  And he in prison groan ?

125

104 *The Captive*: wood-engraving after William Dyce (*Poems and Pictures*, 1846) [BL 1466 i 11]

Dyce. This helps to explain not simply the increasing interest in illustrated books which Burns began to show, but their German style and the choice of artists to embellish them, for, despite all disclaimers, Dyce 'was considered by many of his contemporaries and succeeding generations to be the epitome of Nazarene influence in English art'.[33]

Admittedly this is a matter purely of hypothesis with no documentary evidence to support it – the Dyce Papers contain one routine letter from James Burns and the Burns, Oates and Washbourne archive was destroyed in World War II – but still it does find some support in the circumstances and characters of the two men. Both were Scots, both were Tractarians and both were strongly attracted towards Roman Catholicism, William Vaughan suggesting that Dyce's visits to Rome in the late 1820s and early 1830s were motivated as strongly by religion as by art.[34] He cites a letter from the German Nazarene painter Overbeck to his fellow-painter Eduard Steinle in which Dyce is mentioned as a potential ordinand to the Catholic priesthood at the English College, with whose dean, Dr (later Cardinal) Wiseman, Dyce was on close terms. In fact, Burns himself caused some stir when he became a Catholic in 1847; any danger of Dyce's conversion, meanwhile, had been removed when his father peremptorily ordered him to return to Scotland in 1830.

All these, then, are elements which could have led to a close personal relationship between publisher and author and, given our knowledge of Dyce's artistic tendencies, it is not unreasonable to see his influence in the illustrated books which Burns published. Dyce did in fact contribute designs to some of them and his hand may, perhaps, be seen in Burns's choice of artists for others. Dyce was closely connected not simply with the decoration of the new Houses of Parliament, but with the Prize Committee which awarded the commissions for the frescoes. It is, therefore, perhaps more than coincidence that such illustrators

106 *Song of the Brave Man*: wood-engraving after John Tenniel (*Poems and Pictures*, 1846); for Theodor von Oer's interpretation see fig. 84 [BL 1466 i 11]

as Selous and Tenniel who had been among the prize-winners should have worked for Burns.

Burns's own illustrated publications fall into two distinct categories. On the one hand, there are the 'little' books, a predominantly prose series with greater or lesser degree of embellishment; and on the other, books of verse from square 16mo to quarto in which was developed the style of Burns's most important contribution to the illustrated book of the period – his *Poems and Pictures*, dated 1846 but published for the Christmas season of 1845. In both categories Burns employs the same group of artists who were already influenced by the German shaded outline style, or who were to become so. They included William Dyce himself [fig. 104], C.W. Cope who was to study painting in Munich in 1845 and who already had shown much interest in book illustration as one of the founder-members of the Etching

107 *Sintram and the Little Master*:
wood-engraving after
H.C. Selous (*Illustrations to
Sintram and his Companions*, 1844)
[BL 5544 d 25]

Club, John Franklin, H.C. Selous, John Tenniel, William Bell Scott, F.R. Pickersgill [fig. 105] and Edward Corbould. Of these Selous and Franklin (then in their thirties) and a young artist in his twenties, John Tenniel [fig. 106], made the most regular and perhaps the most interesting contributions to the list.

All three were most closely concerned with the illustration of Burns's series of prose texts of which the nucleus was the English translations from the German romances of Norse mythology and mediaeval chivalry by H.F.K. de la Motte Fouqué. The earliest of these was *Sintram and his Companions* (1842), first published with no other illustration than a reproduction of Dürer's engraving, *Ritter, Todt und Teufel*, as a frontispiece. It was followed in 1843 by *Undine*, containing a miscellaneous set of vignette illustrations, probably printed from Continental casts or clichés. This is perhaps an indication of the publisher's

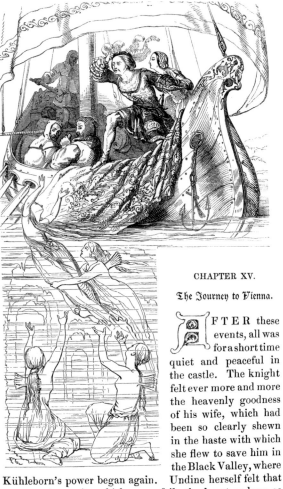

CHAPTER XV.

The Journey to Vienna.

AFTER these events, all was for a short time quiet and peaceful in the castle. The knight felt ever more and more the heavenly goodness of his wife, which had been so clearly shewn in the haste with which she flew to save him in the Black Valley, where Kühleborn's power began again. Undine herself felt that peace and security which never fails the heart so long as

108 Wood-engraved chapter-opening after John Tenniel (la Motte Fouqué, *Undine*, 1845) [BL 1457 d 19]

uncertainty or inexperience on entering what was a new field of activity, although not unusual. In 1844, Burns issued a translation of Alessandro Manzoni's *I Promessi Sposi* in which 'The woodcuts ... are chiefly taken from foreign illustrated editions of the work', while the version of *Peter Schlemihl* printed in *Romantic Fiction* (*c.*1845) uses copies of Adolf Menzel's illustrations.

Burns was, however, no Joseph Thomas and set about commissioning designs for *Sintram* from Selous and for *Undine* from Tenniel. The former were so successful that in 1844 Burns issued them separately as *A Series of Illustrations to Sintram and his Companions ... Drawn on Wood by Henry C. Selous and engraved by Charles Gray* [fig. 107]. They comprise the title and eight full-page chapter openings of which, curiously enough, only two were used, in conjunction with a number of vignettes by Selous, in later editions of the complete text. Meanwhile, Tenniel's series of designs for *Undine* first appeared in 1845 [fig. 108] although, to complicate the bibliographer's task, reprints of the 1843 edition continued to be issued and were generally undated, a particularly irritating habit to which Burns was addicted. These stories form part

109 Wood-engraving very much in the German style after John Franklin (Tieck, *Tales from the Phantastus*, 1845) [BL 1459 c 36]

THAT noble duke, the great
Of Burgundy's proud land,
Felt all his foemen's hate,
And, vanquish'd, bit the sand.

He spoke: " I'm struck ! I bleed !
Where is my valour fled ?
Friends fail me at my need,
My knights are flown or dead;

J. Franklin del.

O. Smith sc.

110 Steel-engraved frontispiece and title-page after Daniel Maclise (Dickens, *The Chimes*, 1845)
[BL C 59 fff 9]

of the first volume of La Motte Fouqué, *The Four Seasons*, and Burns's complete collection of this author eventually comprised five volumes.

If Selous and Tenniel were distinguished by being the acknowledged illustrators of these two tales, the bulk of the unacknowledged work of illustrating the rest fell to John Franklin. From La Motte Fouqué a distinct style of embellishment was developed which was applied to other authors and to other series. Very briefly, it comprised the use of frontispiece and decorated title-page, and of chapter openings with historiated vignette, decorated initial letters and decorated marginal extensions or frames, with integrated vignette illustrations and openings without the vignette. 'Little' books published within the range of 2s. 6d. to 3s. 6d. per volume were embellished on this scale.

However, Burns has always been noted for his cheap editions. The Fireside Library, which eventually numbered nearly forty volumes in a rather more square format than his more expensive series, was issued in attractive paper wrappers at between 9d. for a single and 1s. 9d. for a double volume. In general, illustration was confined to a frontispiece but full embellishment was given to such anthologies as *Ballads and Metrical Tales*, *German Ballads* and *Northern Minstrelsy* (all three undated, but c.1844–5), and to *Household Tales and Traditions*, an undated collection of folk-stories, the vast majority from the Brothers Grimm. The decoration of all these books is German in style. In fact, Burns was not simply a channel for German artistic influence, but for literary influence as well, his authors in translation including not only La Motte Fouqué, but Chamisso, Clausen, Pichler, Musaeus, von Woltman, Hauff and Schiller.

The Fireside Library has always found a place in any discussion of nineteenth-century cheap edition publishing, but less attention has been paid to the illustrative merits of these and Burns's more expensive series of 'little' books. They contain some of the best works of John Franklin [fig. 109], interesting designs by H.C. Selous, and good early Tenniel, when his style was more in the tradition of English book-illustration. In addition, there are typical designs by F.R. Pickersgill, F.W. Topham, C.H. Weigall and, occasionally, John Gilbert, and by no means negligible contributions from William Bell Scott and the Scottish artist

FIRST QUARTER.

HERE are not many peo-
ple—and as it is desira-
ble that a story-teller and
a story-reader should establish a mutual understanding as soon as possible, I
beg it to be noticed that I
confine this observation neither to young people nor to
little people, but extend it
to all conditions of people :
little and big, young and old : yet growing up,

111 Wood-engraved text-opening to Charles Dickens's *The Chimes* (1845) after Richard Doyle showing the influence of the Germanic style of James Burns's publications [BL C 59 fff 9]

B

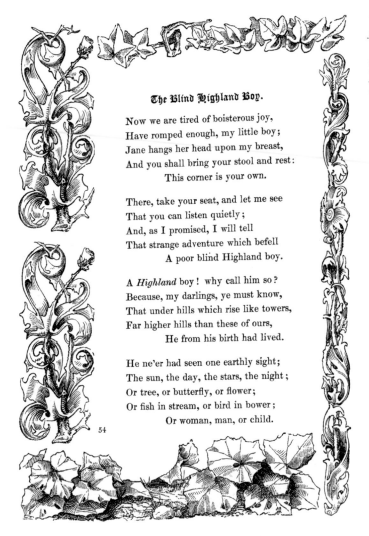

112 Page from *Select Pieces
from the Poems of William
Wordsworth* (*c.*1843),
an early publication of
James Burns, the borders
composed from printers'
stock ornaments
[BL 1467 b 34]

The Blind Highland Boy.

Now we are tired of boisterous joy,
Have romped enough, my little boy;
Jane hangs her head upon my breast,
And you shall bring your stool and rest:
    This corner is your own.

There, take your seat, and let me see
That you can listen quietly;
And, as I promised, I will tell
That strange adventure which befell
    A poor blind Highland boy.

A *Highland* boy! why call him so?
Because, my darlings, ye must know,
That under hills which rise like towers,
Far higher hills than these of ours,
    He from his birth had lived.

He ne'er had seen one earthly sight;
The sun, the day, the stars, the night;
Or tree, or butterfly, or flower;
Or fish in stream, or bird in bower;
    Or woman, man, or child.

54

R.R. MacIan and his wife Fanny. Together they produced books of elegance and charm which assuredly influenced other British publishers, the most striking example being the change in the design of Charles Dickens's Christmas Books.

The first of these five little books, issued between 1843 and 1847, is *A Christmas Carol*. It is illustrated by four *hors-texte* steel-engravings by John Leech and by a number of integrated wood-engravings from his designs, and is typical of the style developed from the 1830s for small format volumes.[35] Nothing, however, could be more different than its successor, *The Chimes* (1844), with its openings so closely reflecting the style of Burns's books down to the use of 'stick' frames. *The Chimes* has a steel-engraved frontispiece [fig. 110], but wood-engraving is used for the rest of its embellishments [fig. 111] and exclusively in the three remaining Christmas Books, of which two use 'stick' frames for some of their subjects.

Striking as this is, Burns's major contribution, not simply to the style of book-illustration but to that important aspect of publishing, the gift book, is his anthology *Poems and Pictures*. This is a notable specimen of book-embellishment which enjoyed immediate success, going into at least two editions, and was reissued by Samson Low in 1860 and by Cassell, Petter & Galpin in 1865. It represents the culmination of a series of related poetic texts in smaller formats which deserve to be considered for this reason as much as for their own merits.

The earliest venture was an undated *Select Pieces from the Poems of William Wordsworth*,[36] a square duodecimo. Roughly a dozen of the vignette head-pieces appear to have been especially designed for the edition, while other head- and tail-pieces are patently derived from printer's stock [fig. 112]. The text is framed by 'stick' and floral borders designed for the conventional duodecimo format, so that separate pieces are required to be inserted at the fore-edge to frame the wider type area. It is as indicative as the 1842 *Undine* of the wish

113 *Behold I stand at the Door*: wood-engraving with 'stick' borders (Williams, *Sacred Verses*, 1843) [BL 1466 e 39]

"BEHOLD, I STAND AT THE DOOR, AND KNOCK."
REV. iii. 20.

A STRANGER in the morning light,
    Without the door He stood,
His locks are wet with dews of night,[1]
    His hair is drench'd with blood.

Lord, art Thou still a stranger, then,
    By love and pity led,
No place among the sons of men
    To lay Thy sacred Head?

Thou bid'st us knock with earnest cries,
    And none on earth so poor
But if he knocks, Thou wilt arise,
    And ope for him the door.[2]

Still Thou for us art listening long,
    To rise and let us in,
We heed Thee not, we do Thee wrong,
    And stray in ways of sin:

For all too well Thy spirit knows
    Short time doth yet remain
Before the eternal door shall close,
    And we shall knock in vain.[3]

Thou waitest, but we do not hear;
    From Heaven Thou comest down;
To us on earth Thou drawest near,
    Thy wandering sheep to own.

Yea, Thou Thyself to us art come,
    And listening at the door,
Seeking with us to make Thine home,
    And dwell for evermore.

[1] Song of Solomon v. 2.
[2] Matt. vii. 7.   [3] Luke xiii. 25.

to enter the illustrated book market without the full resources to do so. Yet, as with prose, so with verse, Burns soon had the matter in hand. In 1843 he issued an anthology of religious poetry for children, Isaac Williams's *Sacred Verses*. It is a pretty book, very German in feeling; the text is framed by 'stick' borders and frequently embellished by those decorated panels so characteristic of German Romantic book design. For illustration *Sacred Verses* depends less upon original designs than upon reproductions of engravings by Albrecht Dürer. Altogether a more confident production, its one peculiarity is that the text is printed upon alternate openings [fig. 113].

Both books were intended for children, an important side to Burns's publishing activities which will find its place in a more general discussion of children's books in the Romantic period.[37] I would only anticipate by saying how important German influences were in this specific field, in the literary rather than the typographic aspect. Burns's contribution here was substantial; he produced some fine children's books, the best being what is really the prototype of his adult *Poems and Pictures*, although it can stand perfectly well on its own and might even be preferred to the more influential anthology.

Nursery Rhymes, Tales and Jingles was published in 1844, a quarto printed by Robson, Levey & Franklyn, again very much in the German style, with 'stick' borders and panels of decoration in the fore-margins [fig. 114]. The illustrations are anonymous, but credited to William Dyce and C.W. Cope in Burns's later catalogue of his illustrated books. They are admirable examples of the shaded outline style and well take the colour which was given to some de luxe copies. All this, however, seems very inadequate praise for a book which has given me a great deal of pleasure to study. If, as I believe, William Dyce was behind James Burns's excursion into the field of illustrated books, this seems as worthy a memorial of that partnership as the half-dozen designs he contributed to the three poems which he illustrated in *Poems and Pictures*.

A description of the book itself can best be left in the hands of a contemporary reviewer whose notice brings out all those points of artistic and religious affiliation between the German Romantics and their British contemporaries which I have endeavoured to establish. The critic himself was a practising, if amateur, illustrator and a knowledgeable writer on contemporary painting – William Makepeace Thackeray – and *Poems and Pictures* won his esteem. In *The Morning Chronicle* of 31 December 1845 he had hailed it as 'the book … than which English typography has produced nothing more beautiful', and he made it the subject of a long review in *Frazer's Magazine* for December 1845. Under the heading 'About a Christmas Book', he wrote:

> This book in particular, just published by Mr. Burns, [is] the very best of all Christmas books. Let us say this, my dear YORKE, who, in other days have pitilessly trampled on *Forget-me-nots*, and massacred whole galleries of *Books of Beauty*…
>
> The charming *Lieder und Bilder* of the Dusseldorf painters has, no doubt, given the idea of the Work. The German manner has found favour with some of our artists – the Puseyites of art, they may be called, in this country, such as Messrs Cope, Redgrave, Townsend, Horsley, &c; who go back to the masters before Raphael, or to his own best time (that of his youth), for their models of grace and beauty. Their designs have a religious and ascetic, not a heathen and voluptuous tendency. There is no revelling in boisterous nudities like Rubens, no glowing contemplation of lovely forms as in Titian and Etty, but a meek, modest, and downcast demeanour. They appeal to tender sympathies and deal with

subjects of conjugal or maternal love, or charity and devotion. In poetry Goethe can't find favour in their eyes, but Uhland does. Milton is too vast for them, Shakespeare too earthy, but mystic Collins is a favourite, and gentle Cowper; and Alford sings pious hymns for them to the mild strains of his little organ.

The united work of these poets and artists is very well suited to the kind and gentle Christmas season. All the verses are not good, and some of the pictures are but feeble; yet the whole impression of the volume is an exceedingly pleasant one. The solemn and beautiful forms of the figures; the sweet soothing cadences and themes of the verse, affect one like music. Pictures and songs are surrounded by beautiful mystical arabesques, waving and twining round each page. Every now and then you light upon one which is so pretty, it looks as if you had put a flower between the leaves.

Thackeray's review catches well the charm which the book had for his contemporaries; but it does more than that. It offers us an insight into that comfortable atmosphere of mid-

114 *Three Jovial Huntsmen*: wood-engraving showing the decorative influence of the *Nibelungenlied* (1840); cf. figs 79 and 93 (*Nursery Rhymes, Tales and Jingles*, 1844) [BL 1210 m 22]

10.

THERE were three jovial
    huntsmen,
  As I have heard them say,
And they would go a-hunting
  All on a summer's day.

All the day they hunted,
  And nothing could they find
But a ship a-sailing,
  A-sailing with the wind.

One said it was a ship,
  The other said nay ;
The third said it was a house
  With the chimney blown away.

And all the night they hunted,
  And nothing could they find
But the moon a-gliding,
  A-gliding with the wind.

One said it was the moon,
  The other said nay ;
The third said it was a cheese,
  And half o't cut away.

The fiend-horse snorts, blue fiery flakes
　　Collected roll his nostrils round;
High reared his bristling mane he shakes,
　　And sinks beneath the rending ground.
Demons the thundering clouds bestride,
　　Ghosts yell the yawning tombs beneath;
Leonora's heart, its life-blood dried,
　　Hangs quivering on the dart of death.

Throng'd in the moon's eclipsing shade,
　　Of fiends and shapes a spectre-crowd
Dance featly round th' expiring maid,
　　And howl this awful lesson loud:
"Learn patience, though thy heart should break,
　　Nor seek God's mandates to control:
Now this cold earth thy dust shall take,
　　And Heaven relenting take thy soul!"

115 *Leonora*: wood-engraving after H.C. Selous (*Poems and Pictures*, 1846): the illustration was omitted from later editions of the book. Did it shock mid-Victorian sensibilities? See also figs 75 and 129 for Neureuther's and Maclise's interpretations of Burger's poem [BL 1466 i 11]

Victorian piety and sentiment which was to exorcise the sensuality and diabolism of the Romantics. This lay ahead and *Poems and Pictures* itself contained illustrations which the publishers who reprinted the anthology in the 1860s thought it wiser to remove. So out went two of the more macabre designs which Edward Corbould had provided for the ballad 'The Wild Huntsman' and H.C. Selous for Bürger's 'Leonora' [fig. 115]. They are, in a sense, exceptional, for as it prefigures the cultural climate of the 1860s, so *Poems and Pictures* symbolizes the death of the Romantic Age in giving the death-blow to the Annuals.

Thackeray had been their sworn enemy and it is only natural that he should contrast the faded splendours of the steel-engraved *Books of Beauty* with the wood-engraved freshness of *Poems and Pictures*. Nor was he alone in making the comparison. The Annual belonged to what had become an outworn tradition of twenty years or more: *Poems and Pictures* was the first of the new style of gift book. In under five years books of which Vizetelly's typo-graphic masterpiece, *Christmas with the Poets*, George Routledge's heavily illustrated editions of the poets in their equally heavily gilded and embossed bindings, or Revd Robert Aris Wilmott's many anthologies are typical examples, had driven the Annual from the market.

James Burns's achievement was therefore considerable and it was packed into the space of five years. In 1847 he was received into the Catholic Church, an event which prompted outraged letters to *The Times*, and sold much of his Protestant stock and copyrights to Edward Lumley. Until his death in 1871 he worked to build what was to become the doyen of English Catholic publishing houses, Burns, Oates and Washbourne. Nevertheless, that short spell of Tractarianism enabled him firmly to establish the German Romantic style of book illustration and design through his publications, to launch a number of important illustrators and, in *Poems and Pictures*, to establish the new pattern of Christmas gift book, one of the most important genres for the Sixties' illustrators.

NOTES

1 E.g. *Buchkunst und Literatur in Deutschland 1750 bis 1850*.
2 Curmer's edition of *Paul et Virginie* (1838) contains seven steel-engravings of which only the frontispiece portrait of Bernardin de St Pierre was included in the English translation published by William Orr in the following year.
3 10 vols by Georg Wigand (1836–40); 2 vols by Theodor Fischer (1841–2).
4 See Appendix II.
5 See ibid.
6 1839, 32.
7 *Artists' Lithographs*, 44; and *Die illustierten deutschen Bücher des XIX Jahrhunderts*, respectively.
8 *Die illustierten deutschen Bücher des XIX Jahrhunderts*.
9 Ibid., no. 2485.
10 Ibid.
11 Quoted by David Irwin, *John Flaxman*, 67–8.
12 Ibid., 68.
13 From c.1820–40: Rudolph Ackermann; Black, Young & Young (later Black & Armstrong); J.H. Bohte; Charles Jügel; George Nott; Williams & Norgate; Hering & Remington.
14 *Fridolin* (1824); *Kampf mit dem Drachen* (1824); *Pegasus im Joche* (1833); *Lied von der Glocke* (1834).
15 *German Romanticism and English Art*, 123.
16 David Irwin, *John Flaxman*, 22.
17 Ibid., 30.
18 *German Romanticism and English Art*, 17ff.
19 Ibid., 158
20 *King of Root Valley* (English trans., unillustrated, 1856).
21 *German Romanticism and English Art*, 174.
22 Ibid., 218ff.
23 *Glances Back*, I, 304–5.
24 *Retrospect*, I, 327, 332.
25 Ibid., 332.
26 Ibid., 330–1.
27 I have been unable to prove or to disprove the truth of this statement from the Longman Archive.
28 *Glances Back*, I, 305.
29 Hall, *Retrospect*, II, 214.
30 *Glances Back*, I, 305.
31 *Retrospect*, I, 331.
32 Ibid., 333.
33 Vaughan, *German Romanticism and English Art*, 189.
34 Ibid., 191–2.
35 See p. 158.
36 British Library Catalogue suggests 1843: probably a year later.
37 See pp. 237–8.

III
SOME BRITISH PUBLISHERS AND ARTISTS

The Publishers

John Van Voorst

Although the styles of embellishment developed in France and Germany are the character-istics of the finest illustrated books of the Romantic period, they need to be seen in the larger perspective of an age which developed an overwhelming hunger for the image. The rising tide of prosperity which flowed from the expansion of manufacture and trade created a new upper and middle class intellectually not so far removed from the aspiring artisan for whom the lavish illustration of Charles Knight's *Penny Magazine* and his part-publications was a deliberate lure. There was an explosion of illustration over the whole publishing trade in Britain, of which we have already considered the effects on three houses – W.S. Orr and Joseph Thomas in the context of the direct influence of French, and James Burns of German Romantic book design. It will therefore help us to understand the environment in which British illustrators worked if we consider the illustrated books issued by those pillars of the London trade, Thomas Longman and John Murray, and briefly trace the fortunes of a major publisher of illustrated books of the period, Charles Tilt, and those of his employee, partner and successor, David Bogue.[1]

116 *The Sky Lark*: wood-engraving designed and executed by John Thompson (Yarrell, *A History of British Birds*, 1, 1839) [BL 7301 1]

These giants should not, however, obscure one small and specialist publisher, John Van Voorst, whose reactions typify those of so many other publishers and whose deliberate policy produced some very fine books. In fact, Van Voorst was to become a scientific publisher specializing in natural history. He was to publish William Yarrell's *History of British Birds* [figs 116, 117] and *History of British Fishes*, similar histories of British starfishes and molluscs by Professor Edward Forbes of Edinburgh, and the works on fossils and comparative anatomy by Professor Owen, the first Superintendent of the Natural History Museum at South Kensington; adding to such general treatises specialized works of local botany or ornithology ranging from Jamaica to Gibraltar, a few travel books, and a strong list of books on Gothic architecture. The general impression which this list was to give was one of solid scholarship and of sound, if perhaps unadventurous, publishing.

Like that of so many of the smaller publishing houses, the history of Van Voorst is obscure, but perhaps, like so many others, the publishing enterprise was built upon a bookselling base. Given the way in which we have seen the list was to develop, we may suspect that the bookselling business was biased towards science and natural history. All the more surprising, then, that the earliest known publications of the firm – dating from 1834 and thus preceding William Yarrell's monumental handbooks – are illustrated books.

To dedicate a new imprint to embellished books is an indication of the strength of their market in the mid-1830s and we can see how successfully John Van Voorst exploited his opportunity if we look back from one of his catalogues of the 1850s. In it, the section headed 'Illustrated Reprints' contains nine titles published between 1834 and 1848 and comprising Dodsley's *Economy of Human Life*, Gray's *Elegy* and Aiken's *Calendar of Nature* (all 1834); Gray's *The Bard* (1837); Shakespeare's *Seven Ages of Man* (1840); Goldsmith's *The Vicar of Wakefield* and White's *Natural History of Selborne* (both 1843); Bloomfield's *Poems* (1845), and Watts's *Divine and Moral Songs* (1848).

All the books are duodecimos except *The Vicar of Wakefield*, a squarish octavo, and all except the Dodsley are illustrated by wood-engraving. John Martin, the Duke of Bedford's librarian who edited Gray's *Elegy*, probably hints at the new technique of lowering the block when, in his preface to the poem, he writes:

> The great improvement which has taken place, within a few years, in the Art of Engraving on Wood, as well as its general adoption, in some measure superseding the use of Copper and Steel, led to the present attempt to apply this mode of embellishment to a poem … which appeared to afford the greatest scope for the talents of the artist.

117 *Puffins and Rabbits*: wood-engraved tail-piece in the traditionally English humorous style (Yarrell, *A History of British Birds*, 1, 1839) [BL 730 1 1]

Yet, although Van Voorst was well abreast of the newest techniques in wood-engraving and applied them to his publications, the style which he adopted was resolutely old-fashioned. This conservatism, so noticeable in the Dodsley with its vignette steel-engravings presented in the manner of John Sharpe's illustrated poets of some twenty years earlier, is a remarkable characteristic of all the wood-engraved books as well. Eschewing the framed page developed by the Germans and the French – a policy perfectly understandable in the 1830s, but eccentric in the next decade – they retain the traditional British layout of open page and vignette head- and tail-pieces. In other words, Van Voorst applies to what are really embellished books those techniques of graphic reproduction and design which served him so well in his illustrated scientific treatises and in so doing demonstrates the vitality of the Bewick tradition in an area which Bewick made especially his own, and of the enduring qualities of British Regency typography.

Where Van Voorst was very much in the mainstream, however, was in his choice of artists for his 'Illustrated Reprints'. Continental painters were not ashamed to work as book-illustrators and the constant complaint of English press critics – often, it is true, with a touch of 'They order this matter better in France' – was the poor standard of draughtsmanship in British books. *The Art Union Journal*, for example, decried British publishers because 'our greatest Painters have not applied their talents to this branch of their profession',[2] by contrast with the French. In fact, Van Voorst had anticipated this ill-founded criticism by following long-established practice and choosing his illustrators from among the leading painters of the day. The Gray's *Elegy* of 1834 and the Shakespeare *Seven Ages* of 1840 were illustrated by no less than twenty-three and nine artists respectively, and their names included Copley Fielding, John Constable [fig. 118], Thomas Stothard, de Wint, Wilkie, Calcott, Chalon and Mulready.

Although both books enjoyed considerable success in their day and went into a number of reprints, their overall effect is disappointing. Not all the painters appear to have understood the requirements of wood-engraving and the only page which I find memorable is William Mulready's contribution to Gray's *Elegy* [fig. 119]. Much happier results were achieved when a more limited number of artists was employed in Bloomfield's *Poems* (1845),[3] but best of all when a single artist was responsible for the entire illustration. This

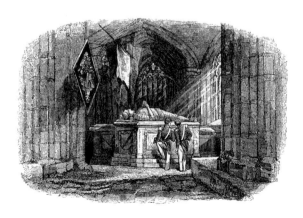

118 Wood-engraved head-piece after John Constable (Gray, *Elegy in a Country Churchyard*, 1834) [BL 11662 b 15(1)]

is what makes George Cattermole's work in *The Calendar of Nature* [fig. 120] so much more satisfying than that of the star-studded cast of its 1834 companion, Gray's *Elegy*. It resulted, too, in two undoubted masterpieces, William Mulready's illustrations to *The Vicar of Wakefield* (1843) [fig. 121] and C.W. Cope's to Isaac Watts's *Divine and Moral Songs* (1848) [fig. 124]. In all the 'Illustrated Reprints' the typography is classical and by and large their artists aim for traditional and tonal effects in their designs. Mulready and Cope are exceptions: both are influenced by the outline style and in overall effect Cope anticipates the work of the Pre-Raphaelite painters Millais and Hunt in Moxon's illustrated Tennyson of 1857.

119 Half-page vignette wood-engraving after William Mulready (Gray, *Elegy in a Country Churchyard*, 1834): curiously, the artist has dressed his figures in contemporary clothing [BL 11662 b 15(1)]

120 *February*: wood-engraved head-piece after George Cattermole (Aiken, *The Calendar of Nature*, 1834) [BL 972 b 27]

121 *Dr Primrose preaching to his fellow-prisoners*: wood-engraved chapter-opening after William Mulready (Goldsmith, *The Vicar of Wakefield*, 1843) [BL C70 C 7]

122 The same scene interpreted by Charles Jacque in a wood-engraved vignette from a bilingual French and English edition of 1838 [BL 635 k 11]

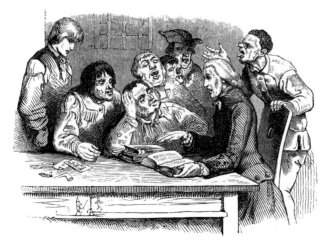

123 How Ludwig Richter saw it: wood-engraved vignette from a German translation of 1841 [BL 1459 g 5]

124 *For the Lord's Day Morning*:
half-page wood-engraving after
C.W. Cope (Watts, *Divine and Moral
Songs*, 1848) [BL 1220 f 33]

Although their range is limited, Van Voorst's books are still some of the most satisfying of the period. They are eminently worthy of study and no one with the slightest interest in nineteenth-century wood-engraving can afford to ignore them since, as with his illustrators so with his engravers, Van Voorst employed the best – men like John Thompson and Samuel Williams among them.

THOMAS LONGMAN AND JOHN MURRAY

To give priority to a publisher whose illustrated books had a sobriety quite at variance with the decorative extravagance of the Romantic books which we have described, is to emphasize yet again that, while Romantic design is the most exciting part of the story of illustrated books at this period, it is by no means the whole story. British publishers and artists were sensitive to and receptive of Continental illustration, and they developed their own variations upon the Romantic theme, especially in the illuminated books designed by Owen Jones and Noel Humphreys. Nevertheless, they continued to produce a great many books in the manner of Bewick and his followers, acknowledging the importance of the image by promoting the vignette head-piece decoration to the rank of half- or one-third-page illustrations.

One appreciates this point more clearly if one considers the range of illustrated books in the list of a major publisher such as Thomas Longman. However, it is important to remember that Longman's standing in the trade gave his firm the pick of the new books. He had a splendid list of biography, history, travel, science and general non-fiction, books which were illustrated as they have always been with portraits and other plates. He drew his profits from books for reading rather than from books whose appeal was primarily to the eye and, although to maintain his position he had to remain sensitive to changes in public taste, he did not have to 'manufacture' books in the way in which the small publisher is compelled to do. Given then the enormous vogue for the image, the new imprints of the 1830s and 1840s would be far more likely to create books in this area and their lists would therefore contain a far higher proportion of embellished books than those of a more established publisher.

Certainly, so far as Longman's are concerned, illustrated books form a very small proportion of the list as a whole. They are, nonetheless, most significant in showing this sensitive response to changes in the market. Longman was, for example, among the first to see the possibilities of steel-engraving and, according to Basil Hunnisett,[4] his links with Charles Heath, one of the pioneers of the new technique, went back to 1818. He issued two of Heath's most celebrated annuals, *The Keepsake* (1832–47) and *The Book of Beauty* (1833–49); he published between 1833 and 1835 *Turner's Annual Tours*, re-issuing the plates with appropriate descriptions in English and French as *The Rivers of France* (1837), and, in the same annual vein, *The Wye* (1839) and *Windsor Castle* (1840) by Leith Ritchie, who had provided the texts for Turner's tours. Longman applied the highly finished 'Book of Beauty' style of steel-engraving, too, to such divers books as G.A. Hansard's *The Book of Archery* (1840), Thomas Moore's *Lalla Rookh* (1838) and, most appropriately since the author Alaric Watts had been editor of one of the most famous annuals, *The Literary Souvenir*, to *Lyrics of the Heart* [fig. 125]. Unfortunately the book itself was an almost total disaster. Announced for 1847, it was not published until 1851, by which time it had outrun both its schedule and its budget and, to crown it all, had eventually to be remaindered.

Thomas Moore was a very different case and his *Irish Melodies* and *Lalla Rookh* were among Longman's most valuable copyrights. The former provided the firm with one of its most spectacular embellished books, the edition of 1846, in which text, borders and vignettes,

125 *Egypt Unvisited*:
squared steel-engraving
after David Roberts
(Watt, *Lyrics of the Heart*,
1851) [BL 11645 f 4]

No, — that hallow'd form is ne'er forgot
Which first love trac'd;
Still it lingering haunts the greenest spot
On memory's waste.
'Twas odour fled
As soon as shed;
'Twas morning's winged dream;
'Twas a light, that ne'er can shine again
On life's dull stream:
Oh! 'twas light that ne'er can shine again
On life's dull stream.

D. Maclise, R.A. del.   *F. P. Becker, sc.*

126 Steel-engraved page after Daniel Maclise (Moore, *Irish Melodies*, 1846) [BL C30 l 1]

127 *The Maid ...
Look'd at him – shriek'd
– and sunk upon the
ground!*: wood-
engraving after John
Tenniel typical of the
Sixties book (Moore,
Lalla Rookh, 1860)
[BL 1347 G 18]

designed by Daniel Maclise, were engraved throughout on steel, very reminiscent of the German *Lieder und Bilder* [fig. 126]. Maclise also designed for wood-engraving in the 1849 edition of *Lalla Rookh* and was, with Birket Foster, the major contributor to Moore's *Poetry and Pictures* (1858). In this way the Longman editions of Thomas Moore epitomize the developments of book-illustration from the little 18mo edition of *Lalla Rookh* published in 1817 with copper-engravings after Richard Westall in the Regency style, to John Tenniel's wood-engraved designs for the same poem, published in 1860 in an edition which is typical of the coming decade [fig. 127].

The change from steel to wood as the accepted medium of engraving is also reflected in two books by Captain Marryat which Longman published in editions illustrated by Clarkson Stanfield. *The Pirate and The Three Cutters* (1836) employs full-page, steel-engraved *hors-texte* illustrations [fig. 163]; *Poor Jack* (1840) a mixture of integrated vignettes and full-page designs engraved on wood, the majority by Henry Vizetelly. Other important books embellished by wood-engraving followed: two volumes illustrated by members of the

Etching Club [figs 169, 170], James Thomson's *The Seasons* (1842) and Oliver Goldsmith's *Poetical Works* (1845); and Macaulay's *Lays of Ancient Rome*, with outline drawings 'from the antique' by George Scharf junior [fig. 128], in 1847, the same year as their most spectacular book in this medium, a translation of Bürger's *Leonora* for which Maclise's designs were engraved by John Thompson [fig. 129]. In all these books a wide variety of Romantic styles is evident, from the strongly Germanic of Maclise to the very French influence apparent in 'Martingale's' *Sporting Scenes* (1840) and Lane's *Life at the Water Cure* (1846). These, as we have seen, were printed by Henry Vizetelly, while the Etching Club volumes show an advance in the page layout introduced in Turner's designs for Rogers's poetry when the illustration was given more prominence by being integrated within the frame of a rule border.

LX.

No sound of joy or sorrow
Was heard from either bank ;
But friends and foes in dumb surprise,
With parted lips and straining eyes,
Stood gazing where he sank ;

128 *Horatius*: wood-engraving after George Scharf junior (Macaulay, *Lays of Ancient Rome*, 1847) [BL 1346 h 28]

Now nearer draws the funeral train,
Like croak of frogs resounds the strain.
Why tolls the bell? who, solemn, say
" Dust unto dust, and clay to clay"?

129 *Leonora*: wood-engraving by John Thompson after Daniel Maclise (Burger, *Leonora*, 1847). Compare with H.C. Selous's interpretation (fig. 115) [BL C30 k 2]

Despite all these books, Longman's lists tend to confirm, too, the persistence of the more traditional British style, as in the series of illustrated books written by William Howitt and published between 1838 and 1842 – *Rural Life in England* (1838), *The Boy's Country Book* (1839), *Visits to Remarkable Places* (two series, 1840–42), *The Student Life of Germany* (1841) and *The Rural and Domestic Life of Germany* (1842). By and large they are all in the English tradition of the wood-cut vignette confined to the head and tail of chapter openings and endings. *The Boy's Country Book* is an engaging example, but the others are fairly routine exercises in this manner. There is little or no sign of Continental Romantic influence – a single page in *The Student Life of Germany* – until we come to *The Rural and Domestic Life of Germany* in which a high proportion of G.F. Sargent's fifty-one designs are integrated into the text.

Thus, side-by-side with exciting new designs in Longman's list march books conceived in a well-established pattern of vignette wood-engraving. They represent in miniature the wider pattern of British publishing. Yet, if Longman's makes a contribution to the Romantic book in Britain, it is less for their books printed with relief or intaglio engravings, fine though so many of them are, than for their lithographic books. They dominated the market in 'illuminated books', that is, books printed by chromolithography, and became the publishers of the two greatest designers in that medium, Owen Jones and Noel Humphreys, in the 1840s.

Like many publishers, colour-plate books are to be found in Longman's earlier lists, books illustrated with hand-coloured copper- or steel-engravings, such as Mrs Hey's *Moral of Flowers* (1833), or her *Spirit of the Woods* (1837), with their fine botanical plates. The period, too, was one of considerable experiment in colour-printing from wood-blocks, culminating in George Baxter's successful multicolour process in 1836. This he eventually applied largely to the production of prints rather than to book-illustration, the latter being left to those like John Leighton and William Dickes who purchased his patent rights, and to Edmund Evans in the 1860s. On a less elaborate scale, however, Henry Vizetelly had shown how effectively page borders could be printed in two and three colours, especially when used in conjunction with chromolithographic title and half-title pages in the books which Owen Jones designed for John Murray.[5] Jones, too, was the designer involved in an early Longman book employing chromolithography – the Baroness de Calabrella's *The Prism of the Imagination* (1843).

The year before, Longman had published a volume of aphorisms by the Baroness, *The Prism of Thought*, with initial letters and arabesque page borders printed in relief, in colours and gold, by Robson, Levey & Franklyn. Admirable though much of their letter-press printing is, they cannot compare with Vizetelly as colour printers. Thus the book, interesting as it is – the initial letters are copied from sixteenth-century Lyonnais models – cannot be accounted successful. For its successor, *The Prism of the Imagination*, chromolithography is employed and, despite the thick card leaves, it is really rather a splendid book. Owen Jones supplied the designs for illuminated titles, story openings and page borders and, in addition, there were a number of full-page tinted lithographic illustrations by Henry Warren.

But can illuminated books really be considered as books in the true sense? Are they not often extremely attractive examples of colour-printing on cards, bound up for the owner's convenience? Perhaps chromolithography is seen at its best when it is an adjunct to relief methods of printing, which themselves marry with a text printed from type. Thus, while *The Prism of the Imagination* may fall just short of complete success, Louisa Stuart Costello's anthology *The Rose Garden of Persia* (1845) shows what can be achieved by this combination [pl. 4]. The title-page and section openings are printed by chromolithography: the borders and ornaments from relief stereo- or polytypes cast from wood-engravings, all relief printing being undertaken by Henry Vizetelly. The narrow octavo format and the richness of the colouring – blue, green, carmine and gold – make this a particularly satisfying book, its decorations being based upon authentic Oriental motifs, traced from manuscripts in the library of the Asiatic Society.[6] Unfortunately, there is no indication as to who designed the book, but given his interest in Islamic art and his connection with the firm, it seems very probable that Owen Jones was responsible for the embellishments.

By now Owen Jones had been joined on Longman's list by the other, and to my mind greater, artist of the illuminated book, Henry Noel Humphreys. Humphreys's first book was the delightful *Illuminated Calendar* for 1845, published in the autumn of 1844. A successor volume appeared the next year, and then, between 1847 and 1850, four biblical works – *The Parables of Our Lord* (1847), *The miracles ...* and *The Maxims and Precepts of Our Saviour* [pl. 5] (both 1848), and *The Book of Ruth* (1850) – interspersed with a piece of mediaevalism, *A Record of the Black Prince* (1849). *Sentiments and Similes of William Shakespeare* followed in 1851 and the tally of illuminated books is completed by *The Penitential Psalms* of 1861. Among them are to be found examples of the very finest chromolithographic embellishment which demonstrate Noel Humphreys's artistry at its best.

His qualities are fine colour sense and an acutely sensitive feeling for his mediaeval and Renaissance models. The latter results in work which is in the grand tradition of manuscript illumination – neither unhistorical pastiche nor slavish copying, but a quite original nine-teenth-century expression of this ancient craft of book-embellishment. (This, incidentally, is in contrast with the French, who produced no artist of Humphreys's calibre and were content – as in the superb *Imitatio Christi* published by Curmer in 1851–7 [pl. 7] – to make meticulous copies of earlier work.) Yet perhaps one of Humphreys's most sterling qualities is that of the natural historian who illustrates Westwood's *British Moths* (1843), *Insect Changes* (1847) and Webb's *British Wild Flowers* (1856) and is one further talent of the palaeographer, numismatist and artist.

While his skills are so apparent in his illuminated books, one may rate as highly the wood-engraved borders which Humphreys designed for Eden Warwick's *The Poet's Pleasuance*, published by Longman in 1847. The printer is Henry Vizetelly who, together with William Dickes, engraved the wood-blocks for these splendid decorations of entwined flowers and leaves, with butterflies, moths and other insects among them. Here is a richness so sadly lacking in his later attenuated style of floral decoration, applied to many books in the 1850s, among them Nisbet's 1857 edition of *The Poetical Works of George Herbert*.

Although it is invidious to compare men who were friends and collaborators, by contrast with Humphreys the painter, behind Owen Jones's decorations seems to lie the more mathematical rigidity of the architect. The motifs of mediaeval decoration are common to builders and to illuminators of manuscripts: Humphreys has the fluidity of the illuminator, but the stiffness of the stonemason may be detected perhaps in some of Jones's work. It suffers, too, when, as in the case of *The Preacher* (1849), it surrounds a text in a Gothic letter which has been tortured to the point of illegibility.

This presentation of Ecclesiastes had been preceded by *The Sermon on the Mount* (1845), Gray's *Elegy* (1846), *The Good Shunamite* (1848) and *The Song of Solomon* (1849). These are all Jones's own work and recall, because they doubtless inspired, so many of the framed texts which decorated the bedroom walls of old-fashioned boarding houses. However, between 1848 and 1851 Jones illuminated three books of verse by Mary Bacon, *Flowers and their Kindred Thoughts* (1848), *Fruits from the Garden and the Field* (1850) and *Winged Thoughts* (1851). All three show rather more freedom, but Owen Jones is not the natural history painter that Noel Humphreys is.

Longman, therefore, dominated the market in illuminated books as the sole publishers of the two leading artists in chromolithography. Yet it was a market subject to surprising and, at this distance of time, not wholly explicable fluctuations. Noel Humphreys's books were published under agreements by which Longman bore the costs of production and shared the profits with the artist. Of the two *Illuminated Calendars*, the first seems to have sold out; yet the second was remaindered. *The Parables of Our Lord* (1847) appears to have been the most successful of all. Two editions, each of 2,000 copies, were sold, Appleton, the American publisher, taking half the second.[7] Yet it was a very different story with the two illuminated books published in the following year. *The Miracles of Our Lord* sold an edition of 2,000 copies, but Longman considered that this had exhausted its potential and there was mutual agreement not to reprint,[8] doubtless because of the failure of its companion, *The Maxims and Precepts of Our Saviour*. Appendix III (p. 296) shows these sales in detail and provides evidence for a similar pattern for Owen Jones's illuminated books, although in this case the sales figures are incomplete. Longman published his books on commission and doubtless Jones dealt directly with a number of customers.

The vogue for illuminated books was therefore relatively short-lived. While it is impossible to determine why particular books sold well and others did not, it would be safe to conclude that there was never more than a comparatively small market for them. Both Jones and Humphreys overestimated its size and its ability to absorb new titles, and by over-production surfeited it to death; this may have affected the sales of Noel Humphreys's serious study of palaeography, *The Illuminated Books of the Middle Ages*. Longman had begun to publish this in parts on the usual shared-profit terms in 1844, but falling sales prompted them as early as 1847 to shift the burden of responsibility for the costs of production to Owen Jones and to account to him thereafter on a commission basis.[9]

While Thomas Longman published the bulk of Owen Jones's illuminated work, he was not his first publisher, that honour belonging to the other pillar of the British trade, John Murray. Murray and Jones were to remain on friendly terms for many years, although their active collaboration was really confined to the decade of the 1840s. This, however, saw the production of what is arguably Owen Jones's finest work, since the books which he designed and embellished for Murray are real books, and not simply specimens, however lovely, of chromolithography. They start with J.G. Lockhart's *Ancient Spanish Ballads* (1841) and continue through *The Book of Common Prayer* (1845) and H.H. Milman's edition of Horace (1849) to a new edition of *Ancient Spanish Ballads* in 1853. In addition, Jones provided for Murray three chromolithographic title-pages in his best Islamic style for the edition of Lane's translation of *The Arabian Nights*, in which the wood-engravings which William Harvey designed for the original royal octavos of Charles Knight's 1839 edition are disastrously cramped to a crown octavo format.

The sixteen letters and notes written to Murray during this period by the artist, surviving in the files of John Murray & Co., offer tantalizing glimpses of the designer at work and of the friendly relations which were established between the two men. The earliest letter, dated 27 November [1839], is strictly business, but within five years a more personal note had crept in, Jones writing to Murray on 29 August 1844 to thank him for 'your handsome and valuable present' and able to return the favour on 26 December of the same year.

> In consequence of the 'tremendous success' of the Sermon, I have only now got my copies by which I fear Mr Longman has the advantage of me in offering you a copy, but I do not wish to be cheated out of my good intentions and therefore beg to offer you another and if as I suspect you will then have two *coats*, I have no doubt you will be able to obey the scriptural injunction to give to him or her that has none.

These friendly relations were maintained and, when sending tickets for the Great Exhibition on 18 January 1851, Jones, who had been commissioned to design the interior décor, could confide:

> … I am happy to say that I have had my own way about the coloring it was settled with the Royal Commission at the beginning of December last with a very small alteration from the plan I proposed it is only the 'lies of the Times' that makes the public think the contrary.

On 3 November 1853 he combines business with pleasure by sending Murray tickets for the Crystal Palace in a letter concerned with the new edition of *Ancient Spanish Ballads* published later in the year, and the series ends with further notes dated 11 March 1854 and 28 May 1857 on domestic matters.

In the first letter of 27 November 1839 we find Jones at work on the chromolithographic plates for the monumental six volumes of Sir Gardner Wilkinson's *The Ancient Egyptians*. He writes to Murray:

> I send you a proof of the Key plate – and some on which I have dabbled a little water color which does not of course pretend to shew the effect they will have when printed but simply the arrangement – this I hope you will bear in mind or you might be fearful of the *result* …

Evidently Murray was satisfied, for next month Jones reported that 'Your messenger will tell you that he found me at work by my midnight lamp upon a stone like old Mortality;[10] to immortalise us both.' Just over a year later, Jones's task was coming to an end and he wrote to Murray on 12 February 1841:

> We are now finishing the printing of Wilkinsons plates (1500) – would it be safe to go on with the other 500 to complete the edition they would not of course form an account till you required them – but if they are *ever* likely to be wanted I would rather do them now that the man is used to the Stone.

In the interim Jones had been engaged for *Ancient Spanish Ballads* and on 7 August 1840 had written to acknowledge 'the receipt of Mr Murray's cheque for £50 on account'. In an undated letter attributed to that year he tells Murray that he 'passed the morning with Warren looking over the book with reference to borders &c and am most anxious to know the alteration you require in the titles'.[11] By 12 February 1841 work was well advanced and in the letter from which I have already quoted Jones requested a further £50 on account.

The letter is interesting, too, in showing that Henry Vizetelly's casting of the engraved borders of *The Rose Garden of Persia* in 1845 had been in accordance with his established practice. Four years before this Jones writes: 'I send you a proof I have just rec[d] from Vizetilly [*sic*] he tells me that they have been waiting for the thaw to polytype the other borders which have been engraved for some time.' Here is an unappreciated hazard of Victorian printing. Polytyping produced a mould by 'dabbing' the engraved wood-block into molten type-metal: if the air temperature of the casting room was too low – as in a freezing February – the operation would become impossible because the metal would solidify too quickly.

Ancient Spanish Ballads is the first of the three books which Jones designed for Murray and is in many ways the most exciting in its use of colour and in the design of its arabesque borders. Islamic art was Jones's first love – his monumental work on the Alhambra (plans, elevations and sections and the details and ornaments), issued in parts between 1836 and 1845, were his first essays in chromolithography – and Islam seems to me a far richer source of Jones's inspiration than European mediaeval art. Nevertheless, the book suffers from defects of design of which Jones himself was probably aware and which he deliberately sought to remedy in his subsequent books.

The major fault – and it is of conception rather than of execution – is the introduction of certain divisive elements which were as apparent to Jones's contemporaries as they are today. One press critic, who was in general most complimentary to Owen Jones himself, wrote: 'The great defect of the book is want of unity … The designs being by many different artists, are often not in accordance with each other, although separately beautiful. The decorations are so various in their style, that they contrast too violently.'[12]

This is all strictly true, but the employment of a number of artists in the same book is a period convention which one can accept without too much difficulty. In fact, the only way in which the artists' work can be said really to disturb the unity of the book is when the designs are printed in tinted wood-engraving as full-page *hors-texte* illustrations. The criticism of the borders is well founded. Each individual ballad is enclosed within a specific set, so that when one ends on a verso, and the next begins on the recto following, a clash is unavoidable, even when both have been designed by Owen Jones. For the really discordant note is struck by the intrusion into Jones's Islamic manner of a set of borders in the French revived-rococo style by François Louis Français. These had been designed for the 'Song for the Morning of the Day of St John the Baptist', for which Français had provided a very French vignette, and however intrusive his 'vine and olive' border may be here, it compounds the initial error of taste to employ it on a number of other pages.

We may, perhaps, detect the hand of the book's printer, Henry Vizetelly, here and in the generally Anglo-French style of the vignette engravings. There is virtually no evidence of German influence except for the occasional and very minor reminiscence in some of Henry Warren's designs, while the fore-margin panels in William Harvey's illustrations to

'Count Alarcos and the Infanta Solisa' owe less to Eugen Neureuther than to Harvey's own engravings in *The Arabian Nights*. But what makes this so satisfying a book in the final analysis are Jones's own borders, superbly printed by Henry Vizetelly in their red and carmine, blue and yellow, green and mauve two- and three-colour pages – and, of course, to Jones's own chromolithographic titles. Any disappointment arises from what may be assumed as less than complete control of the whole design by Owen Jones.

The same, fortunately, is not true of his two other books for Murray and, as a result, *The Book of Common Prayer* (1845) is perhaps the most satisfying piece of design which Owen Jones ever produced. The decorated initials, always a weakness of his chromolithography, gain in clarity from the wood-engraver's burin, while the use of a related design for the borders of each of the far longer sections of the Prayer Book gives both unity and diversity [pl. 6]. The Collects, Epistle and Gospels are illustrated by integrated wood-engravings from outline copies by George Scharf junior of old and modern masters, and of the moderns Overbeck predominates. This bias is consonant with the German influence discernible in the four full-page tinted wood-engravings, three designed by J.C. Horsley [fig. 130] and one by Henry Warren, and particularly in their borders. Employed as *hors-textes*, they are not intrusive as are the full-page illustrations in *Ancient Spanish Ballads*, but provide appropriate frontispieces to the liturgies for Holy Communion, Baptisms, Weddings and the Burial of the Dead. If Owen Jones's Gothic borders cannot quite match his arabesques, individually, the ensemble is far stronger, while the illuminated pages are among his best.

The book is the measure of the sum rather than of the parts and fully achieves the aim set out in a letter to John Murray of 30 March 1848. In discussing the details of Milman's forthcoming edition of Horace, Jones remarks: 'It is very difficult in a few pages to judge of the effect of a book as a whole when it is completed it should be seen in the "mind's eye"'. Adding, 'My endeavour is to connect the whole that the eye should run from the beginning to the end without feeling uncomfortable.'

The Horace itself, dated 1849 but ready in December 1848, is austere by comparison with its predecessors. In this edition only the life of Horace, with which the editor, H.H. Milman, prefaces the Latin text, is surrounded by narrow engraved borders printed in colours and based on Classical models. The text itself is enclosed by two single rule frames, the outer plain and printed in red, the inner black with corner ornaments. Hence Jones wrote:

> I do not think the black corners would be a disadvantage supporting as they would the effect of the coloured titles – and the borders of the life – if you were to reduce the scale of the book to the scale of the cuts the titles and borders would then become fearful blots and spots.

In the event, Murray acceded to Jones's wishes and the Horace is printed in the same royal octavo as the Prayer Book. One associates Owen Jones so very closely with the revival of both Islamic and Christian mediaeval decoration that the book seems almost out of character, yet the austerity of the page layout of the text matches the outline drawings of Classical subjects made by George Scharf junior and printed as integrated wood-engravings. They match, in turn, both the Classical borders of the life of Horace and the chromolithographic title-pages. These last have considerable beauty, their only weakness – and this is Jones's persistent fault – being the weak roman lettering [pl. 8].

I have discussed these books at some length because I feel that Owen Jones's real importance is less as an 'illuminator' (where Noel Humphreys is his superior) than as a book designer, a role which, in the case of *Ancient Spanish Ballads*, includes responsibility for the binding-stamps and end-papers as well. The books which he helped to create for John Murray represent a very considerable achievement and, unlike his own illuminated books, they really are *books*. A complete integration of text, illustration and decoration which satisfies the Romantic aspiration for oriental or mediaeval richness, they yet remain eminently practical and readable objects.

They are, too, a specifically British contribution to the art of the European Romantic book, made by a major British publishing house not otherwise noted for its embellished books. My impression is that Murray quietly adapted his firm's publications to the

130 *The Burial of the Dead*: wood-engraving by John Thompson of J.C. Horsley's design (*The Book of Common Prayer*, 1845) [BL C30 l 2]

LIFE AND POEMS

OF THE

REV. GEORGE CRABBE.

VOL. I.

Drawn by C. Stanfield, A.R.A.   *Engraved by E. Finden.*

House of Crabbe's Father
p. 12

LONDON:
JOHN MURRAY, ALBEMARLE STREET.
1834.

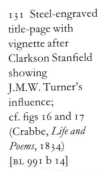

131 Steel-engraved title-page with vignette after Clarkson Stanfield showing J.M.W. Turner's influence; cf. figs 16 and 17 (Crabbe, *Life and Poems*, 1834) [BL 991 b 14]

prevailing demand for more and more illustration, unlike Longman who made aggressive inroads into this new market with the illuminated books of Owen Jones and Noel Humphreys, with the Etching Club's publications and with Daniel Maclise's *Irish Melodies* and *Leonora*. In the 1830s Murray had reacted by commissioning work from George Cruikshank and, in particular, designs for the wood-engravings in his ill-fated Family Library, by adopting for his collected edition of the poems of George Crabbe the steel-engraved frontispiece and vignette title [fig. 131] popularized by Turner and by producing, in 1836, an edition of Lord Byron's *Childe Harold's Pilgrimage* clearly inspired by the editions of Samuel Rogers's poetry with Turner's vignettes engraved on steel.

During the decade 1840–49, when the pressure to produce embellished books was strongest, Murray's response was characteristically guarded and limited to the three books designed by Owen Jones, to Otto Speckter's *Puss in Books* and *The Charmed Roe*, to the re-issue of the Lane/Harvey *Arabian Nights* and to an edition of *Aesop's Fables*, illustrated by John Tenniel and published in 1848 [figs 132, 133]. This last was the most successful of the group and had by 1857 reached its twenty-first printing as one of the cheap editions issued as 'Murray's Reading for the Rail'. Ruari McLean has stated, presumably from evidence in the Murray Archive, that of the three Owen Jones books only *Ancient Spanish Ballads* showed a profit.[13] While this may be true of the first issues of the books concerned, it is interesting to see in 'Mr. Murray's List of Illustrated Works', issued in January 1856, that new editions of all of them were available, together with Speckter's two children's books and the Aesop, while a new edition of *The Arabian Nights* was announced as being 'in preparation'. It seems as though Owen Jones's books had established their popularity and were beginning to show a return on their original high investment.

FABLE LII.

THE

TRAVELLERS AND THE BEAR.

Two friends were travelling on the same road together, when they met with a Bear. The one in great fear, without a thought of his

132 *The Travellers and the Bear*: wood-engraving after John Tenniel (Aesop, *Fables*, 1848) [BL 12305 e 32]

This list is of considerable interest, too, since it so clearly underlines the legacy of the 1840s. In concrete terms this comprised the eight books first published in that decade, even if some of them were less lavishly illustrated. This is true of the 1853 and 1856 editions of *Ancient Spanish Ballads*, deprived of their full-page wood-engravings and with far more economy in the use of colour for the page-borders, and of Sir Gardner Wilkinson's *The Ancient Egyptians*, now abridged in two smaller volumes, which retained the 500 wood-engraved illustrations.

In the abstract, this legacy is the attitude towards illustration in books engendered in the 1840s and expressed in terms of far more lavish use of the image in all classes of book, including those which would always have demanded illustration of some sort. What is significant about this list of Murray's is that the books concerned – such as Robert Curzon's *Visits to Monasteries in the Levant*, or Mrs Bray's *The Life of Thomas Stothard RA*, or the future Dean Stanley's *Historical Memorials of Canterbury*, for example – were presented as illustrated

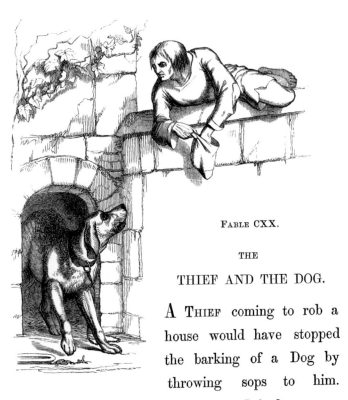

FABLE CXX.

THE

THIEF AND THE DOG.

A THIEF coming to rob a house would have stopped the barking of a Dog by throwing sops to him. "Away with you!" said the Dog; "I had my suspicions of you before, but this excess of civility assures me that you are a rogue."

A bribe in hand betrays mischief at heart.

133 *The Thief and the Dog*: wood-engraving after John Tenniel (Aesop, *Fables*, 1848). Compare the 19th-century design with such earlier versions as figs 7 and 8 depict [BL 12305 e 32]

books rather than as travel, biography, or local history. If, then, the impetus to issue the embellished book had weakened, it had left behind a demand for genuine illustration on a far more lavish scale, and had made the wood-engraving, to be found in virtually all the books on the Murray list, the almost universal medium for this illustration.

CHARLES TILT AND DAVID BOGUE

Both Longman and Murray were general publishers in the widest sense, and their activities in the crucial decade 1840–49 mirror those of the London trade during the full flowering of the Romantic book in Britain, when both French and German influences had been absorbed and when British designers were making their individual contributions to this European style. Charles Tilt's firm, founded in 1827 on the basis of print-selling and which he and David Bogue developed into a book-publishing house, albeit a publisher of illustrated books, provides a clearer picture from this more specialized branch of the trade.

But first, a word about the firm: founded by Charles Tilt in 1827, it prospered under his shrewd direction. He apparently had no children or close relatives to carry on the business when he decided to retire in 1840. Accordingly, he picked one of his assistants, David Bogue, as the man best able to carry on in the tradition of the firm, although he had neither capital of his own nor access to any. Tilt therefore arranged that Bogue should pay the purchase price out of the profits of the business, known during this time as Tilt & Bogue. In 1843 the price had been paid, Tilt retired from the scene, and the firm bore the name of its new owner, David Bogue. He would seem to have been a most sympathetic character who erred on the side of generosity towards his authors, handling George Cruikshank, in particular, with extraordinary understanding and kindness.[14] The firm did not survive the death of Bogue in 1857 – Charles Tilt came out of retirement to help wind up the business – but during the thirty years during which it was in existence it maintained a remarkably consistent policy and line of development.

It is therefore instructive to trace through its catalogues not only how the firm grew and prospered, but how public taste changed between 1827 and 1857. The firm's growth is an important point to bear in mind, particularly where earlier lists are concerned, for Tilt's development follows the common pattern of the bookseller whose publishing activities start with a few modest titles in his own line of business. Hence one must always attempt, not always successfully, to distinguish between the titles on the list which are original publications and those which are simply items of the bookseller's stock which he is anxious to promote.

The basis of Tilt's original business was the sale of prints and he came to dominate, if not to monopolize, the trade in imported French lithographs. He was equally strong in English steel-engravings and appears to have established a close connection with one of the most prominent of the London engraving firms, William Finden, whose *Landscape Illustrations to the Life and Works of Lord Byron* and *Westall's Great Britain Illustrated* are listed, *inter alia*, in a catalogue of 1831. It was, therefore, as a print-seller that he acquired his most important name, George Cruikshank, succeeding James Robins as Cruikshank's regular publisher for the collections of humorous caricatures which he etched after he had turned almost exclusively to book-illustration in 1823.

Humour was, in fact, a strong element in the lists throughout the firm's history, Cruikshank's *Comic Almanack* replacing Thomas Hood's short-lived *Comic Annual* and running from 1834 to 1852. In the late 1840s Bogue was to produce a whole series of 'little' books such as Horace Mayhew's *Model Men*, the 'Natural Histories' of Albert Smith, and other trifles by R.B. Brough, James Hannay, G.P.R. James and A.B. Reach. These continued the firm's comic traditions which go back to editions of William Cowper's *John Gilpin* (1828) and Thomas Hood's *The Epping Hunt* (1829), both illustrated by George Cruikshank, and the artist's own *Comic Alphabet* (1836), his *Ballad of Lord Bateman* (1839) and *Bachelor's Own Book* (1844). Similarly, a children's list developed from Thomas Bingley's moralistic tales of the 1830s to Captain Mayne Reid's adventure stories for boys in the new age of the 1850s.

However, Tilt had founded his firm in the great age of the steel-engraving. Throughout its history both he and David Bogue showed a predilection for the medium, retaining to the last those Galleries of the Graces, of Byron Beauties, of the Bible, or of the Waverley Novels which are so redolent of the 1830s. Bogue even remained faithful to the Annual, taking over the last survivor, *The Keepsake*, in 1848 and publishing it until his death, the elderly customer reassured that it was edited by 'Miss M.A. Power (LADY BLESSINGTON's niece) assisted by the most popular writers of the day'.

Not that the firm was in any way averse to wood-engraved illustrations in its books for, if Tilt the print-seller had connections with the leading steel-engravers of the day, he was equally soundly linked with the finest contemporary printer of wood-engravings, Charles Whittingham the elder. The twenty-four-page *Catalogue of Embellished Books printed at the Chiswick Press* which Whittingham issued in 1834 shows Charles Tilt, along with N. Hailes, as distributor of the full range of his books, including E.T. Bennett's two-volume *The Gardens and Menagerie of the Zoological Society* (1830–31), with what some contemporaries regarded as the over-delicate designs of William Harvey.

The employment of wood-engraving and the greatly increased use of illustrations in books is a phenomenon to which Tilt responded with a projected series of 'Tilt's Embellished Classics'. These were designed – in the hallowed phrases beloved of every blurb-writer – 'to supply a want which has been long felt – EMBELLISHED EDITIONS OF THE STANDARD CLASSIC AUTHORS OF ENGLAND, which while they should merit ... a place in the most select library should at the same time be furnished at a cost sufficiently moderate for popular and general circulation.'

The first two volumes, Cowper illustrated by John Gilbert and Thomson by Samuel Williams, duly appeared in 1841, advertising as being 'in preparation' the poetical works of Beattie, Milton, Falconer, Gray, Goldsmith, Collins, Young, '&c. &c'. However, whether the publishers overestimated the market or underestimated the competition, in the event the first two titles were followed only by a Milton illustrated by William Harvey in 1843 [fig. 134] and, belatedly in 1846, by *The Poetical Works of Beattie and Collins* illustrated by John Absolon. Although the publishers had aimed at 'typographical excellence and beauty of ... illustration', what they produced in most instances was no more than decent pieces of printing in the traditional style, with wood-engravings used as vignette head- and tail-pieces and as half-page illustrations: only William Harvey produced truly Romantic designs for wood-engravings fully integrated with the text.

George Cruikshank had been brought to the firm by Charles Tilt: when he went out of fashion in the late 1840s, David Bogue continued to support the old artist both by publishing his work and by commissioning his designs for the work of such writers as the Mayhew brothers. Bogue also kept the *Comic Almanack* going until 1852, although the market had been contracting for the previous five years at least. He was, however, able to replace him with an artist who was to become equally popular with the great British public – Myles Birket Foster.

Henry Vizetelly in his memoirs [15] claims the credit (really due to Ebenezer Landells) for having discovered Foster and, indeed, his earliest work is the designs for Thomas Miller's

L'ALLEGRO. 195

But come, thou goddess fair and free,
In heaven yclep'd Euphrosyne,
And, by men, heart-easing Mirth;
Whom lovely Venus, at a birth,
With two sister Graces more,
To ivy-crowned Bacchus bore:
Or whether (as some sages sing)
The frolic wind that breathes the spring,
Zephyr, with Aurora playing,
As he met her once a-Maying,
There, on beds of violets blue,
And fresh-blown roses wash'd in dew,
Fill'd her with thee, a daughter fair,
So buxom, blithe, and debonair.
 Haste thee, nymph, and bring with thee
Jest, and youthful Jollity,
Quips, and cranks, and wanton wiles,
Nods, and becks, and wreathed smiles,
Such as hang on Hebe's cheek,
And love to live in dimple sleek;
Sport that wrinkled Care derides,
And Laughter holding both his sides.
Come, and trip it, as you go,
On the light fantastic toe;
And in thy right hand lead with thee
The mountain nymph, sweet Liberty;
And, if I give thee honour due,
Mirth, admit me of thy crew,
To live with her, and live with thee,
In unreproved pleasures free;
To hear the lark begin his flight,
And, singing, startle the dull night,
From his watch-tower in the skies,
Till the dappled dawn doth rise;

134 *L'Allegro*: wood-engraved fore-margin decorations after William Harvey (Milton, *Poetical Works*, 1843) [BL C70 c 8]

The Boy's Summer Book, which Vizetelly printed for Chapman & Hall in 1846. Foster's popularity led to commissions from many publishers, but Bogue appears to have given him special treatment. It was not so much that he commissioned a wide range of illustrations – from J.G. Edgar's books for children to Southey's *Life of Nelson* and the prose and verse of Longfellow (the *Hyperion* of 1855 [fig. 136] is a masterpiece in its way) – but that he published two books of which Foster's designs are the *raison d'être*. Both Milton's *L'Allegro and Il Penseroso* (1855) and Goldsmith's *The Traveller* (1856) are printed in red on the rectos of a thick card on which Foster's designs are etched in black. These are non-books in much the same category as Noel Humphreys's or Owen Jones's illuminated books. Furthermore, they are essentially regressive in style, a repetition of what had been revolutionary when used by Turner in Rogers's poetry in the 1830s and by members of the Etching Club in the early 1840s, but by now distinctly *vieux jeu*. But, to anticipate a later judgement, Foster is old-fashioned and this is perhaps the very reason for his popularity as a watercolour painter, recreating a sentimentalized Golden Age, pre-industrialized English landscape for an industrial, urbanized society [fig. 135].

It was, therefore, appropriate that David Bogue should have been Foster's principal publisher for, throughout the history of the firm, the keynote was, if not conservatism, at least a policy content closely to follow public taste rather than to mould it. Tilt had recognized the demand for French artists' lithographs and had prospered by satisfying it. At the same time he had become an important channel through which French Romantic books became widely available in England, since he and S. Hooper, in association with the original Parisian publisher J.J. Dubochet, had introduced the first genuine *livre romantique*, *Gil Blas*, in

135 *Gathering Palm*: vignette wood-engraving after Birket Foster (Miller, *The Boy's Spring Book*, 1847) [BL 12805 c 9]

and fills the air with mist; and the mountain wind claps its hands and shrieks through the narrow pass. Ha! ha! This is the Devil's Bridge. It leads the traveller across the fearful chasm, and through a mountain gallery into the broad green, silent meadow of Andermath.

Even the sunny morning, which followed this gloomy day, had not chased the desolate impression from the soul of Flemming. His excitement increased as he lost himself more and more among the mountains; and now, as he lay alone on the summit of the sunny hill, with only glaciers and snowy peaks about him, his soul, as I have said, was wild with a fierce and painful delight.

A human voice broke his reverie. He looked, and beheld,

THE DEVIL'S BRIDGE.

at a short distance from him, the athletic form of a mountain herdsman, who was approaching the spot where he lay. He was a young man, clothed in a rustic garb, and holding a long staff in his hand. When Flemming rose, he stood still, and gazed at him, as if he loved the face of man, even of a stranger, and longed to hear a human voice, though it might speak in an unknown tongue. He answered Flemming's salutation in a rude mountain dialect, and in reply to his questions said:—

" I, with two others, have charge of two hundred head of cattle on these mountains. Through the two summer months, we remain here night and day; for which we receive each a napoleon."

Flemming gave him half his summer wages. He was

136 Wood-engraving after Birket Foster (Longfellow, *Hyperion*, 1855) [BL 12733 bb 19]

English translation in 1836, with Jean Gigoux's illustrations printed from polytypes. Yet the transaction strikes one as strictly a business matter, unlike James Burns's espousal of the German manner, which was more a matter of taste, or even Henry Vizetelly's marked Francophilia, where taste and business considerations coincided. Charles Tilt's hard-headed attitudes are again apparent in the market for outline engravings. He saw how popular Moritz Retzsch had become; but Retzsch had established a direct outlet in London. So Tilt simply turned to Paris to obtain the pirated editions with the designs copied in reduction of *The Shakespeare Gallery*, Goethe's *Faust* and Schiller's *Fridolin* and *The Fight of the Dragon*, which he issued *c.*1829.

Similarly, Bogue maintained the French connection and it was he who, in 1849, issued *Gavarni in London*, an effort by his English friends to help the exiled French artist. Bogue expanded the publishing side of the business to include new categories of travel and general books and kept pace with the public taste in the firm's old staples of humour, children's books and practical manuals of painting and drawing. Above all, he remained faithful to steel-engraving and to the Annual. Not until five years after James Burns had pioneered the new type of Christmas gift book, the wood-engraved anthology *Poems and Pictures*, did Bogue respond with one of the finest of the new genre, *Christmas with the Poets*, in 1850–51.

In what has of necessity been an all too brief survey of the illustrated books in the lists of a small sample of British publishers, certain trends become apparent. In the 1820s, and indeed for most of the 1830s, when wood-engraving showed little advantage in terms of printing costs over steel-engraving, and when the demands of the new reading public were only beginning to make themselves felt, the scale of illustration, although growing, was still restricted and steel-engraving held sway in the middle and upper end of the market. Once the technique of lowering the block had established wood-engraving in an unassailable position as the cheapest method of reproducing an artist's designs, and the skill of the facsimile engravers had demonstrated the range of effects of which the medium was capable, there could be little doubt as to the eventual outcome.

The second revival of wood-engraving in Britain which gathered pace from the 1840s onwards would not, however, have taken place on economic grounds alone. Where illustration was limited, say, simply to the frontispiece portrait or to the occasional map or full-page plate, steel-engraving continued for many years to be the favoured means of reproduction, as much from conservatism as from the view that metal-engraving was superior to wood when it came to illustrating rather than embellishing a book. The reason for the revival of wood-engraving was the pressure upon the publishers to satisfy the craving for the image in the great new reading public. The trade in general was subjected to additional competitive pressures from such innovators as Charles Knight, reinforced by the example of the French *livre romantique*. All these combined from the mid-1830s to force publishers to illustrate their books on a hitherto unimagined scale. Wood-engravings could be printed in conjunction with the text at a high impression-rate on a steam-press; steel-engravings required a separate process employing a roller-press with a low impression-rate. Wood-engraving was therefore quick and relatively cheap; steel-engraving slow and, by any account, expensive. Hard economics dictated that there could be no other medium than wood-engraving for the heavily-illustrated book, if it were to be produced at a competitive price.

Yet the publishing trade is nothing if not conservative and, just as traditional styles of design and layout were retained, so throughout the period the steel-engraving remains a constant feature of the illustrated book in Britain. Indeed, it is this diversity of media – steel- and wood-engraving, coupled with printing in colour by chromolithography and from relief blocks – and the cross-fertilization of British, French and German styles of design and layout, which lend an especial attraction to the embellished books of the period.

The Artists

WILLIAM HARVEY AND JOHN GILBERT

The vast increase in the numbers of illustrated books issued as part of a general upsurge of new books and reprints, and the scale of illustration within individual books, all tended to produce conditions favouring the emergence of the professional illustrator. Yet it should not be forgotten that such artists could never have relied for their livelihood upon book-illustration alone. What created the profession was the birth, simultaneously with this massive increase in illustrated books, of a whole new class of publication – illustrated journals and periodicals. Charles Knight's *Penny Magazine* had pioneered the trend in 1832, but what opened the floodgates to illustrated journalism – and hence gave so much employment not simply to artists, but to wood-engravers as well – was the progressive reduction of newspaper Stamp Duty, which began gradually in 1835, dipped sharply in 1842, and was completely abolished in 1855.

Thus the period from the foundation of *The Illustrated London News* in 1842 until the camera took over in the twentieth century was the golden age of the newspaper artist. This proliferation of illustrated journalism meant that, in addition to the wider opportunities available to the trained painter in oils and watercolours – from whose ranks publishers had always tended to recruit their illustrators – the enormously increased demand for designers, particularly for wood-engraving, opened the way for draughtsmen with little or no formal training. In Britain, their number included talented amateurs like John Leech, Alfred Crowquill or William Makepeace Thackeray, but the more significant section comprised the working-class draughtsmen whose talent had attracted them to the one trade in which, to a degree, they could give expression to their artistic instincts – that of engraving.

Such artists were the successors of the countless anonymous artist-engravers of the crude cuts in chapbooks and ballad-sheets and, just as Thomas Bewick and Robert Branston the elder had raised wood-engraving from a folk-craft, so both Bewick himself, his pupils Luke Clennel and Charlton Nesbit and, especially, Branston's pupil John Thurston, demonstrated how the engraver's shop could produce illustrators as talented as many who had had all the advantages of a formal artistic education. Their virtues and limitations are therefore directly attributable to their working environment and, in particular, to the relationship between wood- and copper-engraving at the close of the eighteenth century.

Since copper-engraving was the established medium for graphic reproduction at that time, and since the wood-engravers of the period, including Bewick himself, were by training copper-plate-engravers, it was natural that they should employ the technique and strive to achieve the effects of copper-plate-engraving, both in the actual line of the engraving and in the tints of the print. Bewick and the Newcastle school were perhaps exceptional in that they developed the white-line technique, but the London school of engraving, derived from men like Branston and Thurston who had learned their craft as copper-engravers, naturally took the black line of metal into wood. Thus the black-line technique predominates because, in addition to those who graduated from engraving to draughtsmanship, those artists who were not engravers continued to design for wood as if it were copper. Their work perpetuated the black line and inspired the new breed of professional artist to imitate them. Such is certainly true of one of the first of them, John Thurston, and it also conditions the style of his successor, William Harvey.

Harvey was born in Newcastle-upon-Tyne on 13 July 1796 and was apprenticed to Thomas Bewick, whose favourite pupil he became and for whom he designed and engraved a number of small tail-piece vignettes. In 1817 he came to London where he studied painting and drawing under Benjamin Robert Haydon. He first attracted attention when he reproduced Haydon's painting *Dentatus* on a scale hitherto unprecedented although, with the arrival of illustrated journalism a generation later, such large wood-engravings, composed of a number of separate blocks clamped together, became commonplace. This established him as a highly skilled wood engraver and, although he did some designing – Dr A. Henderson's *The History of Ancient and Modern Wines* (1824), for example – it was probably the first series of James Northcote's *Fables* (1828) which established him in his new role of illustrator.

Harvey's task had been twofold: in the first place to transfer Northcote's own designs to wood to form the principal embellishment at the head of each fable and, secondly, himself to design their initial letters and tail-piece vignettes. From that point he fully established himself as the heir of John Thurston who had died in 1827, and, until his own death at Richmond on 18 January 1866, he was one of the most popular and prolific illustrators of the period. He is, however, an artist whose success was due less to his draughtsmanship *per se* than to its ability to encapsulate contemporary sensibilities. Thus his work will always have a particular appeal to any lover of the Romantic period, because it is so exactly right for that day and age, even in its faults of composition and technique. One can therefore accept Kenny Meadows's jocular assertion that 'beauty was Harvey's evil genius and grace was his damnation';[16] and not attempt to avoid Linton's conclusion: 'Harvey never ... troubled himself about line at all. Fineness, tone and delicacy, fulfilled the purpose of his drawings: the refinement of copper sought for, without the beauty of the copper line in which Thurston was pre-eminent.'[17] Yet the design, so often a mass, if not a mess, of delicate tones, catches the over-exquisite sensibilities of the age and, when the line does emerge, an embellishment of very considerable quality results.

It is, however, difficult within a limited space to do justice to a career as an illustrator which spanned over forty years, from Thomas Bewick's *Fables* in 1818 to Robert Montgomery's *Poems* in 1860, and perhaps even beyond. It included children's books, from Lamb's *Tales from Shakespeare* and Defoe's *Robinson Crusoe* for Baldwin & Cradock in 1831 to the adventure stories of Captain Mayne Reid for David Bogue in the 1850s; contributions to topographical books such as Samuel Carter and Anna Maria Hall's *Ireland* (1841–3) and Charles Mackay's *The English Lakes* (1846); or a *magnum opus* such as Charles Knight's *Pictorial Shakspere* (1842) in which he was principal artist. Harvey bore with Henry Warren the lion's share of illustrating *Ancient Spanish Ballads*, contributed to many an edition or anthology of poetry and was solely responsible for Tilt's 'embellished' edition of Milton (1843) [fig. 134]. While his talents here fall far short of those needed to catch a whiff of the grandeur of *Paradise Lost* – John Martin's mezzotints are still the nearest any artist has approached the poet's concepts – Harvey nonetheless provides some appropriate and attractive marginal embellishments to the minor poems.

If, therefore, one were to select any particular books as representing Harvey's best achievements, I think one would be bound to include the two series of Northcote's *Fables* (1828–33), the two volumes of E.T. Bennett's *The Gardens and Menagerie of the Zoological Society* (1830–31) and *The Arabian Nights* (1839–40). The *Fables* are a classic of traditional British book design; Bennett's book shows Harvey in the tradition of his old master, Bewick. It is true that, as the Victorian naturalist Revd J.G. Wood complained, Harvey's illustrations do tend to be mannered, but Kenny Meadows exaggerates when he attributes this to Harvey's 'well-known love of the graceful [which] caused him to make all his wild beasts turn out their

each of them a thousand lashes;[9] and when thou hast done that, write a bond against them, confirmed by oath, that they shall not reside in the street, after thou shalt have paraded them through the city, mounted on beasts, with their faces to the tails, and hast proclaimed before them, This is the recompense of those who annoy. their neighbours! —And beware of neglecting that which I have commanded thee to do.—So the Wálee did as he was ordered. And when Abu-l-Ḥasan had exercised his authority until the close of the day, he looked towards the chamberlain and the rest of the attendants, and said to them, Depart.

He then called for a eunuch who was near at hand, and said to him, I am hungry, and desire something to eat. And he replied, I hear and obey :—and led him by the hand into the eating-chamber, where the attendants placed before him a table of rich viands ; and

137 Wood-engraved vignette and panel-decoration after William Harvey (*The Arabian Nights*, II, 1840)
[BL 838 k 17]

toes as though they had been taught their steps by a fashionable dancing-master.'[18] Nevertheless, the illustrations show that Harvey could use a line when necessary, and they had more than local significance since Léon Curmer commissioned the artist to contribute similar designs to his own *Jardin des Plantes* (1842). Harvey's persistent failing is to subordinate line to tone and it is the virtue of *The Arabian Nights* that it is illustrated by a series of designs in which Harvey most consistently displays linear rather than tonal strength.

Perhaps the book which showed Harvey at his best would be the three volumes of Charles Knight's part-publication, *The Arabian Nights*, such a choice being motivated not simply by the strength of Harvey's designs but by their setting. *The Arabian Nights* is, in fact, one of the outstanding British Romantic books. The text is open, but Harvey's predilection for tone enables the vignettes to match the density of the type matter. The initial text-page of each volume is a completely integrated design and in general the vignettes are dropped in as half-page or smaller illustrations, with some pages of completely integrated vignettes and others in which the decoration falls as a broad panel along the fore-margin [fig. 137]. This last is a successful feature which Harvey frequently employed in later books such as *Ancient Spanish Ballads* (1841) or the rather disappointing *Pilgrim's Progress* (1850) [figs 138, 139].[19] Superficially it resembles the German style of page-decoration, but in Harvey's case the influence is probably directly from Islamic manuscript models.

If the book is a fine example of Romantic design, it also epitomizes the high ideals of popular education which inspired the Society for the Diffusion of Useful Knowledge and its publisher, Charles Knight. The translator was E.W. Lane (1801–76), who had lived as an Egyptian in Cairo from 1825 to 1828 and 1833 to 1835 and whose *Manners and Customs of the Modern Egyptians* had been published by the SDUK in 1836. A profound Arabic scholar, his great work being his *Arabic Lexicon* of which five volumes were published in 1863 and the remainder posthumously, his selection and translation were made directly from the Arabic and accompanied by extensive and scholarly notes. The whole concept of this popular part-publication says a great deal for the high standards set by Charles Knight and deservedly the translation became the standard text until Sir Richard Burton's full version appeared at the end of the century. As such, it was acquired by John Murray who, from 1846, issued it in various editions. Unfortunately, and to the detriment of Harvey's designs, many of these were in a reduced format.

This takes us rather far from William Harvey whose Continental reputation must have been enhanced or established by his designs. By a curious coincidence, from 1819 the Parisian publisher Ernest Bourdin had been issuing in parts the classic French translation by Silvestre de Sacy simultaneously with Charles Knight. The French edition was designed with integrated wood-engravings in the popular style, but when roughly half the parts had appeared the publishers altered that style abruptly, and the rest of the engravings are clearly and profoundly influenced by William Harvey.

In *The Arabian Nights* Harvey's Romanticism had been checked by the authenticity which the translator, Lane, had been able to impart. The engravings therefore provided a model for other artists, and it is interesting to see this not simply in the work of British artists but in further examples from the French. It is even apparent in the illustrations to the Oriental

138 *The Shepherds on the Delectable Mountains*: vignette wood-engraving after William Harvey in his robust 'popular' style (Bunyan, *The Pilgrim's Progress*, 1830) [BL 1113 c 14]

mountains. So they went forth with them, and walked a while, having a pleasant prospect on every side. Then said the shepherds one to another, "Shall we shew these pilgrims some wonders?" So when they had concluded to do it, they had them first to the top of an hill called Error, which was very steep on the furthest side, and bid them look down to the bottom. So

139 In contrast, the rather anaemic style of the same scene in a wood-engraving twenty years later (Bunyan, *The Pilgrim's Progress*, 1850) [BL 1113 c 34]

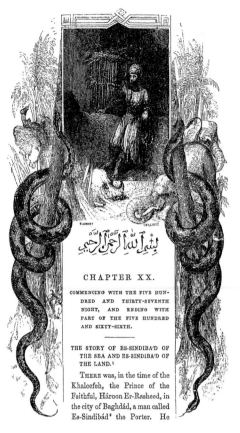

140 Wood-engraved chapter-opening after
William Harvey (*The Arabian Nights*, III, 1840)
[BL 838 k 18]

141 Harvey's design copied by the French
(*Les mille et un jours*, 1844) [BL 838 k 27]

fairy tales in P. Christian's *La morale merveilleuse* (1844), but is best exemplified by *Les mille et un jours* (*Persian Tales*) of the same year. Here F.J. Collignon's designs for the wood-engravings are patently modelled upon Harvey, while decorative motifs and book-openings go even further and are directly copied from his *Arabian Nights* [figs 140, 141].

His Continental imitators, the envious sarcasms of lesser men like Kenny Meadows, and the sheer volume of his work attest to the status which he achieved among British illustrators. It was similar in kind, if not perhaps in degree, to that which George Cruikshank established among caricaturists. Like Cruikshank, Harvey set the style for the younger men of the 1830s and 1840s, and even in artists directly influenced by the German outline school there is a use of tone for which they are indebted to Harvey. His influence was even stronger in the work of the new class of professional illustrator of whom the most important, both as an artist and as a type of Harvey's influence, was John Gilbert.

Gilbert (1817–97),[20] the son of an estate agent, worked for two years (1833–35) as an estate agent's clerk before entering the studio of George Lance who taught him etching and engraving, a grounding in a craft which he very rarely practised – virtually all his designs are for wood-engraving – but which may at the outset have predisposed him towards Harvey's style of book-illustration. He also painted both in oils and watercolours, being elected President SWP in 1872, ARA in the same year, and RA in 1876. His obituarist in *The London Journal* estimated that he had painted some 270 pictures in addition to the fifty exhibited at the Royal Academy, the twenty at the British Artists, and the forty each at the Royal Watercolour Society and the British Institute.

Substantial though this portion of his *œuvre* is, it was as nothing compared with his output as an illustrator. The same obituarist claimed 30,000 designs for *The Illustrated London News* alone and, if the Dalziels[21] considered this exaggerated since Gilbert had ceased to contribute to the periodical many years before his death, *The Illustrated London News*, although the principal outlet for this sort of work, was only one of a number. Gilbert was fortunate to have established himself as an up-and-coming draughtsman at the very time that illustrated journalism burst upon the publishing scene and he was also associated with *The Graphic*, *The Illustrated London Magazine*, *The Leisure Hour*, *The London Journal*, *London Society*, *Once a Week* and *Punch*. Both technically and temperamentally he seems to have been ideally suited to the work and, as Henry Vizetelly admits,[22] it would have been well-nigh impossible to have kept *The Illustrated London News* supplied at the rate of between twenty and thirty engravings in each number without John Gilbert, who 'was a good deal more than head and shoulders above all the rest' of the artists employed.[23] Any assessment, then, of Gilbert's true place in, and most important contribution to British nineteenth-century art will echo Mason Jackson's judgement:

> … Gilbert stands out pre-eminently the great popular illustrator of the Victorian era. He was the first who gave a distinctive character to the illustration of news. He seemed to possess an inborn knowledge of the essentials of newspaper art, and could express by a few freely drawn lines and touches the hurried movement of street crowds or the state and dignity of Court ceremonies … in a way exactly suited to rapid engraving and printing…. His quickness and versatility made him just the man that was wanted…. Nothing came amiss to Gilbert … and he never failed in that most essential quality of a newspaper artist – *punctuality*. It is as the popular illustrator that the name of Gilbert stands at the head of that numerous band of artists who contributed to the foundation of illustrated journalism in this country.[24]

To classify Gilbert as a newspaper artist at a time when the new profession included William Harvey, George Cruikshank, Hablot Knight Browne and John Leech, to name a few, is neither to denigrate his draughtsmanship – the high quality of Victorian magazine illustration is slowly gaining critical recognition – nor to underrate his contribution to book-illustration, although much of this lies outside the limits of the present study. From the mid-1850s onwards he became closely associated with George Routledge, the foremost publisher of illustrated books in the succeeding decade. For him Gilbert designed what are perhaps his most satisfying pieces of book-illustration, the wood-engravings for Longfellow's *Poetical Works* (1856) and for the three-volume Shakespeare of 1858–61, for which he made no less than 832 designs [fig. 142].

142 *Falstaff tipped into a muddy Ditch*: wood-engraved vignette after John Gilbert to illustrate *The Merry Wives of Windsor* (Shakespeare, *Plays*, 1, 1858) [BL 11764 g 16]

143 *Sheerness*: wood-engraved vignette after John Gilbert (Mackay, *The Thames and its Tributaries*, 11, 1840) [BL 796 e 9]

These are in the fully developed style of Gilbert, a style to match the taste of the 1860s, but the developing work of the Romantic illustrator is by no means negligible. It demonstrates that versatility of which Mason Jackson wrote and it shows him moving from the tonal effects of Harvey's influence to the stronger line of the 1860s. Typical of the Harveian style are two books from 1840, Mrs Sarah Stickney Ellis's *Sons of the Soil* and Charles Mackay's *The Thames and its Tributaries*. Both combine the traditional tonality of their designs with the equally traditional British layout of wood-engraved head- and tail-pieces. Charles Mackay's book is a particularly satisfying example of the genre and shows Gilbert, the figure draughtsman, equally competent with landscape [fig. 143]. A similar style is to be found in the two-volume Cowper for Charles Tilt (1841) and in the three sets of illustrations designed for S.C. Hall's *Book of British Ballads* (1841–3) [fig. 144].

The Demon Lober.

And aye when she turned her round about,
 Aye taller he seemed to be ;
Until that the tops o' the gallant ship
 Nae taller were than he.

The clouds grew dark, and the wind grew loud,
 And the levin filled her e'e ;
And waesome wailed the snow-white sprites,
 Upon the gurlie sea.

He struck the topmast wi' his hand,
 The foremast wi' his knee ;
And he brake that gallant ship in twain,
 And sank her in the sea.

Gilbert, del.   J. Bastin, sc.

144 *The Demon Lover*: wood-engraving after John Gilbert (*The Book of British Ballads*, 1842) [BL 2288 g 4]

It was perhaps this contact with the exponents of the shaded outline school which gives greater linear strength to Gilbert's subsequent work, rather than the influence of Tony Johannot, so obviously and so understandably apparent in his illustrations to *Don Quixote* (1842). The shift from tone to line starts around 1843 – it can be seen in the illustrations to Mary Roberts's *Ruins and Old Trees*, for example – but is best traced in the succession of designs commissioned for the Abbotsford edition of Sir Walter Scott's Waverley Novels. Beginning with *The Black Dwarf* (vol. II, 1843) and moving on to *The Fortunes of Nigel* and *St Ronan's Well* (vols VII and VIII, 1845) and *Woodstock* (vol. X, 1846), we can see that gradual development of line at the expense of tone which is the feature of Gilbert's mature style. It is a style which marked the emergence of the Sixties' illustrator and was most successfully demonstrated first in Charles Mackay's *The Salamandrine* (1852).

SAMUEL WILLIAMS AND MYLES BIRKET FOSTER

The career of William Harvey illustrates the way in which wood-engraving afforded an artistic opening for talent deprived of the advantages of formal training, and how the expansion of publishing and the enormous growth in illustrated publications of all kinds gave birth to the professional illustrator. That of John Gilbert stresses the importance to the professional of the illustrated press. In Myles Birket Foster (1825–99) we have, as it were, a second-generation Harvey; but in Samuel Williams, an older man than Harvey, we have an example of how these same conditions benefited both the craftsman and the artist, for Williams enjoyed the highest reputation as a wood-engraver as well as being a respected designer of the illustrations which he himself cut.

Williams was born at Colchester on 23 February 1788 and was apprenticed to a local printer, J. Marsden. There he taught himself both copper- and wood-engraving. He visited London in 1819, when he designed and engraved some 300 cuts for Crosby's *Natural History*, and finally settled there three years later, establishing himself as a highly respected wood-engraver, as did his sister Mary Anne, his brother Thomas and his son Lionel Joseph. Samuel was, however, not only a fine craftsman but, as Linton acknowledges,[25] 'a designer of much merit, frequently engraving his own drawings'. In them Linton traces the influence of the copper-engraving, remarking, 'in his cuts he prefers … the sharp accentuation of blacks with fine grey tints'.

Williams's designs are always attractive and he excels in the more or less sentimentalized vignette of an English rural landscape with figures. Books such as William Howitt's *Visits to Remarkable Places* (1st series, 1840) or *Rural Life of England* (1838); or Tilt's 'embellished' edition of Thomson's *Poetical Works* (1841), or Thomas Miller's *Pictures of Country Life* (1847) were some of the outlets for this talent. Nor should two old-fashioned books of improving verse for children, *The Daisy* and *The Cowslip*, be forgotten; these Williams illustrated in 1830 in as appropriately an old-fashioned a style of refined chapbook engraving.

However, the greatest exponent of the sentimentalized landscape with figures was undoubtedly Myles Birket Foster. Born in Newcastle-upon-Tyne in 1825 to a father who was a friend of Thomas Bewick, he came south to take up an apprenticeship in wood-engraving with Ebenezer Landells, another Northumbrian. Landells was the first to appreciate where his pupil's real talents lay and turned him from engraving to watercolour painting. His bent was towards landscape – in which he benefited from the advice and training of Thomas Creswick – and in the end Foster became one of the most popular and highly-paid of Victorian watercolourists.

But before he was a painter he was a book-illustrator. Henry Vizetelly claimed the credit for spotting the talent of the 21-year-old artist who had shown him a number of his designs on wood.[26] The story gains some credence since his first four commissions are the illustrations for the attractive series of *Boy's Books* (*Summer*, 1846; *Autumn*, *Winter*, and *Spring* [fig. 135], 1847). Thereafter his services as an illustrator were in constant demand, Foster's closest connections at this period being with David Bogue. Among the books which he

145 *The Bell*: wood-engraving after Birket Foster (Longfellow, *Hyperion*, 1855). Very German in feeling in contrast with the French style of fig. 136 [BL 12733 bb 19]

illustrated were some by Longfellow, the most successful being his prose tale *Hyperion* (1855) [figs 136, 145], a good example of the Romantic style printed by Henry Vizetelly. Perhaps the reason for this is that the landscapes are real – Foster and Vizetelly making a tour in Germany to obtain sketches of the actual places mentioned in the book. Unfortunately, *Hyperion* is an exception and the typical Foster landscape is generally imagined. The fact then has to be faced that the artist's imagination understandably flagged after he had been commissioned to produce hundreds and hundreds of idealized English landscapes. Thus, while taken individually there is very considerable charm in a Foster vignette, the tones of the landscape blending well with the density of the type, *en masse* they tend to become cloying and monotonous.

Like John Gilbert, Birket Foster was a transitional artist whose work spanned both the late Romantic and the period of the 1860s, and it was in fact a Sixties' engraver, Edmund Evans, who is the best interpreter of his landscapes. Evans, who is best remembered for his colour printing from wood-blocks, had served his apprenticeship with Ebenezer Landells where he and Foster became close personal friends. It is perhaps this bond which makes Evans so sensitive an interpreter of Foster's designs, an excellent example of this being found in his treatment of the illustrations to William Cowper's *The Task*, published by James Nisbet in 1855.

The effectiveness of this book is enhanced overall by the fact that Foster alone is responsible for its illustration. In those circumstances one is not made aware, by direct contrast with the work of his contemporaries, that in his designs for wood-engraving Foster is doing, perhaps more successfully, what landscape painters including his master Thomas Creswick, had been attempting for the past thirty years or more. The essentially regressive nature of his style and treatment of landscape is typified by the choice medium – the steel-engraving – to reproduce his sets of German landscapes in the two volumes of Henry Mayhew's *The Rhine*. The first volume was published by Bogue in 1856, the second, after his death, by George Routledge in 1858. Both belong to the previous generation.

It is, however, only when one sees Foster's work juxtaposed within the covers of the same book beside that of his contemporaries that one is forcibly reminded just how old-fashioned Foster was in terms of the 1850s and 1860s. This is strikingly apparent in a later volume of Nisbet's illustrated poets, *The Poetical Works of George Herbert* (1857). Here the tonal quality of Foster's contribution contrasts so forcibly with the shaded outlines of J.R. Clayton's vignettes and the fine attenuated lines of Noel Humphreys's initials and floral decorations. Again, in Robert Pollok's *The Course of Time* (William Blackwood, 1857), where Clayton and Foster are the illustrators together with John Tenniel, Foster's landscapes seem positively Harveian beside the outline figures of his fellow artists.

George Cruikshank

Birket Foster was fortunate in that his subject-matter was of continuing appeal, not to say popularity. Those professional illustrators whose staple was humour or fiction were to suffer a very different fate. These artists, whom one may loosely term the caricaturists, were to see both their style – and the steel-etching, the medium by which it was expressed – begin to go out of fashion in the early 1850s and become quite *depassé* by the end of the decade, with the result that illustrators of the eminence of George Cruikshank and Hablot Knight Browne suffered, in varying degrees, neglect and poverty in their old age.

The founding father of their school of draughtsmanship was George Cruikshank (1792–1878). His working life lasted for over seventy years, during which he was wholly or in part responsible for the execution of more than 2,000 individual prints and the illustration of some 860 books. It is this time-span, the amount and variety of his work, as well as the artist's own complex and apparently contradictory character, which combine to make it hard briefly to convey an adequate and balanced view of his achievement.

It should always be remembered that he reached the top in two very different roles, that of political caricaturist and that of book-illustrator. Political caricature came first and very early in life, for he started out as assistant to his father, Isaac, and actually completed his first independent caricature in 1807, at the age of thirteen. By the time James Gilray died in 1815, Cruikshank had made himself ready to step into his shoes, and he held the position of a leading social and political caricaturist from then until 1823, when he turned almost entirely to illustrating books.

Prior to this he had supplied designs for the chapbook publishers and had also illustrated a number of books in a style reflecting the range of his caricature. In the political field there had been 'Dr Syntax's' *Life of Napoleon* (1813) and William Hone's lampoons on George IV and his Tory government (1819–20) and, on the social side, squibs such as the anonymous *The Fashion* (1817) and the immensely successful *Life in London* of 1821. The author was Pierce Egan and the plates had been the joint work of George and his elder brother Isaac

146 *The Young Giant*: vignette steel-etching by George Cruikshank (Brothers Grimm, *German Popular Stories*, 1, 1824) [BL C70 bb 2]

Robert, but George was on his own and the author was David Carey when Cruikshank attempted in 1822 to repeat the success with the rather hack *Life in Paris*.

Thus when, in 1823, he definitely devoted himself to book-work, Cruikshank did so with the reputation of being the leading British comic artist already well established. It was a reputation which his publishers at least were anxious to maintain in *The Comic Almanack*, for each issue of which Cruikshank provided a dozen etchings and a host of designs for wood-engraving between 1834 and 1852; for his own *Comic Alphabet* (1836), *Loving Ballad of Lord Bateman* (1839) with its parody of the outline style, and *The Bachelor's Own Book* (1844); and for the work of others, from the Grimms's *German Popular Stories* (1824–6) [fig. 146], through William Clarke's *Three Courses and a Dessert* (1830) and the books by James Wight and Captain Barker RN [pl. 9] published in that decade, to those of the Mayhew Brothers in the 1850s. But although the comic artist's love of exaggeration and the grotesque pervades Cruikshank's work, the artist was something more than the mere master of caricature.

This quality in him was recognized very early, when *Blackwood's Magazine* reviewed his formal entry into the field of book-illustration, *Points of Humour*, maintaining that, while 'generally speaking, people consider him as a clever, sharp caricaturist, and nothing more … a fact it undoubtedly is – that he possesses genius – GENIUS in the truest sense.…'.[27] And Cruikshank is adjured to 'give up his mere slang drudgery, and labour to be what nature has put within his reach – not a caricaturist, but a painter.'

Although such advice would appear to have been misguided when we remember such efforts in oils of Cruikshank's old age as *The Triumph of Bacchus*, yet in a very real sense he answered the challenge in the painterly qualities of his etchings of the late 1830s and early 1840s. For these, contemporary critics had the same praise which Ruskin had lavished on

147 *The Pawnbroker's Shop*:
steel-etching by George Cruikshank
(Dickens, *Sketches by Boz*, ii, 1836)
[BL 828 f 23]

those in the earlier Grimm, when he wrote that they were 'the finest things, next to Rembrandt's, that, as far as I know, have ever been done since etching was invented.'[28]

Gross and exaggerated as this praise may be, Cruikshank nevertheless must be accounted one of the masters of the art. Unfortunately, his best work went to embellish literary rubbish, and Dickens, who had been happy to launch himself under the artist's banner with *Sketches by Boz* (1836) [fig. 147] and *Oliver Twist* (1838), found in Hablot Knight Browne the pliable illustrator ideally suited to his own artistic intentions. Thus Cruikshank's vast talent fell to the service of William Harrison Ainsworth and the finest of his etched work was devoted to such third-rate fictions as *Jack Sheppard* (1839), *The Tower of London* (1840), *The Miser's Daughter* (1842) or *Windsor Castle* (1843).

In his etchings Cruikshank found the highest expression of his art – of his humour, of his sense of the grotesque, of the macabre, of tragedy, of violence, of drama – yet his designs for

148 *George IV … In love, and in drink, and o'ertoppled by debt*: wood-engraving after George Cruikshank (Hone, *The Queen's Matrimonial Ladder*, 1820) [BL C131 d 13]

wood-engraving should not for this reason be ignored. Despite the distortions which, he himself complained,[29] were introduced into his drawings by the engraver, they are highly characteristic both of the artist and of the book-art of the period. They range from the political caricatures of such squibs by William Hone as *The Political House that Jack Built* (1819) or *The Queen's Matrimonial Ladder* (1820) [fig. 148]; the vignette tail-pieces to David Carey's *Life in Paris* (1822), Captain Barker's *Greenwich Hospital* (1826) [pl. 9], or C.W. Hoskyns's *Talpa* (1852); head-pieces in the classic British manner for Carlton Bruce's *Mirth and Morality* (1834), or the vignettes for John Whitty's *Tales of Irish Life* (1824), William Cowper's *John Gilpin* (1828) or James Wight's *Sunday in London* (1833) [fig. 149]. The *œuvre* is vast and it is impossible to convey its riches in a catalogue of book-titles, however long. While Cruikshank never attempts the striking effects of chiaroscuro achieved in his etchings, his designs for wood-engraving exhibit all his gifts for humorous and incisive observation of the world about him.

In all his art, however, Cruikshank makes one aware that he stands alone among both British and Continental book-illustrators as the direct link between the eighteenth century and the Romantic age. The movement affects him far less than he influences the movement, since he was a book-artist the essentials of whose style had been formed by nearly twenty years of political caricature. Yet while the heritage of Rowlandson and Gilray has been acknowledged in his art, less attention has been paid to the effect upon his character of the environment in which he was raised. As a young man he aped the life-style of the sporting buck of the Regency, and it was the retention of many of the attitudes and attributes of the species – the vanity Cruikshank showed in dress and appearance, for example – into ultra-respectable mid-Victorian England and in the unlikely person of an elderly and rabid partisan of Total Abstinence which so bewildered those who knew him in old age and came to write his biography. It is easy to see the direct links with the eighteenth century and the influence of William Hogarth in Cruikshank's moralizing *The Bottle* (1847) and *The*

149 *Cordial workings of the Spirit*: wood-engraving after George Cruikshank (Wight, *Sunday in London*, 1833) [BL 838 f 18]

150 *Squire Western and his Lady*
Cousins: the steel-etching by
George Cruikshank shows the
artist's feeling for the 18th century
(*Illustrations from Smollet, Fielding*
and Goldsmith, 1832) [BL C58 C 13]

Drunkard's Children (1848); less obvious are the eighteenth-century inheritances in the character of the artist himself. In Cruikshank one is always aware of the century's streak of coarse brutality beneath the surface glitter, which makes him such a good illustrator of historical novels, and perhaps the most authentic for such novelists as Fielding and Smollett [fig. 150]. One therefore regrets that Roscoe's Novelists Library in which the latter appeared (1832) was not illustrated on the scale of Ainsworth's novels in the 1840s.

This eighteenth-century realism, rather than his own manner, was the most valuable gift which Cruikshank bequeathed to his protégé John Leech, nor is it too fanciful to see this same characteristic in the caricaturists and draughtsmen who followed Leech to make *Punch* so useful a source for the social historian. At the same time Cruikshank was not without influence upon the Continent, and especially in France, although few of his designs would seem to have been reprinted in Paris. In 1830 Ambroise Tardieu copied, without acknowledgement, his etchings to *German Popular Stories* for a French translation of Grimm, and in 1833 *Le magasin pittoresque* reprinted his designs for *John Gilpin*. Between 1842 and 1843 the short-lived annual *Le comic almanack* re-issued etchings from the earlier *Comic Almanacks* and supplemented them with wood-engravings from the designs of French artists.

The *Comic Almanacks* may well provide the only readily apparent imitation of one of Cruikshank's stylistic devices by French artists. In them Cruikshank frequently and very effectively introduces into his designs for wood-engraving figures in silhouette. The same device is used as effectively in such *Physiologies* as Marco de Saint-Hilaire's *Physiologie du troupier* (1841), but this is doubtful evidence and Cruikshank's influence is mainly indirect. He, with Rowlandson, was probably seen as a model, if not for style then for satire, when Philipon launched *Le caricature* in 1830. Henry Monnier is known to have admired Cruikshank, whom he met in London *c.*1822–5. Cruikshank inspired his *Esquisses parisiennes* (1827) and *Vues de Paris* (1829), and he may well have influenced elements in Monnier's style for wood-engraving. As early as 1830 Charles Baudelaire was attempting to widen Cruikshank's audience in France,[30] and some twenty years later Gavarni was expressing his admiration for *The Drunkard's Children* and *The Bottle*.

Thus Cruikshank enjoyed the esteem of his peers in France and a certain degree of appreciation from a restricted circle of art-lovers. The same pattern may be repeated on a smaller scale in Germany where he did have one agreeable compliment paid him. In 1835 the etchings which he had made in 1824 for an English translation of Adalbert von Chamisso's *Peter Schlemihl* were copied, and enclosed within rather charming original borders for a reprint of this German classic.

Alfred Crowquill, William Makepeace Thackeray and John Leech

If Cruikshank's Continental influences were mainly indirect, his direct influence upon British illustrators was enormous. In the first place, his preference for copper- and later for steel-etching established the latter as the medium by which British fiction was to be illustrated for the best part of twenty years. In the second, his immense popularity as an artist led virtually all those who worked in the same fields of fiction and humour to copy his style, at least at the start of their careers as illustrators. A striking instance of this is provided by H.C. Selous, whose mature outline style cannot be further from Cruikshank's. Nevertheless, what are probably his earliest book illustrations to the anonymous novel *Tales of a Rambler* (1836), imitate as best they can the style and etching technique employed by Cruikshank in nine rather messy black and white lithographs – a medium Selous was forced to employ since he never, to my knowledge, learned how to etch.

Aside from this general influence, Cruikshank exercised a strong personal influence upon three young amateurs of the 1830s – John Leech, Alfred Crowquill, and William Makepeace Thackeray. Each came from a middle-class background (Leech had had to abandon medicine because of his father's bankruptcy, while Thackeray's first genteel dabblings in journalism were sparked by the failure of the Indian bank in which his inherited wealth was deposited), none appears to have had any but the briefest formal artistic training, and all three would seem to have been taught to etch by the master himself.

All three were helped in various other ways. Crowquill had his designs for 'Cornelius Apel's' *Der Freischutz Travestie* (1824) and for F.W. von Kosewitz's *Eccentric Tales* (1827) etched by George Cruikshank, who later recommended him to Richard Bentley as artist and contributor to *Bentley's Miscellany*. Leech he vainly proposed to Chapman & Hall as the artist to replace Robert Seymour as illustrator of *Pickwick Papers*[31] and then successfully recommended him as a resident artist on *Bentley's Miscellany*. Thackeray's literary career he furthered by putting in his way such commissions as *The Fatal Boots* and *Cox's Diary* in the

Comic Almanacks for 1839 and 1840 respectively, *Sultan Stork* in *Ainsworth's Magazine* (1842), and *The Legend of the Rhine* in *George Cruikshank's Table-book* (1845).

Of the three 'Crowquill', the pen-name adopted by Alfred Henry Forrester (1805–72), looms the smallest. His was an attractive if minor talent, fated in the 1850s and 1860s to be devoted to that of the 'comic' illustrator – mainly of children's books. As such, Crowquill undoubtedly enjoyed considerable success with his contemporaries, but his earlier work is both better and more interesting. He was capable of pleasant if undistinguished landscape sketches for Palmer's *Wanderings with Pen and Pencil* (1846) and some really excellent vignettes for the first edition of W.E. Aytoun's and Theodore Martin's parodies, *Bon Gualtier's Book of Ballads* (1845) [fig. 51], but his most interesting work was that originally published in *Bentley's Miscellany*. It includes good steel-etchings for Henry Cockton's *Stanley Thorn* (jointly illustrated with George Cruikshank and John Leech, 1841) and various prose contributions by the artist, embellished with designs engraved on wood by George's nephew, Percy Cruikshank. These were collected and published in two volumes in 1843 as *Phantasmagoria of Fun*.

Crowquill's earlier comic style generally parodies the German outline school and is climaxed in Crowquill's *Faust* (1834) [fig. 71], a travesty not only of Goethe's poem but of the most popular series of illustrations to it, Moritz Retzsch's outline engravings. In the *Phantasmagoria* a slight French accent is discernible, particularly in the second volume which contains Crowquill's 'Philosophies' … of smoking, drinking, the law, money, etc., imitated from the nearly contemporaneous French *Physiologies* [fig. 151].

William Makepeace Thackeray, having lived, loved and worked in Paris, was both aware and appreciative of the work of the French caricaturists. Writing to Edward Fitzgerald on 8 October 1834, the seasoned critic of twenty-two remarked: 'Yesterday at the Luxembourg I was astonished to see how bad everything was – there is not I think a single good picture among the elite of modern French art – but then in return, the sketches in the novels, the penny magazines &c are full of talent ….'.[32] And in his 'Caricature and Lithography in Paris', a magazine article of 1839 reprinted a year later in *The Paris Sketch Book*, he hails the genius of Honoré Daumier's *Les Robert Macaires* and the enterprise of Charles Philipon, the publisher of this and similar material.

However, in so far as his own style was concerned, one can detect few French influences in Thackeray. His earliest work – if you exclude the satiric designs reproduced as lithographs, *Flore et Zéphyr* (1836) – was

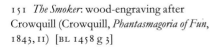

151 *The Smoker*: wood-engraving after Crowquill (Crowquill, *Phantasmagoria of Fun*, 1843, II) [BL 1458 g 3]

etched when Thackeray still mistakenly believed that he could become a professional illustrator – is the very Cruikshankian set of what Henry Vizetelly calls 'execrable illustrations'[33] to Douglas Jerrold's *Men of Character* (1838). This was his sole endeavour for the work of others and when he came to illustrate his own writings, a task to which his artistic talents were now confined, his illustrations are either in the outline style, as in *The Paris Sketch Book* (1840), or parodies of it, in *The Yellowplush Correspondence* and *Catherine* (in *Fraser's Magazine* 1837–8 and 1839–40).

Daniel Maclise was a fellow-Fraserian and one might attribute to his influence, if not to his tuition, the marked improvement in the draughtsmanship of the illustrations to *Comic Tales and Sketches* (1841). Certainly the outline style is one which continued to influence Thackeray and traces of it may be discerned as late as 1848 in *Vanity Fair*, although by then Thackeray had long been working for *Punch* and had thoroughly absorbed the manner of John Leech which influenced his style until *The Virginians* (1857–9). Thackeray is no great artist – his etched work and his designs for wood-engraving lack, as he himself was only too well aware, the spontaneity of the delightful pen-sketches which decorate his letters – but he is by no means negligible and, surely, no writer of his stature has illustrated his own work to such effect?

152 *Behind the Haystacks*: soft-ground etching by W.M. Thackeray (Thackeray, *The History of Samuel Titmarsh and the Great Hoggarty Diamond*, 1849) [BL C71 b 12]

153 *Mr Romford treats Sponge to a little Music*: wood-engraving after John Leech (Surtees, *Mr Sponge's Sporting Tour*, 1853) [BL C70 d 8]

A special quality, which does not depend upon artistic merit, must therefore attach to Thackeray's illustrations. The most successful are perhaps those supplied to such minor works as *Comic Tales and Sketches* (1841); or *The Great Hoggarty Diamond* (1849) for which his friend and protegé, the French artist and engraver Louis Marvy, helped Thackeray to prepare the soft-ground etchings [fig. 152]. In so far, then, as his etchings are concerned, Thackeray's failings in other books may be due in part to his lack of technical expertise.

Such strictures cannot, however, be applied to what is certainly a favourite book, *The Rose and the Ring* (1854). Here Thackeray's designs are engraved on wood and, in addition to the full-page illustrations, a large number are integrated into the text in the Romantic manner. There is nothing remarkable about this in the context of children's books, but there is in the context of Thackeray the novelist. For he stands almost alone in introducing integrated wood-engravings into the texts of three of his major novels, *Vanity Fair* (1848), *Pendennis* (1849–50) and *The Newcomes* (1853–5, illustrated by Richard Doyle) [fig. 160]. Although it could be argued that this is a legacy of his work as a *Punch* artist, as the self-deprecatory chapter initials almost certainly are, I like to think that this is the influence of those sketches in French novels which he so relished as a young man.

Thackeray and John Leech had both been for a very short time contemporaries at Charterhouse, but Thackeray had been very much the senior boy and it was only as colleagues on *Punch* that he and Leech became friends. Leech (1817–64), although Thackeray's junior in years, was very much his senior in art and exerted a strong influence upon the novelist's style of drawing for wood-engraving. Yet something of a question mark hangs over Leech's own style. Although it was black ingratitude on the part of W.J.Linton, for Leech showed a marked preference for him as an engraver, there is considerable truth in his devastating stricture: 'John Leech's style was motivated by his incapacity for determinate drawing. What an Academician would call drawing he had not. I admire his facility in catching character and see improvement from long practice; but he was not an artist.'[34]

It is probably unfair to quote Linton but it would justify a lack of sympathy with Leech's work. It does not always excite in the way that comparable artists such as Phiz and Doyle do. Perhaps one should conclude that his real importance lies in the role which Thackeray gave him, that of 'the social historian of the nineteenth century'. This observation occurs in a long and laudatory notice – Thackeray was never slow to help his friends – in *The Quarterly*

too dark to see the threads ; and when the night closed in, she lighted her feeble candle and worked on. Still her old father was invisible about her ;

154 *The Seamstress*: wood-engraving after John Leech (Dickens, *The Chimes*, 1845) [BL C59 fff 9]

Amusing Himself*:
steel-etching by
John Leech
(Hooton, *Colin
Clink*, 1841)
[BL N2123]

Review of December 1854, of the first of John Leech's *Pictures of Life and Character*. This was
the first of several series, frequently reprinted after Leech's death in the three familiar red-
cloth quarto volumes, which contain this detailed record of the dress, social habits, attitudes
and prejudices of the English middle-class in nearly 3,000 caricatures from 1841 to 1864. If
I am insensitive to the artistic merits of this contribution to *Punch*, I hope I can at least
acknowledge the link provided by Leech in the transmission of the down-to-earth realism
of Hogarth to draughtsmen such as Keene, Du Maurier and Belcher in the pages of the
magazine.

This is not to say that Leech worked exclusively for magazines or exclusively for *Punch*; he
was also to be found in *The Illustrated London News* and *The Sporting Review* among others, and

he illustrated over fifty books. Best known of these are the novels of R.S. Surtees [fig. 153], which, as a hunting man himself, Leech must have found particularly congenial. Other work included the novels of his friend and fellow medical student Albert Smith, as well as the work of other friends and colleagues, Douglas Jerrold's *Mrs Caudle's Curtain Lectures* (1846) and Charles Dickens's *A Christmas Carol* (1843). His designs for *Punch* were, of course, engraved on wood [fig. 154]; most of the illustrations of the books we have mentioned were etched on steel. Indeed, what are probably his best essays in this genre were executed under George Cruikshank's eye for *Bentley's Miscellany*: the plates for R.H. Barham's *Ingoldsby Legends* (3 vols, 1840–47), C. Hooton's *Colin Clink* (1841) [fig. 155], and Charles Whitehead's *Richard Savage* (1842).

Of his designs for wood-engraving, mention should be made of those for the third and subsequent editions of *Bon Gualtier's Book of Ballads*; for Percival Leigh's *Comic Grammars* (both English and Latin, 1840) and his *Jack the Giant Killer* (a Vizetelly/Orr Comic Nursery Tale, 1843); Gilbert A'Beckett's *Comic History of England* (1847) and *Comic History of Rome* (1851); and for a collection of Albert Smith's contributions to *Bentley's Miscellany*, *The Wassail Bowl* (1843). While none of these may be great art, they all contain that most engaging ingredient of British illustration of the period – verve and exuberant high spirits.

HABLOT KNIGHT BROWNE (PHIZ) AND RICHARD DOYLE

This exuberance is the keynote of the early work of Hablot Knight Browne (1815–82), whom Thackeray rightly calls 'the dashing designer', Phiz. Apprenticed to the engraver William Finden, Browne never completed his indentures but, in 1834, set up with Robert Young, who had served his time with Finden, as independent etchers and engravers, Browne being responsible for the artistic and Young for the technical side of the business. Young was, indeed, to specialize in the biting-in of steel-etching, both for Browne and for other artists, including Richard Doyle whose plates for Thackeray's *The Newcomes* were bitten-in by Young.

Meanwhile, Browne's great opportunity came when, as resident artist on Chapman & Hall's literary magazine *The Library of Fiction*, he was called upon to replace Robert Seymour, that artist having committed suicide before two issues of *Pickwick Papers* had appeared. The tremendous success of this first novel made the reputations of both Charles Dickens and of Phiz – the name which Browne adopted to complement Dickens's Boz. Although Phiz is primarily remembered as Dickens's illustrator, his work for Dickens formed part only of the many commissions for illustrations in both books and magazines which this success brought him.

Browne, whose early work both in *Pickwick Papers* (1837) and in *Nicholas Nickleby* (1839) shows the strong influence which Cruikshank exerted on almost all the young illustrators, soon developed a more individual style, its merits, Thackeray wrote when reviewing Charles Lever's *Our Mess* in *Fraser's Magazine*, being that 'He draws a horse admirably, a landscape beautifully, a female figure with extreme grace and tenderness, but as for its humour, it is stark naught; nay, worse, the humorous faces are a bad caricature.' [35]

Thackeray's is a surprisingly modern reaction – how many people have been put off Phiz for life by having been exposed at too early an age to Dickens with his original illustrations – to a convention of the grotesquely comic which Thackeray himself observed. Yet, if it can be accepted, there is considerable merit even in this side of Phiz's book-art. It is part of the enormous sense of life and of fun which is to be found in novels like W.J. Neale's *Paul Periwinkle* (1841) [fig. 156], for example, or in the rackety shapeless fictions of the now-forgotten best-selling Irish novelist, Charles Lever. Set on the Continent and in Ireland, in peace and in the Napoleonic Wars, they gave Phiz just the sorts of subjects in which he revelled – hunting, fighting, drinking, crowd scenes, violent activity – and all of which he etched with the greatest gusto.

Nor was his art static either in range or in technique. In 1847 Parry, Blenkarn & Co. commissioned from him a frontispiece and vignette title-page for their reprint of Harrison

156 *The 'Prosperity' going down*: steel-etching by Phiz (Hablot Knight Browne) (Neale, *Paul Periwinkle*, 1841) [BL 1208 k 34]

Ainsworth's *Old Saint Paul's*. Possibly inspired by the mezzotint effects achieved by John Franklin when he first illustrated the book in 1841,[36] Phiz began to experiment in the same style. These so-called 'dark' plates first occur in Charles Dickens's *Dombey and Son* (1848) and in Albert Smith's *The Pottleton Legacy* (1849), and Browne continued to develop the technique throughout the 1850s – the best examples being in Charles Dickens's *Bleak House* (1853) [figs 157, 158] and in Augustus Mayhew's *Paved with Gold* (1857).

In addition to this inspired use of the ruling-machine to achieve the effects of darkness, by developing the technique of 'stopping-out', Browne managed as startling and opposite effects of light in Charles Dickens's *Little Dorrit* (1857), for example, and in Charles Lever's *Davenport Dunn* (1857–9). Yet the most forcible demonstration of Browne's development may be found in another of Ainsworth's novels. The illustrator had established a connection with the novelist in 1844, when Cruikshank resigned from *Ainsworth's Magazine* and Phiz replaced him as resident artist. Among the novels which Browne illustrated was *Mervyn Clitheroe*, begun in 1851, temporarily suspended, and finally completed in 1858. Between its covers may be found the vignette steel-etchings executed when Ainsworth embarked upon *Mervyn Clitheroe*, in stark contrast with the squared etchings – which include many of Browne's finest 'dark' plates – etched when the volatile novelist resumed work.

157 *Lady Dedlock in the Wood*: a 'light plate' etched on steel by Phiz (Hablot Knight Browne) (Dickens, *Bleak House*, 1853) [BL C58 i 17]

158 *The Morning*: a 'dark' plate etched on steel by Phiz (Hablot Knight Browne) (Dickens, *Bleak House*, 1853) which may well show the influence of John Franklin (see fig. 178) [BL C58 i 17]

Of the early Victorian illustrators, Browne seems to have been sadly underestimated, especially in his designs for wood-engravings [fig. 159].[37] One reason, perhaps, is that he, like George Cruikshank, suffered particularly badly from the change in taste which gathered momentum from the mid-1850s and brought with it decisive changes in both the style and medium of book-illustration. Browne's altered status is typified by his summary dismissal in 1864 by Charles Dickens after nearly thirty years of close collaboration, to rub salt into the wound inflicted by an even more summary rejection by Anthony Trollope half-way through the part-issue of his novel *Can You Forgive Her?* in 1863. Yet his work for Dickens had been in many respects the most interesting and significant use of illustration in the entire Romantic period.

Just as the British were almost alone in illustrating original as opposed to reprinted fiction, so Dickens alone of British novelists seems fully to have realized the potential of the illustration as an adjunct vital to the writer's art at the particular period and for the particular audience for whom he was writing. As the late Mrs Q.D. Leavis has pointed out, Dickens's readership was only recently literate and had certainly not yet become accustomed to creating the mental image from the printed word.[38] What they had was the tradition of Hogarth's prints, veritable pictorial novels, and they were closely attuned to the pictured symbol. Dickens therefore used illustrations as an extension of his text, not simply to give his characters visible form, but to reinforce in pictorial symbols the point which his prose was designed to make. He therefore demanded, and in Phiz obtained, an artist who was willing and able to subordinate his own vision to that of the novelist. The result is that Phiz's is not merely the most authentic representation of the novelist's conception of his characters, but the full realization of one aspect of the Romantic book – the enrichment of the lives, not of a small cultural elite, but of the people at large, in the marriage of text and image.

Hablot Knight Browne deserves to rank very high among the draughtsmen of the old school of British caricaturists, even though his art far transcends caricature. The same may be said of Richard Doyle (1824–83) in respect of the new, for Doyle is a fascinating example of a draughtsman of the outline school who uses the style both in parody and in earnest.

The son of 'H.B.', the political caricaturist John Doyle whose elegant lithographs succeeded George Cruikshank's savage copper-etchings in the public esteem, young Dicky Doyle was taught draughtsmanship by his father. In 1843 at the age of 19, a letter of introduction enabled him to impress the editor of *Punch* so forcibly with his talent that he was engaged as one of the magazine's regular artists. To Doyle is due the fourth cover which *Punch* wore for over a hundred years, from its introduction in 1844. While never a cartoonist on the scale of John Leech, he provided a host of witty initial letters and vignettes which mocked the artistically fashionable outline style, and this parody was particularly effective in a series entitled 'Manners and Customs of ye Englyshe' designed to illustrate

159 *The Death of Quilp*: wood-engraving after Phiz (Hablot Knight Browne) (Dickens, *The Old Curiosity Shop*, 1840) [BL 838 i 17]

Percival Leigh's *Mr Pips hys Diary* (1849). Nor was it less deadly when Doyle was invited to provide the illustrations to Thackeray's Christmas book for 1849–50, *Rebecca and Rowena*, a skit on Sir Walter Scott's *Ivanhoe*.

Doyle owed this commission to his friendship with Thackeray and to the fact that the novelist had been seriously ill in the autumn of 1849, and so had been unable to follow his custom of illustrating his own work. Doyle's other Thackeray commission, the illustrations to *The Newcomes* [fig. 160], came about through the novelist's wish to spend the winter of 1853–4 in Rome with his daughters, and his consequent inability to supply both text and illustrations for the part-issues of the novel. Both men had recently resigned from *Punch*: Thackeray in 1851, because of its attacks on the Emperor Napoleon III, and Doyle a year earlier, deeply offended, as a Catholic, by the magazine's strident 'No Popery'. Thackeray might be suiting his own convenience, but he was equally anxious to help a friend and,

160 *London super Mare*: steel-etching by Richard Doyle (Thackeray, *The Newcomes*, I, 1854) [BL 12654 r 1]

although he regretted at first entrusting the illustrations to a third party and grumbled at the result, he was delighted with the end-product, writing from Paris to Percival Leigh on 12 April 1854: 'I have seen for the first time the engravings of the Newcomes .... He [Doyle] does beautifully and easily what I wanted to do and can't.'[39]

Although Doyle's masterpiece is generally regarded as being the designs for the wood-engravings printed in colour by Edmund Evans in William Allingham's *In Fairyland*, the illustrations in *The Newcomes* are on any account fine work and certainly overshadow many of the very respectable number of designs executed for publishers during the Romantic period. They included such children's books as *The Fairy Ring*, a selection from the Brothers Grimm translated by Edgar Taylor and extravagantly overpraised by Thackeray,[40] the Countess Montalba's *Fairy Tales from All Nations* (1849), and John Ruskin's *King of the Golden River* (1851) [fig. 161], the best of the three and most typical of the German influence upon Doyle's draughtsmanship.

Other noteworthy books include his contributions to the later editions of *Bon Gualtier's Book of Ballads*, and to Thomas Hughes's *The Scouring of the White Horse* (1859) [fig. 162], with its fine double-spread title-page and other vignette designs engraved by W.J. Linton. Finally, the products of Doyle's busy social life and membership of the Dickens circle should not be overlooked. These are his contributions to three of Dickens's Christmas Books – *The Chimes* (1844), *The Cricket on the Hearth* (1845) and *The Battle of Life* (1846). The Christmas Books

161 Wood-engraved frontispiece and title-page after Richard Doyle (Ruskin, *The King of the Golden River*, 1851) [BL 12805 h 8]

162 Wood-engraved double-spread title-page after Richard Doyle (Hughes, *The Scouring of the White Horse*, 1859) [BL 12632 d 27]

show the quality of Doyle's draughtsmanship when he was using the outline style in earnest and not in parody. The wood-engraved embellishments on the opening page of *The Chimes* complement rather than disgrace the steel-engraved frontispiece designed by that British master of the outline style, Daniel Maclise [figs 110, 111].

In order to draw attention to the way in which the expansion of book publishing in the Romantic period and the simultaneous birth of illustrated journalism created conditions under which artists could earn a living almost entirely by their work for the press, I have devoted considerable space to the first generation of the professional illustrators. Many of them had had little formal training, and yet they created a wealth of etched and engraved work which is probably still undervalued critically because it was spent upon so much purely ephemeral literature or upon then popular writers whose work has not stood the test of time. Equally, conditions so favourable to the creation of a new class of artist favoured, as never before, the use of the talents of professional painters in the embellishment of books.

This encouragement operated in a variety of ways. The cult of the Annual opened a new market to the established painter for the reproduction of work of all sorts – landscape, portrait, genre, historical or religious. Of these, the landscape had probably the widest circulation, reproduced by steel-engraving in the Annuals and in the many books of topography and travels which were such a feature of the period, as well as into collected editions of poets such as Byron and novelists such as Sir Walter Scott.

Then there was the constant critical pressure upon the publishers to employ recognized and respected painters as illustrators. Publishers such as John Van Voorst naturally adopted this practice, but other houses were constantly bullied by the reviewers' drawing such unflattering (and often unfair) comparisons between the work of British illustrators and those in France and Germany. This tendency towards elevating book-embellishment into a recognized artistic genre received the support of painters who followed the German example. Such a group as the members of the Etching Club, for example, produced a whole series of books in the spirit if not in the style of the German painters of the *Lieder und Bilder*. Finally, the expansion of the illustrated press, both in books and magazines, offered wider opportunities for young painters with a name still to be made to earn both money and reputation from their designs for illustration.

THE LANDSCAPE PAINTERS

The popularity in Britain in the nineteenth century of landscape painting is exhibited in the numbers of bound volumes of artists' aquatints and lithographs which were issued. It pervades book-illustration in general and is demonstrated in the Annuals and in the large number of books of travel and topography in which the steel-engraving so admirably translated the atmospheric effects of the watercolour. In the first category, *Heath's Picturesque Annual* provides both a useful example of the genre itself and its very title names the aesthetic movement responsible for this interest in landscape. The second provided an inexhaustible market for the landscape painters, two of the most prolific being Thomas Allom (1804–72) and William Henry Bartlett (1809–54). Allom followed illustrations to books of English topography with those for Robert Walsh's *Constantinople* (1838–40), and George Wright's *China* (1843) and *France Illustrated* (1844); Bartlett travelled and painted in the Low Countries, Germany, Switzerland, Italy, European Turkey, Asia Minor, the Near East, Canada and the United States to supply the material for the steel-engravings in a series of books on these areas. Although both artists provided large numbers of conventional *hors-texte* illustrations in that most typically British medium of the period, the steel-engraving, they made little contribution to the art of the Romantic book.

In this respect J.M.W. Turner, that greatest of English Romantic painters, was completely opposite and, as we have seen, his embellishments to Samuel Rogers's poetry and to Sir Walter Scott's prose profoundly influenced the design of books in Britain. Yet this was a contribution quite disproportionate to the number of illustrations involved, and the bulk of Turner's designs published in books were issued as full-page squared steel-engravings in Annuals and works of topography or travel. This would be true also of the book-illustrations provided by the majority of British landscape painters during the period. Of course, there were exceptions in the book-illustrations of such an artist. Turner himself provided designs for a six-volume Milton (1835) and for Thomas Moore's *Alciphron* and *The Epicurean* (1839) for the shrewd and pushing young publisher John Macrone. George Cattermole (1800–68), although primarily an architectural and topographical painter and illustrator, accepted a commission to provide designs for Aiken's *Calendar of Nature* (1834) [fig. 120] from John Van Voorst and for Charles Dickens's *Master Humphrey's Clock* (1840–41).

A very similar judgement would be formed of William Clarkson Stanfield's book-illustrations. Stanfield (1793–1857), who was known in his day as 'the English Vandevelde', had the rather unlikely background for a painter of land- and seascapes of being a merchant seaman with a talent for drawing. In 1812 he was seized by the press-gang and, after serving on HMS *Namur*, was discharged as unfit. While at sea he had sketched and had painted scenery for the ship's amateur theatricals; he now undertook the task professionally, first in his native Edinburgh then, from 1822, in London, where he became one of the foremost stage-designers of the day. Meanwhile he worked at his painting, being elected RBA (1824), ARA (1832) and RA (1835).

As a successful landscape painter Stanfield contributed to *Heath's Picturesque Annual* and, as such, was commissioned by John Murray to provide the Turneresque frontispieces and vignette titles for the collected edition of George Crabbe [fig. 131]. His high professional standing – and his Scottish birth – brought him the commission to provide designs for the bulk of the steel-engraved *hors-texte* illustrations in the Abbotsford edition of Sir Walter Scott's Waverley Novels (1842–7). It says much for Stanfield's status as a painter, and for the status of the steel-engraving in Britain, that both should have figured so prominently in the publisher's advertising. This was, perhaps, the greatest illustrated part-issue, in scale at least, of the Romantic period in Britain for, in addition to the steel-engravings, the twelve volumes eventually absorbed no fewer than 2,000 designs for integrated wood-engravings.

Drawn by C. Stanfield. R.A   Engraved by J. T. Willmore.

163 *Cutting away the Masts*: steel-engraving after Clarkson Stanfield (Marryatt, *The Pirate and The Three Cutters*, 1836) [BL C151i3]

164 Full-page
vignette steel-
engraving after
Thomas Creswick
(Ritchie, *Ireland
Picturesque and
Romantic*, 1, 1837)
[BL PP6910]

The exceptions to the pattern in Stanfield's career as a book-illustrator stem primarily from the work which he undertook for his personal friends and in particular for Charles Dickens and for Captain Marryat. For his novels Dickens always employed Hablot Knight Browne (Phiz), but for his Christmas books he turned to artists in his immediate social circle. Thus John Leech was solely responsible for *A Christmas Carol* (1843) and contributed to the other four; Stanfield alone of the other artists – including Daniel Maclise, Richard Doyle, Frank Stone and John Tenniel – contributed to all four of the remaining Christmas books.

Stanfield was an old friend of Charles Dickens, and his scene-painting talents were at the disposal of Dickens's company of amateur actors, but an older friend was Captain Marryat, for Marryat had befriended Stanfield when he was serving as a seaman on the *Namur*. Accordingly, in 1836, he provided designs for a vignette title and eighteen full-page illustrations for the two *novellen* issued together as *The Pirate and The Three Cutters* [fig. 163], and in 1840 drawings for full-page vignette illustrations to *Poor Jack*. The latter were engraved on wood and, while the vignettes are generally effective, the full-page illustrations do not stand comparison with the steel-engravings of the earlier book. Yet, disappointing though they may be, they hardly deserve the denunciation of *The Art Union*

Journal, which stated that this 'attempt to deteriorate the arts, on the part of one of the most influential publishing houses of the metropolis [Longman] deserves its most severe censure.'[41]

Perhaps the fault lay with the designer rather than publisher, printer or engraver. Henry Vizetelly, who cut most of the blocks for *Poor Jack*, complains in his memoirs that Stanfield, 'like many other painters, found the difficulty of drawing on the boxwood block with the necessary neatness and precision almost insurmountable', and in consequence 'John Gilbert was employed to transfer many of his drawings.'[42] Notwithstanding, he continued to supply designs for wood-engraving, notably for Dickens's Christmas books, for Mrs S.C. Hall's *Midsummer Eve* (1843/8) and for Edward Moxon's celebrated illustrated edition of Tennyson (1857).

One landscape painter, however, who seems to have been interested in the art of the printed book and not simply in the publishing trade as an outlet for reproductions of his paintings, was the Birmingham-born pupil of J.V. Barber, Thomas Creswick (1811–69). Although many of his book illustrations appeared in the conventional guise in Annuals and topographical books, Creswick was a member of the Etching Club and contributed to all its publications. One can therefore view his book-illustrations in a slightly different light from those of his confrères.

Of Creswick's conventional work, one should note his illustrations to Thomas Roscoe's *North Wales* (1836) and *The Wye* (1839) and to Leith Ritchie's *Ireland Picturesque and Romantic* (2 vols, 1837–8) [fig. 164]. The fine steel-engravings in these latter volumes were afterwards used in Mr and Mrs S.C. Hall's three-volume *Ireland* (1841–3) and in Mrs Hall's attractive guide-book, *A Week at Killarney* (1843). It was doubtless from this connection that Creswick was invited to contribute both to the husband's *Book of British Ballads* (1841–3) and the wife's

165 *View of Broxbourne, on the River Lea*: wood-engraved vignette after Thomas Creswick (Walton, *The Compleat Angler*, 1844)
[BL 1040 e 40]

197

Midsummer Eve (1843/8), although in both cases his 'aids' were minimal. He retained his popularity as a landscape painter and was one of the artists whose work was chosen for reproduction by coloured wood-engraving in *Poetry of the Year* (1853).

The same popularity is to be seen in the commissions which he received for book-illustrations from *Childe Harold's Pilgrimage* (1836) to the Tennyson of 1857. As a landscape painter he naturally expressed himself tonally and therefore his designs for wood-engraving depend upon tint more than upon line. This gives them a somewhat old-fashioned air in the Tennyson and they are best seen in some of his earlier books. While always expressive, I have found him at his best in conjunction with John Absolon in the traditional vignette designs for that very lovely edition of Izaak Walton's *The Compleat Angler*, published by Charles Tilt in 1844 [fig. 165].

HENRY WARREN, NATIONAL PAINTERS AND MEMBERS OF THE ETCHING CLUB

While there was a very obvious opening for the landscape painter as a book-illustrator and embellisher, opportunities arose for other specialists as well. An interesting case is that of Henry Warren (1798–1879) who had built a reputation for oriental genre painting without ever having travelled to the East. He found the Zoological Gardens supplied him with animal models, while the theatrical costumier could give his human models the necessary touch of local colour. Nonetheless it was this speciality which presumably led him to share with William Harvey the commission to supply something like 80 per cent of the designs for J.G. Lockhart's *Ancient Spanish Ballads* (1841) [fig. 52], to supply those for steel-engraving for *The Tales and Poems of Lord Byron* (W.S. Orr, 1848) [fig. 166], and to contribute to the illustration of *The Four Gospels* (Chapman & Hall, 1847–9). It is certainly the reason for his presence among the many artists engaged in illustrating the Abbotsford edition of Scott's

166 *The Young Giaour*: steel-engraved vignette after Henry Warren (Byron, *Tales and Poems*, 1848) [BL 11656 f 67]

Waverley Novels, since his share is confined to the specifically Oriental scenes in *The Talisman* (vol. IX, 1846) and *Count Robert of Paris* (vol. XI, 1847).

It would, however, be wrong to think that Warren's subjects were exclusively Oriental. He illustrated the Baroness de Calabrella's *The Prism of the Imagination* (1844) and supplied the design 'Baptism' for Murray's *Book of Common Prayer* (1845), where it is interesting to observe the greater delicacy of detail achieved by Vizetelly's tinted wood-engraving by comparison with the tinted lithographs used in *The Prism*. He was also connected with both James Burns and with S.C. Hall, contributing to the *German Ballads* (1845) of the one, and to the *Book of British Ballads* (1842) of the other [fig. 167]. Yet perhaps his most interesting Western illustrations, both from the medium and the subjects, are the oval steel-engravings which

Robin Hood's Death and Burial.

He then bethought him of a casement door,
   Thinking for to be gone,
He was so weak he could not leap,
   Nor he could not get down.

He then bethought him of his bugle-horn,
   Which hung low down to his knee,
He set his horn unto his mouth,
   And blew out weak blasts three.

Then Little John, when hearing him,
   As he sat under the tree,
' I fear my master is near dead,
   He blows so wearily.'

Then Little John to fair Kirkley is gone,
   As fast as he can dree ;
But when he came to Kirkley-hall,
   He broke locks two or three :

Untill he came bold Robin to,
   Then he fell on his knee ;
' A boon, a boon,' cries Little John,
   ' Master, I beg of thee.'

' What is that boon,' quoth Robin Hood,
   ' Little John, thou begs of me ?'
' It is to burn fair Kirkley-hall,
   And all their nunnery.'

' Now nay, now nay,' quoth Robin Hood,
   ' That boon I'll not grant thee ;
I never "hurt" woman in all my life,
   Nor man in woman's company.

' I never hurt fair maid in all my time,
   Nor at my end shall it be ;
But give me my bent bow in my hand,
   And a broad arrow I'll let flee ;
And where this arrow is taken up,
   There shall my grave digg'd be.

H. Warren del.   Evans sc.   337

167 *Robin Hood's Death and Burial*: wood-engraved panel-decoration after Henry Warren (*The Book of British Ballads*, 1842) [BL 2288 g 4]

decorate Mrs Sarah Stickney Ellis's three-decker novel, *Social Distinctions* (1848–9) [fig. 168]. They mark the versatility of an artist of considerable talent and of some importance as a Romantic illustrator.

The custom of entrusting the illustration of a book to a group, rather than to a single artist, had the effect of allowing painters not otherwise associated with book-illustration to contribute a limited, and in most cases a very limited, number of designs to a given publication. This served to placate critics whose constant complaint was the poverty of British draughtsmanship, and it enabled publishers to benefit disproportionately from the association with a popular painter's name. From the historian's point of view, however, it tends to cloud the issue by bringing into the ranks of the book-illustrators artists who were, strictly speaking, easel painters and whose contribution to book-illustration was infinitesimal by comparison with the professionals.

168 *The Child answered not*: steel-engraving after Henry Warren (Ellis, *Social Distinctions*, III, 1849)
[BL 12620 c 25]

A more legitimate device was to associate national painters with books of national interest. We have seen how Cadell made a feature of the contributions of a Scottish painter, Clarkson Stanfield, to the Abbotsford edition of Scott's Waverley novels, in which he involved other Scots painters not normally associated with book-illustration – among them J. Burnet, R.S.J. Lauder, W.L. Leitch, Paul Paton and William Simson. Irish books benefited from the same policy: the Irish painter Henry Macmanus RHA (1810–87) being a case in point. He was among a number of Irish artists whom the Halls commissioned to provide illustrations for their three-volume *Ireland* (1841–3), and he was again commissioned, along with such professionals as William Harvey, John Gilbert and Phiz, to illustrate William Carleton's *Traits and Stories of the Irish Peasantry* (1843–4). These seem to be among his very few excursions into book-illustration, except for his own *Bob Norberry* (1844) and *Sketches of the Irish Highlands* (1863).

We have discussed hitherto the ways in which painters became involved in the illustration of books, and when we consider the productions of the Etching Club we have an instance of painters actively engaged in this genre. The Club, in the words of its founder Charles West Cope, 'was at first only a small society. We met at each other's room in turn, once a month, and experimented in etching for an hour or two, and then had a simple supper limited to bread and cheese.'[43] The members comprised Cope's friends from his days at Sass's Academy: Charles Stonhouse, the pupil of Sir David Wilkie, and the sculptor John Bell; Richard Redgrave whom he had met at the Royal Academy Schools, and the engraver Charles Lewis. They would seem to have progressed to the publication of their designs through their need as struggling young painters to supplement their income, and their numbers expanded. Their original group now embraced Richard Redgrave's brother Sam – their Honorary Secretary – Thomas Webster, Thomas Creswick, H.J. Townsend, J.F. Tayler, J.P. Knight, J.C. Horsley and Frank Stone. (Later members included Samuel Palmer, J.E. Millais and Holman Hunt.)

The overall impression left by their publications is that given by the similar work of German painters – collections of designs inspired by works of literature, with the emphasis far more strongly placed upon the design than the text. This is most certainly true of Oliver Goldsmith's *The Deserted Village* (1841), of *Shakespeare's Songs* (1843), and of *Etched Thoughts* (1844), all published on commission by Longman, and of the later volumes which were published by Joseph Cundall, Thomas Gray's *Elegy* (1847) and John Milton's *L'Allegro* (1849). Two more substantial volumes, however, both published on commission by Longman, James Thomson's *The Seasons* (1843) [figs 169, 170] and Oliver Goldsmith's *Poetical Works* (1845) [fig. 171], for which members of the Club designed the wood-engravings, are among the best examples of British Romantic book design, the vignettes integrated with the text and the whole framed by narrow single-rule borders.

Of the regular contributors to the Club's publications Thomas Creswick can most properly be termed a book-illustrator, by contrast with Charles Stonhouse whose only illustrations appear to have been those for the Club's books, and the genre painter Thomas Webster (1800–86) whose work amounts to no more than half-a-dozen designs in three of the Club's books and to a single design for John Van Voorst in the Robert Bloomfield *Poems*

(1845). John Bell, the sculptor, contributed to three of their publications, best and most extensively with his outline drawings to Thomson's *The Seasons*, and was also one of the many artists engaged by the Halls for their *Ireland*.

Given their circumstances, it is hardly surprising that other members should have been engaged in S.C. Hall's projects. Both Richard Redgrave and J.H. Townsend contributed to *The Book of British Ballads*, and the latter to *Ireland* as well. Similarly, C.W. Cope's connection with the group of artists assembled by James Burns may help to explain the presence of J.C. Horsley, Richard Redgrave and H.J. Townsend among the contributors to *Poems and Pictures* (1846). And this is the keynote of their activity as illustrators: all, with the possible exception of J.C. Horsley, were commissioned almost exclusively by publishers who, as a matter of policy, looked to painters to illustrate their books. Thus Cope, Horsley and Tayler

Screaming, the dreadful policy arraigns,
Inhuman and unwise.   The sullen door,
Yet uninfected, on its cautious hinge
Fearing to turn, abhors society.
Dependants, friends, relations, love himself,
Savag'd by woe, forget the tender tie,
The sweet engagement of the feeling heart.
But vain their selfish care : the circling sky,
The wide enlivening air is full of fate ;
And, struck by turns, in solitary pangs
They fall, unblest, untended, and unmourn'd.

169 Wood-engraved page-decorations after John Bell (Thomson, *The Seasons*, 1843) [BL 1347 h 1]

worked for John Van Voorst, while Cope and Tayler were commissioned to illustrate the Abbotsford edition of the Waverley Novels, Cope making designs for *The Betrothed* (vol. IX, 1846) [figs 172, 173]and Tayler for *The Abbot* (vol. V, 1844) and for *Redgauntlet* (vol. X, 1846).

It is difficult to assess accurately the influence of the Etching Club's publications upon commercial book-illustration, but it was, perhaps, analogous to that of the private press movement during the twentieth century – pervasive rather than patent, and helping towards the improved standards of draughtsmanship which are the feature of the illustrated books of the 1850s and 1860s. Apart from their more esoteric volumes, they produced two very fine pieces of commercial book-illustration in the Thomson and the Goldsmith, and it is significant that Thackeray should couple the latter with *Poems and Pictures* as an example of 'typographical excellence'.[44] Like Burns's artists, and as was natural for painters upon whom

Tends on the little island's verdant swell,
The shepherd's sea-girt reign ; or, to the rocks
Dire-clinging, gathers his ovarious food ;
Or sweeps the fishy shore ; or treasures up
The plumage, rising full, to form the bed
Of luxury.   And here a while the muse,
High-hovering o'er the broad cerulean scene,
Sees Caledonia, in romantic view :
Her airy mountains, from the waving main,
Invested with a keen diffusive sky,
Breathing the soul acute ; her forests huge,
Incult, robust, and tall, by Nature's hand

170 *Gathering Ovarious Food*: wood-engraving after Richard Redgrave (Thomson, *The Seasons*, 1843) [BL 1347 h 1]

171 Wood-engraving after Frederick Tayler (Goldsmith, *Poetical Works*, 1845) [BL 11660 bb 25]

172 Wood-engraved chapter-heading after C.W. Cope (Scott, *The Betrothed*, 1846) [BL 14581 9]

German Romanticism was the predominant influence, the majority of the Etching Club illustrators affected a more or less shaded outline style. John Bell was the most German of them all and in 1844 issued an album of outline engraved *Compositions from Morning and Evening Prayer*. Thus they accentuate the tendency initiated by painter-illustrators to move away from Harvey's tints towards a style which, if equally derived from copper-engraving, could express itself on wood in the manner of the German Renaissance masters.

So far as the work of individuals is concerned, this must largely be a matter of personal taste. If one forgets the attitude towards nude painting which won him the nickname of 'Clothes' Horsley in the 1880s, one will find that his sentimentalities do not cloy, while the three designs reproduced as tinted wood-engravings in John Murray's *Book of Common Prayer* (1845) [fig. 130] are fine and appropriate. His colleague C.W. Cope, even on the basis of his very limited output, may be classed among the best of nineteenth-century illustrators. His style is the shaded outline, his contributions to the Etching Club's publications and to *Poems*

173 Wood-engraved
chapter-heading
after C.W. Cope
(Scott, *The Betrothed*,
1846) [BL 1458 i 9]

Chapter the Tenth.

They bore him barefaced on his bier,
Six proper youths and tall,
And many a tear bedew'd his grave
Within yon kirkyard wall.
THE FRIAR OF ORDERS GREY.

and Pictures are distinguished, his illustrations to *The Betrothed* stand out from the rest, while in Isaac Watts's *Divine and Moral Songs* he produces work of a classic simplicity which makes it one of the most satisfying of illustrated books in the Romantic period [fig. 124].

WILLIAM MULREADY AND DANIEL MACLISE

If his youthful work as illustrator of William Roscoe's *The Butterfly's Ball* (1807) and similar books for children are excluded, William Mulready's (1786–1863) contribution to the embellished book is even more slender than that of C.W. Cope. Yet it is all of very high quality and includes one of the finest of nineteenth-century illustrated books. Apart from his illustrations to the Abbotsford *Peveril of the Peak* (vol. VIII, 1845) and four designs in Moxon's Tennyson (1857), all his other work was commissioned by John Van Voorst. Mulready was one of the many artists involved in the Gray's *Elegy* of 1834 and the Shakespeare's *Seven Ages of Man* of 1840. His single design in the former strikes an odd note by depicting the figure in contemporary nineteenth-century dress, but he alone of the artists shows any concept of book design and, instead of the exiguous vignettes provided by most, Mulready gives a generous half-page to produce the only satisfying page of wood-engraving and text in the entire book [fig. 119].

It is, however, in Oliver Goldsmith's *The Vicar of Wakefield* (1843) [fig. 121] that Mulready achieves his masterpiece, which contemporary critics recognized as such and applied as a standard to later wood-engraved books.[45] In the thirty-two half-page vignette chapter headings, sympathetically engraved on wood by John Thompson, the line is delicate yet firm, the composition masterly. Yet the overall effect is difficult to analyse. While clearly influenced by the prevailing fashion among painters for the outline drawing, and perhaps retaining the impress of Stothard's later manner, there is a quality of timelessness about them which removes them from any period style. This timelessness is the keynote of Mulready's best work and is apparent in two of his four designs – 'The Sea Fairies' and 'The Deserted House' in Moxon's Tennyson – which, in contrast with the work of the other illustrators, look forward in style to the late-Victorian and Edwardian age.

This remoteness may well reflect Mulready's partial withdrawal from the artistic world, the failure of his marriage with John Varley's sister, and to a feeling of disappointment, failure and neglect. Henry Vizetelly recalls him in 1849 'living in seclusion in Linden Grove, Bayswater. There was about him none of the Irish sprightliness of the old days when he stood up with the gloves against Gentleman Jackson, Byron's pugilistic preceptor, and when Mendoza, the jew bruiser, was his intimate friend.'[46]

By contrast, his fellow-Irishman Daniel Maclise (1806–70) was very much of the literary and artistic world, a member of the Dickens circle and a notable Fraserian. To accompany William Maginn's biographical sketches, Maclise contributed a series of portraits of the artistic and literary celebrities of the day in *Fraser's Magazine*. They constitute an important visual record of the period and, as such, were twice collected and re-issued later in the century.[47] Portraits of his friends William Harrison Ainsworth and Charles Dickens were engraved and often used by them as frontispieces to their novels – which explains why he is sometimes bracketed with Phiz as an illustrator of *Nicholas Nickleby* or *Martin Chuzzlewit*, for

174 *Come down,*
O maid...: wood-
engraving after Daniel
Maclise (Tennyson,
The Princess, 1860)
[BL 1347 f 7]

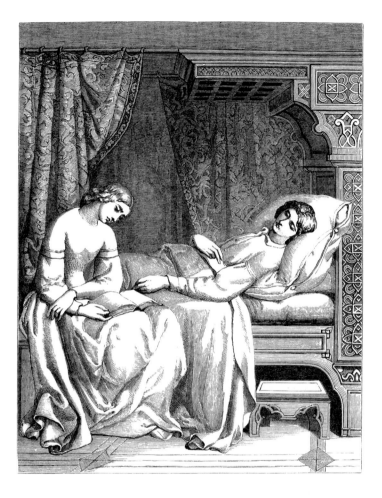

example – and his paintings were reproduced in the Annuals. Here the very British medium of steel-engraving masks the strongly German strain in his draughtsmanship so apparent in the work directly commissioned as book-illustration.

This element in his style would appear to be the response of something within Maclise's own artistic make-up, for he stood apart from the more obvious centres of German influence. True, the Art Union in 1850 issued reproductions of his frescoes of Shakespeare's *The Seven Ages of Man*, and true, his work appears in the Halls's *Ireland*. This is, however, fortuitous, since it was among the steel-engravings which they took over from Leith Ritchie's *Ireland Picturesque and Romantic*. Certainly he never contributed to S.C. Hall's *Book of British Ballads*, and escaped with a single design for the wife's *Midsummer Eve*. Nevertheless, when one considers his book-illustrations, all in the shaded outline style, from Thomas Moore's *Irish Melodies* in 1846 to Tennyson's *The Princess* in 1860 [fig. 174], the temptation to class Maclise as a Germanist is almost irresistible. Of his designs for Bürger's *Leonora* (1847), a contemporary critic wrote: 'In style we know no German work that surpasses this – essentially German in character – or equals it in the beautiful execution of the wood-engraving.... Since Mulready's still unrivalled "Vicar of Wakefield," no English illustrated book has appeared which we would rank with this.'[48]

However, most modern students would, I think, consider it far less German than the earlier *Irish Melodies* [fig. 126], which of all British books most obviously resembles *Lieder und Bilder*. That it does so is due to the reinforcement of the Germanism of Maclise's outline designs by their reproduction by intaglio engraving, the German plates being engraved on copper, the British on steel by 'Mr. Becker's process'. F.P. Becker engraved the text – a characteristic, too, of *Lieder und Bilder*, assisted by others, including Charles Lewis, Thomas Landseer, F.W. Topham, and the artist himself who was responsible for five of the large designs. The publishers, Longman, commissioned the designs for the coloured papers which covered the case binding, from Owen Jones with whom they were closely connected at this time.[49]

The decorative borders which surround the pages of *Irish Melodies* and the large and small vignettes which are incorporated into them are a *tour de force*, unfortunately diminished by the engraving of the text in open letters. This gives the pages an overall grey look, the more apparent because the Appendix is printed from type. There is no density of the text itself to stand out in contrast with the delicacy of the borders nor to match the black tones which lend emphasis to the outlines of the vignettes.

A far more effective exercise in the same style, therefore, is the translation of Bürger's ballad *Leonora*, published in the following year with Maclise's designs for borders and vignettes engraved on wood by the great John Thompson [fig. 129]. This is a much slighter volume, with only six vignettes to the 51 large and 110 small designs of *Irish Melodies*, in the same handsome small quarto format, bound in coloured paper boards designed, again, by Owen Jones. Nevertheless, it is much more effective as a *book* because the short text is conventionally printed from type and has a colour so sadly missing from the more imposing volume. However, despite these strictures, *Irish Melodies* must rank among the finest British Romantic books and with *Leonora* forms a fitting tribute to Maclise's grand manner as a book-illustrator.

Nor was he less successful in a more modest role as contributor to books illustrated by a group of artists, such as the Moxon Tennyson (1857) or Thomas Moore's *Poetry and Pictures* (1858), but perhaps his happiest efforts on a small scale were his contributions to his friend Charles Dickens's Christmas Books. Although he shared in only two of the five, he designed a most attractive frontispiece to *The Chimes* (1845), engraved on steel [fig. 110], and a frontispiece and two integrated vignettes, engraved on wood, for *The Battle of Life* (1846).

Book-illustration was really a side-line for all these painters and their output cannot compare in sheer volume with the professionals. Nevertheless, their work was of real importance, not simply for itself, but because of the influence which it exerted upon younger artists and upon such professionals as John Gilbert, in this way determining the style of book-art in the later 1850s and 1860s. Nor was it unremunerative and it is worth noting that, while George Cruikshank in his heyday was paid no more than twelve guineas per etched plate by Richard Bentley, Longman, never extravagant in his rewards to artists,[50] gave Maclise ten guineas per *design* for each of the large vignettes in *Irish Melodies*, with a further fifteen, the standard rate, for each of the five plates which the artist himself engraved. So far as Mulready is concerned, the entries in his Account Book which relate to payments from John Van Voorst[51] are not specific and may relate as much to payment on account for *The Vicar of Wakefield* as to payment for work done on *The Seven Ages of Man*. However, by the time Moxon came to commission the illustrations for his Tennyson, Mulready was the grand old man of British painting, and was paid at the rate of 20 guineas per design.[52]

THE GERMANISTS: JOSEPH NOEL PATON, F. R. PICKERSGILL, JOHN TENNIEL, H.C. SELOUS AND JOHN FRANKLIN

In painting, the other Germanizing influence was William Dyce and if, like Maclise, his style represents a response to rather than the influence of German art, in practice it disseminated that influence. In terms of book-illustration it worked most strongly through and in the artists associated with James Burns. The principal members of the group comprised two older painters, the Irishman John Franklin (*fl.* 1800–70) and H.C. Selous (1803–90), and two younger artists, John Tenniel (1820–1914) and F.R. Pickersgill (1820–1900). In all four cases the Germanizing influence of William Dyce was reinforced by their close association with the Art Union and with its moving spirit, Samuel Carter Hall, where they were joined by a young Scottish painter who did not belong to the Burns stable, Joseph Noel Paton.

So far as their subsequent reputations are concerned, Franklin, having won almost immediate recognition – contemporary criticisms in the *Athenaeum*, for example, are almost invariably friendly if not laudatory – sank into total obscurity until relatively recently.[53] With the rest, the general neglect of the Romantic period of British book-illustration has led to a concentration of interest upon their later work, and their early and often very interesting achievements have gone unnoticed. Tenniel is simply seen as the *Punch* artist – he joined the staff when Richard Doyle resigned in 1850 and succeeded as principal cartoonist on the death of John Leech in 1864 – and if as a book-illustrator, then just as the illustrator of *Alice*. Pickersgill and Paton are essentially 1860s artists, but their early work bears consideration and, although ten years their senior and with a far larger body of work dating from the 1840s, Selous is probably best remembered for his designs for Cassell's illustrated books, John Bunyan's *The Pilgrim's Progress* and *The Holy War* (1863) and the three-volume Shakespeare of 1864.

Of these artists, Pickersgill and Paton are typical of the outline style. Neither was particularly productive of book-illustrations in the period, and in fact, apart from two albums of outline engravings – *Compositions from Shelley's Prometheus Unbound* (1844) and *Compositions from Shakespeare's Tempest* (1845) – before 1860 Paton seems to have supplied work for only two books. *Silent Love* (1845) is the fourth edition of the poems of a Paisley apothecary, James Wilson, who died in 1807, for which Paton engraved a frontispiece and ten full-page illustrations. Printed and published in Paisley, the result is a pretty little book which shows the outline style at its best [fig. 175], in simple small-scale compositions rather than in the pompous landscape folios of the Art Union premium books [fig. 72]. Far more ambitious are the thirty-nine designs for Mrs Hall's *Midsummer Eve* (1843/8) comprising full-page and vignette illustrations engraved on wood [fig. 176]. They are excellent examples of Paton's work and rival what are probably his best-known designs, the illustrations undertaken in conjunction with his brother Walter for the 1863 edition of W.F. Aytoun's *Lays of the Scottish Cavaliers.*

F.R. Pickersgill, ultimately less successful as a painter than Paton, was even at this stage more involved in book-illustration than he, through his connection with James Burns. In 1844 Burns published an edition of the Jacobean playwright Philip Massinger's *The Virgin Martyr* with a frontispiece and five full-page wood-engravings from Pickersgill's designs, and employed him with some frequency thereafter to design frontispieces for his Fireside Library such, for example, as those for C. von Woltman's *The White Lady* and for the two volumes of Plutarch's *Lives.* Pickersgill then became one of the major contributors to *Poems and Pictures* (1846). Prior to this he had illustrated a single British ballad for Samuel Carter Hall, and subsequently his work can be found scattered throughout the illustrated books of the 1850s.

In 1850, the Dalziel brothers commissioned from him designs for a series of New Testament subjects to be published by Chapman & Hall in cheap shilling parts. The inspiration for this project was Alfred Rethel's *Aus ein Todtentanz*,[54] and the wood-engravings were similarly printed on a flat yellow background which, although giving the outlines some body, is so much less effective than Vizetelly's style of broken tint as a means of suggesting tone and colour. Although the project was a commercial failure and the first issue, *Six Compositions from the Life of Christ* [fig. 177], had no successors, the contact thus established with the Dalziels brought many commissions in the 1860s to illustrate their art editions.

Pickersgill is a correct if sometimes clumsy practitioner of the outline and shaded outline styles. Despite his competent draughtsmanship, however, he conspicuously lacks a talent developed by the other three Burns artists and so essential a feature of Romantic book design, that of conceiving a page as a related unit, with text, decorations and vignette(s) integrated into a balanced and satisfying whole. This is very apparent in the designs of the older artists H.C. Selous and John Franklin, and is one of the precocious virtues of John Tenniel.[55]

175 *Eros*: outline wood-engraving after Joseph Noel Paton (Wilson, *Silent Love*, 1845) [BL 11622 df 28]

and distorted dwarf, carrying in both hands a huge china bowl, stood by his side, and on tip-toe offered him to drink: at first Randy motioned

him away; but there arose from the bowl a very fragrant steam; and the dwarf asked if he feared to drink to his young lady's health, of the mountain dew, sweetened with the richest honey of the wild bee—'mountain dew '—name which libels the purest and holiest draught that Nature sends to Earth from Heaven! And as THE WOODCUTTER's good spirit had been half vanquished by the spirit of evil that taught him to overvalue his own strength, and the enemy had power over him—HE DRANK—and slept.

The day was passing rapidly, and though Geraldine missed the

176 In contrast with fig. 175, a two-block wood-engraving in the traditional style after Joseph Noel Paton (Mrs Hall, *Midsummer's Eve*, 1843) [BL 12620 c 29]

Tenniel's artistic background was very similar to that of some of the caricaturists whom we have discussed. Apart from a few lessons at the Royal Academy Schools and at the Clipstone Street Academy, he was very largely self-taught. His abilities and ambition set him to submit a series of outline drawings inspired by the story of Griselda to the Art Union's premium book competition and, more importantly, designs for the frescoes for the new Houses of Parliament to the official Prize Committee. In the latter he was successful and as a result went to Munich to study fresco painting in 1845.

Although already influenced by the Germanism of the Art Union – he illustrated one British ballad, too, for S.C. Hall – and that of Burns's circle, his work for Burns had, up to this point, been in the very effective style developed by Selous and Franklin. This blended German linear strength with the tints of the British tradition of Harvey to produce designs for wood-engraving in which the vignette still retained areas of black sufficiently dense to match the density of the type-matter. Add to this Tenniel's feel for the design of the integrated page and some very attractive work results. It is best exemplified by the designs for *Undine* (1845) [fig. 108], but present in *Poems and Pictures* (1846) [fig. 106] and in the frontispieces of such Fireside Library titles as Schiller's *William Tell* or La Motte Fouqué's *The Magic Ring* (1846).

On his return from Germany, Tenniel's enthusiasm for the shaded outline style found expression in an edition of Aesop's *Fables* published by John Murray in 1848. Text, and

177 *The Entombment*: outline wood-engraving after F.R. Pickersgill (*Six Compositions from the Life of Christ*, 1850) [BL 742 g 14]

vignettes engraved on wood by Leopold Martin, are surrounded by a single narrow rule frame and, by and large, are simple half-page illustrations, giving Tenniel little opportunity to show his talent for integrated design. There are exceptions as, for example, in the fables of 'The Fox and the Grapes' or of 'The Travellers and the Bear' [fig. 132], which integrate illustration and decoration, or 'The Miller and his Sons' which integrates illustration with type-matter. The book deserves its high reputation, too, for in it we get the best of both worlds – Tenniel's earlier, more tonal style for his animals, and his newer outline style for his humans. Apart from *Alice in Wonderland* and *Through the Looking Glass*, this is perhaps his best book, its only serious competitor being the very fine series of designs in the 1860 edition of Thomas Moore's *Lalla Rookh*. Tenniel's contributions to illustrated books of the 1850s, such as Martin Tupper's *Proverbial Philosophy* (1854), Byron's *Childe Harold* (1855) or William Cullen Bryant's *Poems* (1855), exemplify his outline style in which the figures are not always exempt from a certain heaviness and clumsiness, this failure to maintain a consistent standard of draughtsmanship being particularly noticeable in Robert Pollok's *The Course of Time* (1857).

If *Punch* and *Alice* have drawn attention away from Tenniel's early work, the general neglect of book-illustration in the 1840s may be blamed for a similar treatment of H.C. Selous. Tenniel was to leave him far behind in the 1860s, but when both were being commissioned by James Burns, the nine-year age-gap made all the difference, and it was the older artist who set the standards for the younger. Again the pattern is much the same. After the aberration of the Cruikshankian lithographs for *Tales of a Rambler* (1836), Selous adopted the German style and in 1844 his outline drawings for John Bunyan's *The Pilgrim's Progress* [fig. 72] won the Art Union's premium for which Tenniel's *Griselda* had been entered. Like Tenniel and Pickersgill, he too yielded to Hall's blandishments to illustrate a British ballad, but he played a more important role than they in Burns's publishing programme. His contribution to *Poems and Pictures* [fig. 105] may be far smaller than Pickersgill's, but he was as deeply involved in the Fireside Library. He produced, among others, a splendid set of designs for 'Valentine and Orson' in *The Book of Nursery Tales* (third series, 1845) and the important part he had earlier played in illustrating the romances of De La Motte Fouqué, one of the staples of the list, was recognized when, in 1844, Burns issued Selous's designs for *Sintram and his Companions* as a separate publication [fig. 107].

Yet of all the artists in the James Burns/Art Union/Samuel Carter Hall ménage, the most brilliant and the most neglected is John Franklin. Born in Ireland, he entered the Royal Dublin Society Schools in 1819 and exhibited at the opening of the Royal Hibernian Academy in 1826. Coming to London, he worked as a portrait painter with a line in architectural and historical subjects. His first 'book' illustration was a series of outline engravings inspired by *The Ancient Ballad of Chevy Chase* (1836). By this time Franklin must have entered at least the fringes of Harrison Ainsworth's circle, for the novelist was sufficiently impressed by his work to want him to illustrate his new novel, *Crichton*.

This was doubtless due to the fact that when, in 1836, Ainsworth's publisher John Macrone had brought out a new edition of the earlier novel, *Rookwood*, illustrated with vignette etchings by George Cruikshank, the author should have had cause to complain. 'They are anything but full subjects and appear to be chosen as much as possible for light

178 *The Plague Pit*: steel-etching by John Franklin (Ainsworth, *Old St Paul's*, 1841) [BL N1540]

work', he wrote to Macrone on 8 March 1836.[56] Unfortunately, Macrone's ill-health and consequent financial difficulties led to the transfer of the novel to Richard Bentley who issued it unillustrated in February 1837. In the meantime, what may well have been Franklin's sample drawings were separately published in the winter of 1836 as an album of outline engravings entitled *Tableaux from Crichton*.[57]

The *Athenaeum*, which had been most complimentary to the outline engravings to *The Ancient Ballad of Chevy Chase*, did not like this new set at all. The critic, in fact, dismisses it in words which clearly show the reputation which Moritz Retzsch enjoyed in Britain and the way in which he could be used to belittle British practitioners of his style. Of Franklin the critic scornfully remarks that 'many of his heads, attitudes and costumes, are almost, if not altogether, borrowed from Retzsch.'[58]

Ainsworth, however, would appear to have been satisfied, but he now entered upon a period of collaboration with George Cruikshank, he as editor, Cruikshank as artist of *Bentley's Miscellany*. Only when he had left the one and fallen out with the other was he able to commission Franklin to illustrate a novel for him, *Old Saint Paul's*, notwithstanding that Cruikshank may (as he claimed) or may not have suggested the plot to the novelist. The illustrations were needed for the volume publication of the novel in 1841, subsequent to its serialization in *The Sunday Times* which had paid the unprecedented sum of £1,000 for the rights, and Franklin provided eighteen steel-etchings of monumental quality. They are as fine as anything produced during the period, not excepting Cruikshank's work, with their dramatic chiaroscuro which so well captures the sinister atmosphere of London in the Plague and Great Fire.

It seems curious that so talented an artist should not have continued in this vein, but Ainsworth patched up matters with Cruikshank and, no doubt preferring to have the doyen of book-illustrators to assist his tinsel creations, dropped Franklin as ruthlessly as he was to discard Tony Johannot. Yet Franklin was not without his influence upon the illustration of other novels including Ainsworth's own. When Hablot Knight Browne came to illustrate a new edition of *Crichton* (1848) he clearly modified his usual style in deference to Franklin's earlier outline engravings, while the influence of *Old Saint Paul's* is even more dramatic. Browne's first 'dark' plates [fig. 158] date from 1848, the year after he had been commissioned to supply frontispiece and vignette title for a re-issue of the novel with Franklin's

179 *Dives and Lazarus*:
wood-engraving
after John Franklin
(*The Parables of Our Lord*,
1851) [BL L16 d 2]

180 *Jack the Giant-Killer*: wood-engraved half-title after John Franklin (*The Book of Nursery Tales*, 1st series, 1844) [BL 1210 l 29]

etchings. The coincidence is too striking to be accidental and there can be little doubt that Browne was inspired by Franklin's successful efforts to reproduce in steel the effects of the mezzotint [fig. 178].

The rest of Franklin's career follows a pattern with which we are already familiar, but, just as he was the most outstanding artist in the group (his 1851 *Parables of Our Lord* is his masterpiece) [fig. 179], so his contributions to the publications both of Hall and of Burns were the most substantial. As Hall acknowledged, he supplied the lion's share of the illustrations to *The Book of British Ballads* (1841–2) [fig. 102] and also contributed to *Midsummer Eve* (1843/8). Apart from this strong tie he was, as an Irish painter, a natural choice for the Halls's *Ireland* (1841–3) and for the same reason was among those painters chosen to illustrate William Carleton's *Traits and Stories of the Irish Peasantry* (1843–4).

He was an equally strong support to James Burns, his designs featuring in the romances of La Motte Fouqué, the Scottish ballad collection *Northern Minstrelsy* (1845) and other volumes of the Fireside Library, *Poems and Pictures* (1846) and, most effectively, in the children's series *The Book of Nursery Tales* (three volumes, 1844–5) [fig. 180]. Indeed, his standing as a book-illustrator was such that he was commissioned to illustrate the Abbotsford editions of *Ivanhoe* (vol. IV, 1844) [fig. 181] and *The Talisman* (vol. IX, 1846). Furthermore, it was perhaps the excellence of his illustrations in *The Book of Nursery Tales* coupled with his general standing which led Joseph Cundall to invite his collaboration on that attractive series of children's books, *Gammer Gurton's Story Books*, which he produced between 1843 and 1847. It was a tribute to Franklin's achievements as a book-illustrator that he should have been associated in the project with the painter-members of the Etching Club.

It is fitting to close this account of the major British book-illustrators of the Romantic period with the Irish artist John Franklin. Reviewing his contribution to *Poems and Pictures*,

181 *Isaac the Jew in the Dungeon*: wood-engraved chapter-heading after John Franklin (Scott, *Ivanhoe*, 1844) [BL 1458 i 4]

The Old English Gentleman.

'LL sing you a good old song, that was made by a good
old pate,
Of a fine old English gentleman who had an old estate,
And who kept up his old mansion at a bountiful old
rate,

182 *The Old English Gentleman*: wood-engraving after John Franklin (*Poems and Pictures*, 1846)
[BL 1466 i 11]

the critic of the *Athenaeum* had written that Franklin 'reminds us, as usual, of his profound erudition in the contemporary vignette-art of Germany; like Mr. Carlyle, he has studied that which is German so deeply, that it has become a part of himself.'[59] Thus he absorbed those Continental influences which were to have so decisive an effect upon later British book-art and at the same time produced work which is completely individual and can stand comparison with the best of any country in the period.

NOTES

1 Information based upon the firms' catalogues and lists.
2 March 1839, 32.
3 Thomas Webster (1); T.S. Cooper, J.F. Tayler and J.C. Horsley (4 designs each).
4 *Steel-engraved Book Illustration in England*, 143.
5 *See* also pp. 149ff.
6 Longman Archive, Impression Book I, 11.
7 Ibid., Divide Book IV, 421, 427.
8 Ibid., 336.
9 Ibid., Divide Book III, 266; Commission Book VIII, 302.
10 Allusion to the itinerant antiquary in Sir Walter Scott's novel of this name.
11 Jones refers to the artist Henry Warren, see pp. 198–200.
12 *The Athenaeum*, no. 731, 30 October 1841, 827.
13 *Victorian Book Design*, 90.
14 Buchanan-Brown, *The Book Illustrations of George Cruikshank*, 23–4.
15 *Glances Back*, I, 352.
16 Ibid., 17.
17 *The Masters of Wood Engraving*, 201.
18 Vizetelly, *Glances Back*, I, 17.
19 It is interesting to compare Harvey's 1850s style with the more robust Regency designs for Major's edition of 1830 (see figs 138 and 139).
20 Knighted 1872.
21 *The Brothers Dalziel*, 80.
22 *Glances Back*, I, 231–2.
23 Ibid., 238.
24 *The Pictorial Press*, 355–6.
25 *The Masters of Wood-engraving*, 188.
26 *Glances Back*, I, 309.
27 Vol. XIV, no. 78 (July 1823), 18–26.
28 *The Elements of Drawing* (2nd edition, 1860), 350.
29 *Letter to George Hancock* (*A Handbook for Posterity*, vii).
30 *La mode*, 2 October 1830.
31 Dickens also recommended Leech. The latter was engaged to replace Phiz as resident artist on Chapman & Hall's short-lived magazine, *The Library of Fiction*.
32 *Letters and Private Papers*, I, 276.

33 *Glances Back*, I, 140.
34 *The Masters of Wood-engraving*, 204.
35 February 1844, 153ff.
36 See pp. 214–5.
37 See p. 283.
38 'The Dickens Illustrations: their Function' (Chapter VII, F.R. and Q.D. Leavis, *Dickens the Novelist*, London, 1970).
39 *Letters and Private Papers*, III, 362.
40 *The Morning Chronicle*, 26 December 1845: Thackeray always liked to give his friends a helping hand, but 'Callot is a barren inventor beside this young artist' is surely taking it a little too far.
41 February 1840, 23–4.
42 *Glances Back*, I, 160.
43 *Reminiscences*, 135.
44 *The Morning Chronicle*, 31 December 1845.
45 See, for example, p. 208.
46 *Glances Back*, I, 348–9.
47 As *A Gallery of Illustrious Literary Characters* (1873) and as *The Maclise Portrait Gallery* (edited by William Bates, 1883).
48 *The Athenaeum*, no. 1002, 7 January 1848, 17.
49 Longman Archive, Impression Book II, 20v.
50 Buchanan-Brown, *The Book Illustrations of George Cruikshank*, 21, compares payments by Longman and Murray.
51 29 September 1840; 12 January 1841; 20 January 1842 (Mulready Papers, Victoria & Albert Museum).
52 22 August 1856; 21 March 1857 (ibid.).
53 Vaughan, *German Romanticism and English Art*, 169–71.
54 Dalziel, *The Brothers Dalziel*, 52.
55 Knighted 1893.
56 Ellis, *W.H. Ainsworth and his Friends*, I, 278.
57 Title-page dated 1837 as is customary.
58 No. 508, 22 July 1837.
59 No. 951, 17 January 1846, 71.

IV

ACHIEVEMENT AND DECLINE

Social Criticism

Romanticism, by exalting the role of the individual, and the Industrial Revolution, by creating the whole complex of a new urban society, between them shaped the conditions which could elevate the novel to an art-form, a form which classically explores the relation of the individual to the society in which he lives. In seeking to comprehend the totality of that social structure, Balzac's *La comédie humaine* presents in the work of one man what so many lesser writers attempted to do in hosts of minor novels and pieces of reportage. These mark the revival of character-writing and provide, both textually and visually, a meticulous documentation of the age, published in formats as typical of the Romantic period.

Not that the great illustrated edition of *La comédie humaine* which Hetzel published in twenty volumes between 1842 and 1855 is a typical example of such Romantic book design, for the illustrations take the form exclusively of full-page wood-engravings. The artists commissioned to provide them include some of the great names in Romantic book-illustration – Daumier, Gavarni, Johannot and Monnier among them – but much of the success of the enterprise was due to the work of a young draughtsman, Bertall, who contributed over half the hundred or more designs employed.

Bertall, the name used by Albert d'Arnoux (1820–82), did the lion's share of the work but, as a comparative tyro, got less recognition in the publisher's publicity than he deserved. Nevertheless, he was an illustrator who was to grow in stature as the century progressed and who has been characterized by Henri Béraldi as 'a highly

183 *Three Sheets in the Wind*: wood-engraving after Gavarni (*Le diable à Paris*, II, 1846) [BL 12352 g 30]

220

original artist whose wit is unstained by malice; one of those sterling characters who have had the rare privilege of entertaining and amusing their contemporaries; something for which we should be truly grateful – given the prevalence of bores.'[1] As a caricaturist he found a ready market for his wit in such periodicals as *L'illustration*, *La semaine*, *Le grelot* or *Le journal pour rire*: his involvement in the illustration of *La comédie humaine* emphasizes his importance from the outset of his career as one of the artists who recorded visually what Balzac was attempting to set down in his novels – the infinite complexity and variety of nineteenth-century urban life.

In this role, and doubtless because he was so very much the younger man, there is a tendency for the less obtrusive merits of his work to be obscured by the bigger names which so often keep it company. This is certainly true of his contributions to Hetzel's two-volume miscellany, *Le diable à Paris* (1845–6), where the splendid full-page wood-engravings of Gavarni's Parisians of all classes and professions [fig. 183] tend to overshadow the many witty and delicate in-text vignettes contributed by Bertall [fig. 184]. In fact, the first volume reprints one of his most delightful achievements in this vein – Eugène Briffault's *Paris dans l'eau*, where an imaginative layout displays the Parisians of the 1840s fishing, boating and swimming in the Seine.

Doing justice to Bertall is not by any means to denigrate his better-known contemporaries, and notably Gavarni, the name adopted by Sulpice Gabriel Chevalier (1804–66) as a direct result of the Salon of 1829 miscataloguing his painting 'Vue de Gavarni' and giving the artist the name of the place. Starting life as a government surveyor in south-west France, his first work as an artist was to design fashion-plates for Emile Girardin's *La mode*. Although he contributed largely to the periodicals, it is significant that Gavarni was not a member of Philipon's team on *La caricature*, for he had none of the Republican acid of Daumier or of Grandville. Up to 1848 Gavarni is the light-hearted social historian and satirist, his Parisian characters being issued in innumerable single lithographs and collected

184 *In the Chamber of Deputies*: wood-engraved vignette after Bertall (*Le diable à Paris*, 1, 1845) [BL 12352 g 30]

sets. While Daumier is his master artistically, Gavarni must rank as the chief historian of the lighter side of Louis-Philippe's Paris. The range of his vision is enshrined in the two volumes of *Le diable à Paris* which contain over two hundred full-page wood-engravings through which, and under the general heading of 'Gens de Paris', working-class, bourgeois, bohemian and criminal Paris is paraded.

Gavarni's style exhibits great facility and his output was prodigious – over 2,100 separate lithographs alone.[2] His name was soon made and then publishers were eager to see it on the title-pages of their books. Thus Gavarni becomes associated with a substantial number of publications to which his contribution was small in proportion to that of others, a good example being *La comédie humaine*, to which he contributed fourteen designs and the unacknowledged Bertall fifty-seven. This had the effect of spreading Gavarni's very extensive output of designs for wood-engraving over a very large number of individual books. These include children's literature (contributions to both *Le livre des enfants* and *Le nouveau magasin des enfants* and, in 1843, twenty-two lithographs for a translation of Canon Christoph Schmid's internationally popular stories) and adult fiction (including Eugène Sue's novels, his best work appearing in *Le juif errant* [1845]) [figs 185, 186].

It is, however, to his record of the passing social scene that he owed his immense popularity and his work is thus a great feature of the countless books on contemporary society so popular during this period. Gavarni was a leading contributor to *Les français peints par eux-mêmes* (1840–42) [figs 21, 48; pl. 10] and supplied much of the extra illustration in *Les anglais peints par eux-mêmes*, the French translation of *Heads of the People*: his designs are in Louis Huart's *Muséum parisien* (1841) and Paul de Kock's rival volume, *La grande ville* (1844). Gavarni and Bertall show their artistic superiority to Emy, Frère and Lorsay in *Les étrangers à Paris* (1844) and his popularity makes Gavarni one of the most frequent contributors to the *Physiologies* [fig. 199] which enjoyed such a vogue between 1841 and 1843.

At this period Gavarni has a facility and surface attraction which conceals a certain lack of depth to his work. This is exposed by contrasting his engaging but superficial work with that of his slightly younger contemporary, Honoré Daumier (1804–79). Sometime lawyer's clerk and bookseller's assistant, Daumier was first appreciated as a political caricaturist by Charles Philipon who employed him on *La caricature*. There, his savage attacks on Louis-Philippe, as 'Gargantua', earned him six months in prison. After the re-introduction of press censorship in 1835 he turned to more general social satire, attacking the bourgeois world of finance and the

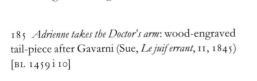
185 *Adrienne takes the Doctor's arm*: wood-engraved tail-piece after Gavarni (Sue, *Le juif errant*, 11, 1845) [BL 1459 i 10]

law in *Les Robert Macaires* (1839). Daumier's real artistic importance is that of the painter and lithographer and his book-illustrations are in some sense subsidiary. Nevertheless, he did design fairly extensively for wood-engraving [figs 187–9] and his illustrations may be found alongside those of Gavarni in the books by Huart [figs 190, 191] and de Kock mentioned above, as well as in Eugène Sue's *Les mystères de Paris* (1843–4) [figs 192, 193] and in several of the *Physiologies* (1841–3). All bear the strong individual impress of this major nineteenth-century artist.

As strong an individuality may be found in the book-illustrations of Henry Monnier (1799–1877), a man of such varied talent – artist, writer and actor – that in no single role did he make the mark to which he seemed entitled. His designs are to be found in his own *Scènes populaires* (1836–9), realistic dialogues of everyday life, and in a wide variety of single

186 *Jacques Rennepont*:
wood-engraving after Gavarni
(Sue, *Le juif errant*, III, 1845)
[BL 1459 i 11]

187 *The Phrenologist*: wood-engraved head-piece after Honoré Daumier (*Les français peints par eux-mêmes*, III, 1841) [BL 1457 k 10]

188 *The Parisian –
a countryman at heart*:
wood-engraved
head-piece after
Honoré Daumier
(*Les français peints par
eux-mêmes*, III, 1841)
[BL 1457 k 10]

189 *Public Counsel
for the Defence*:
wood-engraved
vignette after
Honoré Daumier
(*Les français peints par
eux-mêmes*, II, 1840)
[BL 1457 k 9]

190 *Mr Gullible*:
wood-engraving after
Honoré Daumier
(Huart, *Muséum parisien*,
1841) [BL 12330 i 12]

191 *Old Soaks*:
wood-engraving after
Honoré Daumier
(Huart, *Muséum parisien*,
1841) [BL 12330 i 12]

vignettes or series of illustrations which start with *L'art de payer ses dettes* (1827), include the lithographs of *Voyage en Angleterre* (with Eugène Lami, 1829) and conclude with a contribution to *La comédie humaine* (1842–55).

At a time of close cultural and social ties between Britain and France, Monnier seems the most overtly Anglophile and, among French caricaturists, the most patently influenced by English caricature. The contacts which he made during his and Lami's visit in the 1820s would seem to have included George Cruikshank, to whom Monnier dedicated his *Distractions* (1832). Yet the most obviously English influence to be seen, in the two-volume edition of Béranger's *Chansons* published by the Baudouin brothers in 1828, is not Cruikshankian. Monnier's small squared designs, reproduced as coloured lithographs, have more than a flavour of Rowlandson, whose work was known well enough for a translation

192 *Polidori-Bradamanti*: wood-engraving after Honoré Daumier (Sue, *Les mystères de Paris*, I, 1843) [BL 1458 k 13]

193 *Screech-owl and
the Schoolmaster*:
wood-engraving after
Honoré Daumier
(Sue, *Les mystères de
Paris*, 1, 1843)
[BL 1458 k 13]

of William Combe's *Dr Syntax* to have appeared in 1821, the original etchings copied by lithography. The Béranger is, on all counts, a typical instance of the way in which the French Restoration book aped the classic English style, down to the tail-piece decorations, either engraved from Devéria's designs or drawn from the printer's stock of polytype vignettes.

For wood-engraving Monnier was to develop a more robust style which may owe more to Cruikshank, and some of his best work is to be found in *Les français peints par eux-mêmes* [figs 22, 47, 194, 195] and in the *Physiologies*. Monnier's strong, not to say harsh line, his bold use of solid black tints, give his work a rough strength which contrasts with the *chic* of Gavarni, and may owe something in feeling, if not in form, to the English caricaturists whose work Monnier admired. His biographer Champfleury sums up the essential difference between the two when he writes:

> This painter of fashion-plates [Gavarni] could not escape from the world of his own imagination, peopled by puppets dressed in the height of Parisian fashion. Monnier, an artist far less attractive to a mass-audience which wants only to be entertained, cast his cold glance at the real world and the dance of its puppets, and this is one aspect of his work which appeals to the more critical observer.[3]

Thus Monnier with his strength complements the savage line of Daumier and the elegance of Gavarni, and the three combine to depict a society in all its aspects and in a way which is Balzacian in its thoroughness.

Nor was this type of social analysis represented in the books illustrated by Daumier, Gavarni and Monnier, for example, confined to France, but is apparent to a lesser degree in English books of the period. If one takes a single illustrator as an example, one observes that between 1837 and 1840 Phiz was involved in designing for at least half-a-dozen books which fall within this category. They comprise Edward Caswall's *Sketches of Young Ladies* (1837),

194 *The Sick-nurse*: wood-engraving head-piece after Henry Monnier (*Les français peints par eux-mêmes*, 1, 1840) [BL 1457 k 8]

195 *The Postillion*: wood-engraved head-piece after Henry Monnier (*Les français peints par eux-mêmes*, 1, 1840) [BL 1457 k 8]

Charles Dickens's companion pieces *Sketches of Young Gentlemen* (1838) and *Sketches of Young Couples* (1840), James Grant's *Sketches in London* (1838) and, in the following year, *A Paper of Tobacco* by 'Joseph Fume' (W.A. Chatto) and *A Handbook of Swindling* by 'Captain Barabbas Whitefeather' (Douglas Jerrold). Dickens's first published book, *Sketches by Boz* (1836), collects his *Morning Chronicle* articles in this vein, but the very obvious British counterpart to contemporary French character-writing is *Heads of the People*.

Issued in parts between 1838 and 1840 and published in two volumes in 1840–41, it clearly belongs to the same category as *Les français peints par eux-mêmes*, which it resembles in sketches of characteristic social 'types'. The text, written by a number of different authors including Leigh Hunt, Thackeray, Douglas Jerrold, Laman Blanchard, William Howitt, Mrs S.C. Hall and Mrs Gore, is accompanied by equally characteristic designs by Kenny Meadows. These were engraved on wood by John Orrin Smith to be printed as full-page vignette illustrations. No attempt was made to match the wealth of integrated vignette illustration, the decorated initials or head-pieces of the French series, nor can Kenny

Meadows's scratchy and meagre line match that of the French artists. *Heads of the People* is a very British book, as are the others mentioned, with their steel-etched *hors-texte* illustrations; nevertheless, they all express this contemporary obsession with social structure. Yet, just as Balzac makes explicit the fascination with the complexities of urban society implicit in Dickens's novels, so character-writing and its concomitant graphic representation of social types features more strongly in France than in England, their full flowering being found in the *Physiologies* published between 1841 and 1843.

In all, the series runs to roughly a hundred individual titles, and their numbers, the numbers of their authors and of the artists who illustrated them present obvious problems for brief description. Their usual format was 32mo and they ran to around 130 pages each. They were issued in a distinctive yellow paper wrapper with wood-engraved vignette and their embellishments comprised decorated head-pieces and initials and up to a hundred integrated wood-engraved vignettes. Their most prolific authors were Maurice Alhoy and Louis Huart and their most distinguished Balzac himself. Their subject-matter was the full range of (Parisian) society – tailors, musicians, lawyers, civil servants, schoolboys, soldiers, woman in all her aspects (the Parisienne, the unhappiest woman in the world, the grisette,

44

papier mesquin , la pièce où se tient le garçon de bureau est meublée d'un poêle , d'une grande table noire , plumes , encrier , quelquefois une fontaine ; enfin une banquette , sans nattes pour les pieds de grue du public. Le garçon de bureau , assis dans un bon fauteuil , repose les siens sur un paillasson.

Le bureau des employés est une grande pièce plus ou moins claire , rarement parquetée. Le parquet et la cheminée sont spécialement affectés aux chefs de bureau , de division , ainsi

45

que les armoires , les bureaux et les tables d'acajou , les fauteuils de maroquin rouge ou vert , les glaces , les rideaux de soie , et autres objets de luxe administratif. Le bureau des employés a un poêle dont le tuyau donne dans une cheminée bouchée , s'il y a cheminée. Le papier de tenture est uni , vert ou brun. Les tables sont en bois noir.

L'industrie des employés se manifeste dans leur manière de se caser. Le frileux a sous les pieds une espèce de pupitre en bois ; l'homme à tempérament sanguin-bilieux n'a qu'une sparterie. Le lymphatique qui redoute

196 *Civil Servants*: wood-engraved vignettes after J.L. Trimolet (Balzac, *Physiologie de l'employé*, 1841)
[BL 012314 de 22]

the lorette), the married man, the adventurer, the Englishman, the provincial in Paris, the old maid and the bachelor, the debtor and creditor, the politician, and the criminal. As Caboche Demerville wrote in the preface to *Les petits français peints par les grands* (1842):

> We have for some time been living under the dominion of the *Physiologies*. Assuredly no age has been so encyclopaedically described as our own ... with its eruption of character sketches and this general daguerréotyping of all classes of society.

As we have said, the three major artists involved were Daumier, Gavarni and Monnier, who also wrote the text of *La physiologie du bourgeois*, but Traviès was also a notable contributor. Among the lesser artists, mention should be made of Trimolet [fig. 196], Maurisset, Markl,

197 *The Rash Traveller*: wood-engraved vignette after Janet-Lange (Alhoy, *Physiologie du voyageur*, 1841) [BL 012314 de 20]

12

quelquefois par ses goûts volages et ses inclinations tant soit peu libertines.

BIROUSTE SC

Mais une fois qu'il a vu briller son neuvième lustre, il comprend ce qu'il doit et à lui-même et à la société. Il prend femme, et jouit de tou les agréments de la vie conjugale. C'est ains qu'agit un homme bien intentionné.

15

Mais lorsque vous verrez un particulier de quarante ans ne pas demander la main d'une

demoiselle ou d'une veuve quelconque, ne pas faire publier ses bans à la mairie, ne pas prendre les habitudes débonnaires, la redingote à la propriétaire, les souliers de castor et la canne à bec de corbin du mari modèle, lorsque vous le verrez persister à porter des bottes vernies, à s'habiller chez Zang ou chez Humann, à lorgner les femmes au spectacle ou dans la rue, à faire belle jambe et fine main... vous pourrez dire à coup sûr : « Voilà un célibataire. »

198 *The unmarried man* [l.] *and the true Bachelor* [r.]: wood-engraved vignettes after Henry Monnier (Couailhac, *Physiologie du célibataire et de la vieille fille*, 1841) [BL 012315 aaa 41]

Janet-Lange [fig. 197], Emy, Alophe, Lorentz and Vernier. All provided appropriate and often exciting vignettes for what is a most attractive series of little books, so attractive, in fact, that it is difficult among so many to select particular examples of the genre. However, I would suggest among those which repay study are L. Couailhac's *Le célibataire et la vielle fille* (Monnier, 1841) [fig. 198], James Rousseau's *La portière* (Daumier, 1841), Louis Huart's *La grisette* (Gavarni, 1841) [fig. 199] and Etienne de Neufville's *La femme* (Gavarni, 1842) and *Le théâtre* (Emy, 1841) [fig. 200].

The majority of these little books were published by Laisné, Aubert and Lavigne, but their popularity was such that they were imitated by a number of other Parisian publishers including Warée, Terry, Fiquet, Lachappelle and, most notably, by Desloges. In addition, the title 'Physiologie' was applied to what were really guide-books, such as Madame Valérie de Frezarde's *Jardin des Tuileries* (Charpentier, 1841) and to her *La palais et jardin du Luxembourg* (Lachappelle, 1842); or to P. Bernard and L. Couailhac's *Le jardin des plantes* (1841), for which Léon Curmer used a number of small vignettes engraved for the splendid two-volume guide which he published in the following year. Nor was their appearance confined to France. The Barcelona publisher Juan Oliveres issued nine titles in Spanish

22

A Nancy, toutes les femmes se ressentent encore heureusement du séjour de la cour du roi Stanislas : — elles ont conservé un cachet de distinction tout particulier ; et là les pieds sont éminemment aristocratiques, ainsi que la tournure et l'ensemble de la toilette.

Aussi les brodeuses de Nancy ne sont-elles pas moins occupées à se faire *fin pied* que

23

fine taille, et le tout au profit des heureux élèves de l'École forestière.

Si de l'est de la France nous sautons au midi, nous devons admirer les brunes Arlésiennes aux yeux fendus en amande et à la chevelure d'ébène.

Enfin, pour finir, citons, avec tous les éloges qui leur sont dus, les célèbres *épinglières* de Toulouse, ainsi nommées non parce qu'elles font des épingles, mais parce qu'elles en ont toujours une très-grande pour faire leur

199 *Working Girls*: wood-engraved vignettes after Gavarni (Huart, *Physiologie de la grisette*, 1841) [BL 1094 f 5]

un nègre et tourmente sans cesse le directeur pour se faire jouer.

Enfin il y a l'auteur qui ne peut travailler sans collaborateur. Ce collaborateur, il le prend, quand il ne peut pas faire autrement, parmi les clercs d'huissier qui débutent dans le flon-flon ; mais sa grande ambition est d'arriver à travailler avec un auteur bien posé, bien nanti, bien pansé. Il n'y a pas d'efforts qu'il ne fasse pour atteindre ce but. Vous savez l'histoire de

XIII.

LES AUTEURS.

—

Il y a l'auteur qui a cinquante mille livres de rente, auquel le directeur va demander des pièces, qui fait ses conditions, pour lequel on réserve les meilleurs acteurs et qui, outre ses droits et ses billets, touche une prime sous le nom de *lever de rideau*.

Il y a l'auteur médiocre qui travaille comme

ce vaudevilliste qui, sachant que l'un de ses

200 *Playwrights*: wood-engraved vignettes after H. Emy ('Un journaliste', *Physiologie du théâtre*, 1841) [BL 012331 de 14]

translation, illustrated from polytypes or electros of the original French engravings. They do not, however, seem to have transplanted well, and copies in their original yellow paper wrappers dated 1848 may be found with a cancel-title dated 1868.

In England the influence was less direct – I have traced no translation – and probably appears first in the pieces which Alfred Crowquill wrote and illustrated for *Bentley's Miscellany* and later reprinted in his *Phantasmagoria of Fun* (1843) [fig. 151] – 'The Philosophy of ... Smoking ... Drinking ... Physic ... Money ... Law ... Marriage ... Idleness ... Time'. They are, however, very different in format and in length and the influence is indirect. Similar indirect influence may be seen in Thackeray's 'The Snobs of England' and in Horace Mayhew's *Model Men* and *Model Women and Children* first published in *Punch*. Thackeray's series was published in 1848 as *The Book of Snobs* and in the same year David Bogue issued Horace Mayhew's work in volume form.

The latter owe considerably more to the *Physiologies*, since Bogue had already begun to publish a British series of 'Natural Histories' in direct imitation of the French. These were an immediate success, the first of them, Albert Smith's *The Natural History of the Gent* (1847), selling 10,000 copies within a very short time,[4] and they continued to sell well since they were to feature, ten years later, in the catalogue of Bogue's 'successor', William Kent. A further four titles came from Albert Smith's pen, Angus B. Reach wrote two and *The Bal*

201 Wood-engraved vignette after G.S. Hine (Reach, *Natural History of Bores*, 1847) [BL 12352 b 39]

masqué came from 'Count Chicard'. In all, eight titles appeared in 1847–8 and the series closed in 1849 with *The Natural History of Evening Parties* which Albert Smith had originally written for *Bentley's Miscellany* and which had already been reprinted in 1843 in *The Wassail Bowl*, a collection of other material by Smith which had first appeared in the magazine.

Two artists are primarily responsible for the wood-engraved illustrations in the 'Natural Histories'– G.S. Hine [fig. 201] and Archibald Henning [fig. 202]. Hine (1811–95), who had served his apprenticeship as a stipple-engraver and later worked as a wood-engraver for Ebenezer Landells, was to turn to landscape and figure painting in watercolours from the mid-1850s. He was elected to the Royal Institute of

68   HUMBUGS.

but not particularly flattering pen-and-ink sketch of the personal appearance of the respectable Mr. Mizzle who payed his way.

The butcher acknowledges to being "stuck" for £70, and the baker for a little matter of £50, both in consequence of transactions for temporary loans. Who will deny that Mr. Mizzle ran his respectability gig to some purpose?

HUMBUGS.   69

When a man sets up a respectability gig, he should be careful as to what stable he runs it from. A very inferior vehicle will pass muster if it hails from Hackney, Clapham, or any such serious and rather theological locality; but if a native gentleman hand up his card, inscribed

"Mr. Frederick Flash, Quadrant," or a foreign gentleman introduce himself as "M. Le Comte

202 *Mr Muzzle* [l.] *and Mr Frederick Flash* [r.]: wood-engraved vignettes after Archibald Henning (Reach, *Natural History of Humbugs*, 1847) [BL 12352 b 39]

Painters in Water Colours in 1864 and became its Vice-President in 1887. Archibald Henning, son of the sculptor John Henning (d. 1864), was a somewhat disreputable and Bohemian figure, tarred by the brush of working for that notorious scandal-sheet, *The Town*. Although neither matches the draughtsmanship of the *Physiologies*, the 'Natural Histories' are engaging imitations of their French models. In these circumstances it is unfortunate that the best set of illustrations, those of John Leech for *The Natural History of Evening Parties*, should be ruined almost beyond repair by the small format of the series. They had been designed for the double octavo columns of *Bentley's Miscellany* and, although to scale with the 16mo *Wassail Bowl*, are quite out of proportion to a 32mo.

If deliberate imitations of the *Physiologies* fall short of their French originals, from the mid-1840s British publishers produced a number of 'little' books of undeniable appeal. Many of the best designs in them are due to Phiz and show the artist's unacknowledged skill in designing for wood-engraving. My favourite is *Saint Patrick's Eve* (1845), illustrated by steel-engraved *hors-texte*, full-page plates and by wood-engravings which are a model of the

THIRD ERA.   201

stood, a vast pro-
cession could be seen
moving on foot and on
horseback. Some,

in country cars, assisted up the steep ascent by men's strong

203 *The Steep Ascent*:
wood-engraving after Phiz
(Hablot Knight Browne)
(Lever, *St Patrick's Eve*, 1845)
[BL 1457 C 19]

integration of text and embellishment [fig. 203]. One particularly interesting device, which is also to be found in the edition of *Paul et Virginie* illustrated by Bertall and published in Paris in the same year, is to frame a vignette occupying most of the type-area by the running head and a full line of text type at the foot.

Saint Patrick's Eve is in much the same format as *The Wassail Bowl* and is therefore somewhat larger than the *Physiologies*, but Phiz was equally at home in the smaller format of such humorous books as *Nuts and Nutcrackers* (*c*.1845), again illustrated by a combination of steel-etched *hors-textes* and integrated wood-engravings. He also designed for books wholly illustrated by wood-engraving, of which the most attractive is A.B. Reach's *A Romance of a Mince-Pie* (1848). This may be a slight and rather silly story, but it does provide an excellent example both of Phiz's draughtsmanship and of well-integrated illustration.

Children's Books and Artists

The French evolved a new style of book design to satisfy a new kind of readership. Although this style modified the presentation of text and illustrations in books for the traditional market throughout Europe, its primary appeal was directed through cheap but heavily illustrated editions at this new working-class and petit-bourgeois readership and, through 'embellished' editions, at the newly rich who lacked a background of inherited wealth and culture. At the same time publishers realized that a simultaneous revolution in accepted attitudes towards children and child-education, which derives ultimately from Rousseau, presented a rich and virtually untapped vein. To chart the growth of the theories and practices of child-education in the period is beyond the scope of this book, and I would simply point to the effects which they had upon the publishing trade by contrasting the catalogues of one British publisher at an interval of thirty-three years.

In Charles Tilt's catalogue of 1832 and under the heading 'Interesting Works for Young People' are listed nine titles. They include William Cowper's *John Gilpin* with Cruikshank's illustrations and an edition of Isaac Watts's *Divine and Moral Songs* illustrated by Thomas Stothard; there is an imitation of *The Butterfly's Ball*; two volumes of fiction; *Curiosities for the Ingenious*; *A brief Compendium of the History of England*; *A Letter to a young Piano-forte Player*; a volume of religious verse by Revd C.B. Taylor, and a most improving anthology, *The Pious Minstrel*. In contrast, the thirty-page catalogue issued in 1856 by Tilt's successor, David Bogue, contains no less than five pages devoted to 'Juvenile Works'. It is not, however, the sheer number of children's books which calls for comment – after all, one would expect this when comparing the list of a five-year-old business with one which had grown and prospered for nearly thirty years – but the natures of the two. The books in the 1832 catalogue represent the days when children had little choice between such improving literature as Tilt features or the charming chapbooks of Harris, his rivals and successors. Bogue's catalogue reflects an entirely new attitude towards children's publishing and effectively its structure is that of any similar list for the next hundred years or more. There is fiction, in Bogue's case led by Captain Mayne Reid's adventure stories for boys; non-fiction, with Henry Mayhew's books of popular science and J.G. Edgar's biographies; fairy-tales, including an edition of Grimm illustrated by E.H. Wahnert, and George Cruikshank's Fairy

Library; and picture-books for young children, from the semi-educational Harry and Little Mary Books to the six nursery rhymes of the Indestructible Pleasure Books.

Quite clearly a revolution had taken place and if we were to attempt to pinpoint it, we should find that the early- and mid-1840s were the crucial years. One of the key figures of the 1840s was Joseph Cundall and for a proper appreciation of his role reference must be made to the section 'Towards a check-list of books published, edited or written ...' by him in Ruari McLean's biography.[5] It is, however, sufficient for our purposes to note that either under his own imprint, or under the imprint of Cundall & Addey, or in association with other publishers, he was responsible for ensuring that so many of the books for this new children's market were produced to a very high standard.

It was therefore only natural that when Henry Cole,[6] dissatisfied with the books available for his own children, decided to create something better, he should go to Cundall for professional advice and assistance. Together they produced 'The Home Treasury' of children's books illustrated very largely by members of the Etching Club, and the same group of artists worked on Cundall's own series of texts edited by the pioneer folklorist W.J. Thoms, 'Gammer Gurton's Story Books' [fig. 204]. The Little Mary and Indestructible Pleasure Books were joint-publications with Bogue, while something of the quality of Cundall's work can be seen if one compares the delicacy of the reproduction by lithography of John Absolon's designs in the Cundall series of Myrtle story books (1845–6) with the way

204 Wood-engraved frontispiece after Frederick Tayler (*Gammer Gurton's Story Books* 1843–7). Note the influence of the illuminated manuscript in the fore-margin decoration of the text page [BL 12835 b 9]

236

THE INVISIBLE PRINCE.

ONCE on a time there was a King who had an only son, named Furibon. He was dwarfish in stature, and of a malicious disposition, and although the King his father was sensible of his son's de-

in which the same artist's work is printed in a very similar series published by W.S. Orr, *c.*1844.[7]

John Absolon (1815–95) seems as deeply involved as an illustrator as Cundall was as a publisher of children's books. He draws correctly, but he leaves me completely unmoved. Clearly he had great appeal for his contemporaries, for he was a very popular and prolific illustrator, especially of children's books. He must, therefore, rank as one of the more important British Romantic book illustrators.

Because of the quality of his publications, Cundall must bulk very large in any account of British children's books at this time: he should not, however, occupy the stage completely. We have seen how James Burns issued one of the most beautiful children's anthologies, *Nursery Rhymes, Tales and Jingles* (1844) [fig. 114], but his *Book of Nursery Tales* (three series, 1844–5) [fig. 205] is another fine piece of Romantic book design. Burns's books show the

full application of integrated text, decoration and vignette illustration, in the German
Romantic style, and these traditional tales contain fine work by his house artists, and
especially from John Franklin [figs 180, 206], H.C. Selous and John Tenniel.

The importance which children's publishing had assumed is indicated by the participation, albeit on a limited scale, by John Murray. In 1844 he issued *Puss in Boots*, a translation
of *Das Märchen vom gestiefelten Kater* published the year before by Brockhaus, copying in
lithography Otto Speckter's original engravings [fig. 207]. In 1846 came *The Fairy Ring*,
translated from Grimm and illustrated by Richard Doyle, and in 1847 *The Charmed Roe*, again
with lithographic copies of Speckter's original designs.

If Murray may be said to have set the seal of respectability upon children's publishing,
equally significant is the fact that all three books were of German origin and that two of
them were illustrated by a German artist, for it underlines the important part which
Germany played in giving this new direction to writing for children. That one of the titles

should be a selection from Grimm emphasizes the importance to children's literature of the pioneering work undertaken by the Brothers in recording the oral traditions of Germany. Their contribution to philology was enormous, but so was the pleasure which they brought to subsequent generations of children by making fairy-tales socially acceptable. This permitted traditional stories to enter by the front door of respectable publishing rather than by the back door of the hawker's chapbook, and it also created a recognized genre for imaginative writers for children.

First and greatest of these was Hans Christian Andersen whose work is the literary high-point of this early period of modern children's literature. From his native Denmark his books travelled to Germany, and from Germany to Britain, with the curious result of giving a slightly inflated artistic reputation to one of his earliest German illustrators, Count Franz von Pocci. Despite an output of professional dimensions of books which he either wrote or illustrated or of which he was both author and artist, and of songs and music for which he provided the designs, he leaves the overall impression of being the amateur artist. A very

207 Copper-engraving after Otto Speckter (*Das Märchen vom gestiefelten Kater*, 1843) [BL 12430 g 6]

talented amateur, it is true, whose designs have great charm and a grotesque humour, but set him beside a professional like Ludwig Richter in a book like the collection *Alte und neue Studenten-, Soldaten- und Volkslieder* (1847), and you will see the difference; just, for example, as you will see the difference between the professional, Richard Doyle, of *The Newcomes* and the amateur, Thackeray, of *Pendennis*.

Pocci's illustrations to Andersen were used in two of the early collections of the Danish writer's stories, *A Danish Story-book* (Cundall, 1847) and *The Dream of Little Tuk* (Grant & Griffith, 1848), while the third, *The Shoes of Fortune* (Chapman & Hall, 1847), has copies of Otto Speckter's designs. Pocci's work also appears in *Charles Boner's Book* (1848), a collection of stories and poems by one of the translators of Andersen. Here the designs are reproduced by wood-engraving and there is a strength and delicacy of line lacking in Pocci's preferred medium, lithography. This is the form in which the bulk of his work was published, in charming little booklets of traditional fairy stories such as those of Snow White (1839) or of Bluebeard (1845) [fig. 208], or in poems and stories for children both written and illustrated by the Count.

Pocci himself belongs to the Catholic revival – he was a South German from Munich – and his work contains a strong element of piety [fig. 209]. It is therefore interesting, in the

208 *Bluebeard*: lithographs by Count von Pocci for his *Blaubart* (1845) [BL 554 b 64]

209 *The Good Book*:
lithograph by Count von
Pocci for his *Geschichten
und Lieder*, I (1841)
[BL 788 b 15]

context of the influence of German Romanticism upon such Anglican High Church artists
as William Dyce, to observe the way in which the dangerous Romanism of Pocci's *Spruchlein
mit Bilder fur Kinder* (1846) is foiled. This pretty little book was translated as *Rhymes and Pictures
for Children*, printed by Ambrose Masson, significantly, at Littlemore, and published by
Parker in 1850. Pocci's original illustrations undergo a subtle transformation. Without its
onion dome, the Bavarian church takes on a reassuringly English air and the wayside shrine
loses its crucifix to become a stile. The Madonna is transformed into her Son, and the child
no longer kneels to say its prayers before a picture of the Sacred Heart, but the Divine
Monogram – in Greek letters, too, to avoid any taint of Jesuitism.

This is, however, a point of somewhat special interest: of more immediate concern is the
effect which the study of folklore had upon children's literature. In France, where a selection

from Musaeus, with appropriate illustrations from the German edition of 1842, was to be published in 1846 as *Contes populaires de l'Allemagne*, there had been a revival of interest in the seventeenth-century writers of fairy-tales, Charles Perrault and Madame d'Aulnoy. Mesdames Voiart and Tastu had used these as the principal sources for *Le livre des enfants* (1836–8) and, among the editions of Perrault's *Contes* which were re-issued at this time, the selection published by Curmer in 1843 is notable as being wholly engraved on steel. Although the overall effect is disappointing in the half-hearted way in which text and embellishments are integrated, there are some very attractive designs by Charles Jacque and by the engraver Louis Marvy.

Original writing for children in this genre was stimulated, too, and *Le nouveau magasin des enfants* published by Hetzel between 1843 and 1857 contains work by Balzac, Alexandre Dumas, Jules Janin, Charles Nodier and by the publisher himself, under his pen-name of J.P. Stahl [fig. 210]. Just as *Le livre des enfants* had found a British publisher in Joseph Thomas, so a selection of individual tales from Hetzel's series was published in twelve separate volumes as 'Picture Story Books by Great Authors and Great Painters' by Chapman & Hall in 1846. Of these Alexandre Dumas's *La bouillie de la comtesse Berthe*, issued by Chapman & Hall in their series as *Good Lady Bertha's Honey Broth* with Bertall's original illustrations [fig. 53], was also published in English translation by Jeremiah How in 1846 as *The Honey Stew* with six hand-coloured, full-page wood-engravings from the designs of Harrison Weir [pl. 11].

The series title adopted by Chapman & Hall epitomizes the changed status of the children's book which had been effected by the mid-1840s, a change which can be graphically illustrated by contrasting the perfunctory chapbook style of George Cruikshank's illustrations crudely engraved on wood for William Gardiner's *Original Tales of my Landlord's School* (1821) with the extraordinary exercises in miniature etching seen in his plates for the Mayhew Brothers's *The Good Genius who turned everything into Gold* (1847), or in his own Fairy Library (1853–4) [fig. 211].

Cruikshank serves as an excellent example because his long working life spans the two eras of children's publishing, from chapbook to respectability. Respectable publishers now employed recognized artists and nearly every illustrator of note in Britain or on the Continent at some time or other received commissions to design for children. In England John Absolon tended to specialize in this class of work, in Germany Otto Speckter and Ludwig Richter became well known as illustrators of children's books, but in France, where so many artists

210 *The Anglers of the Île-St-Louis*: wood-engraved vignette after A.J. Lorentz (*Le nouveau magasin des enfants*, reprinted 1860) [BL 12806 g 43]

worked in this field, it is very hard to distinguish any particular artist as a specialist children's illustrator. Yet if one were to single out one specific draughtsman for his contribution to French children's book-illustration, that artist might perhaps be Bertall, whose work as a caricaturist and social commentator we have already noted. So far as children's books are concerned, his career spans the age of *Le nouveau magasin des enfants* of the 1840s to that of *La bibliothèque rose* of the 1860s and beyond. Indeed, this series was kept in print up to and probably well beyond World War I, so that illustrations designed by Bertall, for example for their edition of Hans Andersen of 1856, could continue to appear in the thirteenth impression published in 1905.

His children's illustrations retain that quality of comical exaggeration inseparable from caricature, but without those excesses of the grotesque which turn to downright ugliness in

211 *Jack climbing the Bean Stalk*:
etching by George Cruikshank
for his *Fairy Library*, 1853–4
[BL C70 b 9]

243

the work of his contemporary, Cham, or in that of such British artists as Crowquill. Perhaps Bertall is at his best in this genre in the many designs which he contributed to *Le nouveau magasin des enfants*, among which those for Alexandre Dumas's adaptation of E.T.A. Hoffmann, *Histoire d'un casse-noissettes*, should be noted. Finally – and although it belongs to the literature of childhood rather than being strictly speaking a children's book – the designs which he produced for Havard's modest edition of *Paul et Virginie* in 1845 should not be forgotten.

Romantic Book Design

The Romantic period produced many consciously magnificent books, yet what is perhaps its most important contribution to fine printing – the integration of text and image – may be best seen in some of its most typical printed ephemera, the little books of social satire such as the French *Physiologies*. The peculiar attraction of these small-format books is the harmonious balance which they achieve between type and engraving, thus making the work even of journeymen artists look better than it really is. The secret, I suppose, is that in small formats what is effectively a half-page illustration does not dominate the whole page in the way it tends to do in an octavo, and the density of black tends more frequently in a small-scale engraving to coincide with the density of the letterpress. It is this match which is so crucial to the success of any book: its achievement sets the seal upon good book design; its absence can condemn an illustrated book, despite the merits of its embellishments as independent specimens of draughtsmanship.

The need for this balance is, I believe, inherent in the nature of black-line wood-engraving for, while the white-line method is essentially a process of diminishing the black in the surface of the block, the black-line builds it up. Thus the white-line engraving will always be able to match the density of the page of type, however solid it is set, while the black-line will have to depend upon its tints to match it. However much it sacrificed to linear strength, Harvey's predilection for tints answered this need and reached the same solution as Bewick's white-line method, if from the opposite direction. Both styles, however, had a grave economic disadvantage – they required careful and time-consuming engraving and neither the time nor the skilled engravers were always available in the new mass-market conditions and under the enormous pressure of serial publication.

The problem arose at the outset, and Jean Gigoux records in his memoirs that once the publisher Dubochet realized what a gold-mine he had in the serial publication of *Gil Blas*, he applied the pressure:

> He hung around me all day, as well. No sooner had I sketched my design on the wood, than he took the block away for engraving, without giving me time to finish it. This annoyed and even humiliated me, since one of my guiding principles has always been to finish a job properly. Dubochet was a perfect slave-driver so far as the poor engravers were concerned. The smallest accident cost them dear, and often he had them up in front of the local magistrate. I should emphasise that he paid them very little, for he often employed apprentices rather than trained craftsmen. So, to give these poor folk less trouble, I simplified my designs as much as I could, and *I was as sparing as I could be of my tints* [my italics].[8]

Nor was this problem confined to France and, looking at it from the engraver's standpoint, W.J. Linton wrote:

> Drawings such as those of Leech and Gilbert and Cruikshank, and Seymour of earlier time, … well suited the hasty sketches needed in Hone's *Political Tracts* and *Punch*. That as sketches they satisfied the special occasion, that there is a charm in this loose free handling, that they were quickly drawn and easily – only too easily engraved, that they were satisfactorily cheap to the publishers, – is true; yet no less were they detrimental to the *art* of engraving.[9]

Thus Linton underlines the three economic features of the black-line engraving – speed of execution by the artist, speed of working by the engraver, and reduction of cost to the publisher.

But Linton also admits the 'charm' of the 'free loose handling' so very characteristic of Jean Gigoux's designs for *Gil Blas* and which is not so apparent when, as in *Lettres d'Abailard et d'Héloise* (1839), he 'finished the job properly' and did not 'spare the tints'. It is also characteristic of Tony Johannot's designs for the medium and through him of much of French book-art of the period. Not that it is without its dangers, which may be summed up in one word – greyness. This is less apparent in engravings upon a small scale, but the French fashion of using the wood-engraving as a full-page illustration, and the increasingly large formats employed, tend to aggravate the problem. It becomes all too patent when both wood and steel are used for full-page plates. Perhaps the most graphic example is provided by Perrotin and Garnier's edition of Victor Hugo's *Notre Dame de Paris* (1844), where the steels, so clearly showing Cruikshank's influence, have so very much more powerful an effect than the somewhat grey wood-engravings.

Moreover, the same danger lurks in the integrated wood-engraving, too. When the page is not enclosed by a framing rule border, effects, depending upon a harmonious balance between the density of black in the engraving and the type-matter, can be made or marred by the size of type used and by the amount of leading between the lines of text. It is the

212 *The Bugbear: the government's stage censor*: wood-engraved vignette after C.J. Traviès (Huart, *Muséum parisien*, 1841) [BL 12330 i 12]

213 *A Bench-full of Bores*: wood-engraved vignette after Henry Monnier
(Huart, *Muséum parisien*, 1841) [BL 12330 i 12]

214 Spread from Jules Janin's *La Normandie* (1844) [BL 1443 k 8]

perfect balance between the weight of the typography and the vignettes in Jules Janin's *L'âne mort* (1842) which makes me rate this book as one of Tony Johannot's best. Yet perhaps the clearest illustration of the point under discussion comes from contrasting the success and failure of two very similar books – Louis Huart's *Muséum parisien* (1841) with Paul de Kock's *La grande ville* (1844). Both treat the same subject – Paris and Parisian society in its widest sense; both are embellished with integrated wood-engravings by much the same group of artists – Daumier [figs 190, 191], Traviès [fig. 212], Monnier [fig. 213], Gavarni and Grandville; both adopt the same royal octavo format. Yet Huart's book is immensely satisfying to handle, and a notable piece of Romantic book design, while de Kock's is a commonplace, run-of-the-mill production.

With so much in common, why should the one succeed and the other fail? The answer lies in the larger type and more generous leading of the *Muséum parisien* which give type-matter a proportion of white to match that in the 'loose free' style of the vignettes. The text of *La grande ville* is more solidly set in a smaller type-face and this has the tendency to isolate the vignettes so that they become a disruptive rather than an integrating element in the typographic design.

Debarcadère de Rouen, le jour de l'inauguration, 3 mai 1843.

ROUEN.

SON HISTOIRE. — SES MONUMENTS. — SON INDUSTRIE. — SON COMMERCE. — SES GRANDS HOMMES.

Mais vous avez mis pied à terre. Ici, vous redevenez un voyageur vulgaire, et bien vous en prend. Vous pouvez regarder à loisir, et promener tranquillement vos souvenirs, entraînés tout à l'heure, sans trêve ni relâche, sur les pentes de cet impitoyable coursier qui s'appelle la vapeur. La terre que vous foulez est une terre historique, s'il en fut. Avant d'être un chef-lieu de département, et bientôt un faubourg de Paris, cette ville de Rouen a été la capitale d'une grande province, pour ne pas dire d'un vrai royaume; elle a été l'un des centres les

215 Spread from Jules Janin's guide-book, *Voyage de Paris à la mer* (1847). The steel-engraved view of Rouen is no longer isolated on its page in this smaller format, although the sides of the the wood-engraving have had to be shaved to accommodate the block to the narrower line-width [BL 10170 bb 41]

Disruption is, of course, the greater danger when vignette wood-engravings are used unintelligently, and it would be pointless to ignore the fact that all too often publishers and printers are guilty of this fault. Frequently they sin in the interests of economy, since it is manifestly less complicated, and hence cheaper, to insert vignettes between solid blocks of type, rather than to drop into the type area, with the tricky short-line setting which this involves. However, then, the problem of matching density of black in type and vignette is further complicated by the need to achieve a proper balance between vignette and type-area. It is not so much a matter of depth: all too often the vignette is too narrow in proportion with the measure of the line so that the extra white margin which results creates a wide line of demarcation between the two type-areas which the vignette should unite.

This is common to all books of the period but is best illustrated by topographical books, where Romanticism modified the conventional presentation of text illustrated by *hors-texte* plates by introducing the integrated wood-engraved vignette. Two of Jules Janin's books, *La Normandie* (1843) and *La Bretagne* (1844), receive this treatment. Both contain full-page illustrations, many of which are finely engraved on steel by J.J. Outhwaite, agreeable wood-engraved vignettes and, in the case of the book on Brittany, most attractive hand-coloured costume-plates, and coats of arms reproduced in gold and colours by chromolithography. Yet both, when all is said and done, are really rather dull books, in which the wood-engraved vignettes intrude to break the even texture of the printed page.

Interestingly enough, many of the vignettes engraved for *La Normandie* were re-used in 1847 for another and far more modest venture by Janin – a guide-book for the newly-opened railroad from Paris to Rouen, and for the continuation of the journey by steamer to Le Havre. *La voyage de Paris à la mer* has a number of new illustrations – both full-page steels engraved by Outhwaite and wood-engraved vignettes – but what is of special interest is the way in which the old vignettes now integrate so well with the text. The result is that this modest little guide is a very much more satisfying book than the more imposing topography in which so much of the illustration originally appeared. It therefore underlines the importance of scale and suggests how much better wood-engraving by its very nature served the smaller formats [figs 214, 215].

Nor was this a phenomenon peculiar to French book design. Although the wood-engravings are better integrated in Mr and Mrs S.C. Hall's *Ireland* (1841–3), there are enough pages, where their presence is divisive, to show the universal nature of the problem. As in the case of *La Normandie*, so from this three-volume book steels and wood-engravings were abstracted to illustrate Mrs Hall's guide-book, *A Week at Killarney* (1843). Once again the guide-book is in a slightly smaller format – a square demy octavo as compared with the royal octavo of *Ireland* – but the contrast is less striking because the parent volumes are not so commonplace as Janin's.

Two years later the Halls' publisher, Jeremiah How, issued what is one of the most engaging of Romantic guide-books, F. Knight Hunt's *The Rhine Book*. In much the same format as *A Week at Killarney*, it perhaps has the advantage to the modern taste of being illustrated throughout by wood-engravings from the designs of Harrison Weir and G.F. Sargent, so that it has a homogeneity lacking in the other book [fig. 216]. Certainly the quality of the individual vignettes in *The Rhine Book* is no higher – probably the reverse – yet by some

216 The rule border
of this page from
Mrs Hall's *A Week at
Killarney* (1843)
draws the vignette
wood-engraving
and the text-type
into a visual unity
[BL 797 e 23]

DRUIDICAL WORKS.   95

other ponderous remains may be seen; and a serpentine passage of considerable length, formed by parallel lines of huge masses of stone, can be traced from the shore, terminating in the Red Bog, a tract of low ground at some distance. The opposite side of the road from that on which the church stands is crowded with Druidical works, which it is impossible for us to particularise; one, however, called by

the country people "Labig yermuddagh a Grana,"—that is, Edward and Grace's Bed,—is here represented.

This was probably a tomb. It had been a complete oblong chamber, formed by great stones, and covered over with vast flags. The length of this sepulchral chamber was thirteen feet and a half, the breadth six feet. An old woman resided in it for many years, and on her death the covering stones were thrown off, and it was left in its present state by "money-diggers, who found only some burned bones in an ould jug, that surely was not worth one brass farthing." Above this tomb a tabular rock, upwards of ten feet in circumference, rests upon four supporters; and not far distant there is a singular natural formation called "Carrignanahin, or the Mass Rock." It is full of chasms and hollows, and is said to have received its name from a priest having regularly celebrated within one of its recesses the ceremonies of the Roman Catholic church, at a period when that religion was proscribed.

The eastern shore of Lough Gur abounds also with mighty vestiges of Druidical

strange alchemy the whole book comes together to demonstrate how the Romantic period could turn a practical manual into an elegant and visually exciting object.

What very largely helps Jeremiah How to achieve this end is the employment of a rule border to surround the text and the vignettes in both books, and this simple stylistic device seems to me to be absolutely crucial to the success of the Romantic book. As I have stressed, there is a real danger in books of larger format that the introduction of vignettes can disturb the colour of a page unless, as is the case in Léon Curmer's edition of *Paul et Virginie* and in Christopher Wordsworth's *Greece*, the style of the engraving can match the density of the type-matter and the amount of white space at the side of the wood-block is carefully controlled.

What the rule border does is to reduce the page area to the type-area, in which letterpress and the black-line of the engraving, the leading between the lines of type and the white areas within and around the vignette, all become a single black-and-white illustration framed by the rule border. To strengthen this effect, the width of the vignette is sometimes allowed to exceed the measure of the line and to break the frame created by the rules. Paradoxically, this has the effect of making the frame itself part of the total image and results in an even better integrated page [figs 96, 97].

The framing rules are subservient to type and vignettes and are probably at their most effective when at their simplest although, at a time when decoration was at a premium, there is a tendency to use a swelled or decorated rule and to insert rosettes or other ornaments at the corners. Since British practice seems to have favoured the 'open' page, at least for prose works, direct comparison can be made between editions employing the same set of embellishments. If one sets side by side the 'open' English translation of René Lesage's

217 Page from René Lesage, *Le diable boîteux* (1840) with the wood-engraving after Tony Johannot [BL 12511 i 7]

Le diable boîteux and the 'enclosed' French original, one can see how much better Tony Johannot's designs integrate with the text when both are framed by a rule border [figs 217, 218].

The rule border is so important a feature of Romantic book design that it would be satisfying if one could give it a direct line of descent, from Strixner's lithographic reproduction of Dürer's decorations for the Emperor Maximilian's prayer-book in 1808, through Neureuther's engravings of a selection of Goethe's *Balladen und Romanzen* in 1829–30 [fig. 74] to the 1835 edition of *Gil Blas* [fig. 6]. But I do not think matters are as simple as this. The rule is not the typical style of German border. Naturally, it was used and used extensively, but the characteristic frame for the pages of German Romantic books was the 'stick' [fig. 219]. Again, one wonders whether a series of artist's engravings, of consequently

ASMODEUS ; OR,

secret for three whole days ; but when the news of the fire at Miedes reached Siguença, as every body thought it strange that all the servants of the Sicilian should have perished in the flames, she naturally took it into her head also that the fire was the work of Guillem himself. To revenge her lover's death, therefore, she sought the signor Don Felix, your father, and related to him all she knew. Don Felix, alarmed at finding you were in the hands of a man capable of everything, accompanied the lady to the corregidor, who on hearing her story had no doubt of Stephani's intentions towards you, and that he was the diabolical incendiary the woman suspected. To make inquiries into all the circumstances of the case, the corregidor instantly dispatched orders to me at Retortillo, where I live, directing me to repair with my brigade to this chateau, to find

218 Page from the English translation (*Asmodeus or the Devil on Sticks*, 1841) where the absence of framing rules makes it looser and visually less effective [BL 838 k 11]

186

limited circulation, could have so influenced book-designers whose eyes, as we have shown, were fixed westward across the English Channel, rather than eastward across the Rhine.

The stronger probability is that the employment of the single rule in French books is purely fortuitous and merely a manifestation of a parallel development. There was a general spirit of Revivalism abroad, and nothing would be more natural than to reproduce a feature characteristic of European seventeenth-century typography. The rule border is, then, a characteristic of French Romantic book design which was exported to England in the same way as the 'stick' border came from Germany. It was not so widely used in Britain but remained one of the features of the up-market Christmas gift volumes of poetry in the 1850s and 1860s, at a time when it was abandoned in France for all except cheap popular reprints.

In addition to the 'stick' border, the Germans developed the decorative panel, or

Die drei Tellen.

Es schlafen die drei Telle
Im edlen Schweizerland,
In einer Felsenzelle,
Im Rütli an dem Strand,
Wo noch die Welle brausend
Vom Vierwaldstätter-See;
Da schon ein halb Jahrtausend
Sie ruhn in stiller Höh'.

219 *The Three Tells*: wood-engraving after H.F. Pluddemann (*Deutsches Balladenbuch*, 1852). By the 1850s there seems to have been a tendency to enclose the page within rule borders in the French style, although the image itself retains the typically German 'stick' border [BL 11521 g 1]

slip [fig. 220]. This is a notable feature of Romantic book design which was most success-fully imitated by Germanists in Britain, Owen Jones and Noel Humphreys creating, in opposition, original work on the same principle. In France Léon Curmer very effectively used the frame of wide decoration round the pages of his editions of *Les saints évangiles* (1836) and Bossuet's *Discours sur l'histoire universelle* (1839) [pl. 1]. In both cases his designers seem to have based themselves very firmly upon such later mediaeval manuscript models as the *Heures* of the Duc de Berri.

In this they were wise, for the same perverse ingenuity which we observed in Paulin's edition of *Les évangiles* (1837) most unfortunately infects the work of Vivant Beaucé (1818–76). He specialized in the design of decorative title-pages and chapter-openings for which he produced work of great charm and genuine distinction. This gave him a modest

220 *My Anne is like a red, red Rose*: wood-engraving after Otto Speckter (Groth, *Quickborn*, 1856). The typically German panel decoration is on a page enclosed by characteristically French double-rules [BL 11526 h 2]

international reputation and he contributed to the Anglo-French *Les beautés de l'opéra* (1845) [fig. 221]. This history of the Paris opera and description of some of the most popular works in its repertory is illustrated by French [figs 222, 223] and British artists – among them Henry Warren – with full-page steel-engravings and with vignette wood-engravings cut by French and British craftsmen, the latter including Samuel and Thomas Williams and Henry Vizetelly. The borders, good examples of Beaucé's style, are printed in colours, in clear imitation of *Ancient Spanish Ballads*. However, Beaucé is no Owen Jones; the book tries hard, but must be adjudged a failure.

Similarly ill-directed ingenuity may be seen in the part-issue by Chapman & Hall of an imposing folio *Four Gospels* between 1847 and 1849, when the death of Charles Heath closed the project and curtailed the planned issue of the remaining books of the New Testament.

221 *Le Diable boiteux*: wood-engraved page decorations after Vivant Beaucé (*Les beautés de l'Opéra*, 1845) [BL Hirsch 1842]

Henry Warren and the French artist Henri Valentin designed the bulk of the vignette illustration, and the borders were the responsibility of Beaucé. They are in many respects a *tour de force*, for his designs are based upon the content of the pages which they surround. They must, however, be adjudged failures upon a massive scale since, unlike the Germans and the British Germanists, they are conceived as illustrations rather than as decorations. The essential fault of this French school of design, typified by Beaucé, is to forget that the function of the border is essentially decorative, something of which the British and the Germans never lost sight.

Whether, then, as a plain single or double rule, as a 'stick' or more elaborate piece of decoration, the frame is the characteristic feature of Romantic page layout. This has the effect of producing a succession of single pages, with the natural result that the printer-

222 *La Sylphide*: page decoration engraved on three wood-blocks after Jules Collignon (*Les beautés de l'Opéra*, 1845) [BL Hirsch 1842]

designer of the period does not pay sufficient attention to the double-page opening. A major weakness, certainly to modern eyes which are used to judging the impact of such an opening, is that while each separate page may be well balanced, they clash in juxtaposition. This is particularly true of 'open' pages: the 'enclosed' page lessens the jarring impact of the fault which it has tended to produce.

In so far as the book typography of the period is concerned, while it is in no sense a period of particular distinction except for the revival of old-face types by Charles Whittingham the younger in England and by Louis Perrin in France, printers in both countries could feel that they were the immediate heirs of such great names as William Bulmer, Thomas Bensley and Pierre Didot the younger. The consequence is the maintenance of high standards of press-work and of unobtrusively good typography producing a

223 *La Juive*: wood-engraved decorated page after Célestin Nanteuil (*Les beautés de l'Opéra*, 1845) [BL Hirsch 1842]

224 Wood-engraved
head-piece and
section-opening
after F.L. Français
(Bernardin de St-Pierre,
Paul et Virginie, 1838)
[BL 1458 k 9]

clear, readable page. As the century progressed, increasing mechanization produced lower standards, especially in cheap editions intended for a mass-market. In the period under discussion, however, the typography of the text supplied a sober background to the visual excitement of the vignettes, and the Romantic exuberance only found expression in the letter-forms of the display faces used on the title-page and in the use of decorated initial letters.

The most imaginative effects were produced by historiated and decorated initials, from simple letter-forms to the elaboration and even over-elaboration of head-piece and marginal extension incorporating the initial [fig. 224]. Frequently, such designs were directly inspired by mediaeval manuscript models and, as might be expected, German Revivalism produced some excellent examples, particularly fine specimens being designed by Ludwig Richter for the three volumes of Count Athanase Raczynski's *Histoire de l'art*

LIVRE HUITIÈME.

CHAPITRE PREMIER.

GIL BLAS FAIT UNE BONNE CONNOISSANCE, ET TROUVE UN POSTE QUI LE CONSOLE DE L'INGRATITUDE DU COMTE GALIANO. HISTOIRE DE DON VALERIO DE LUNA.

'ÉTOIS si surpris de n'avoir point entendu parler de Nunez pendant tout ce temps-là que je jugeai qu'il devoit être à la campagne. Je sortis pour aller chez lui dès que je pus marcher, et j'appris, en effet, qu'il étoit depuis trois semaines en Andalousie, avec le duc de Medina Sidonia

Un matin, à mon réveil, Melchior de La Ronda me vint dans l'esprit; et, me ressouvenant que je lui avois promis à Grenade d'aller voir son ne-

225 Decorative book-opening after F.L. Français (Lesage, *Gil Blas*, 1835). Although the decoration breaks the inner rule border, the outer border integrates the engraving with the text. The echoes of the mediaeval manuscript in the initial letter are typical of the Romantic period [BL G18301]

moderne en Allemagne (1836–41). Work in a very similar idiom may be found in French books – Madame Amable Tastu's *Des Andelays au Havre* (1843), for example – but whether this is the result of direct influence it is hard to say. My impression is that French illustrators – unlike their British counterparts – remained relatively unaffected by the style of German Romantic book design. Lorentz, it is true, seems to echo Richter in his illustrations of such children's books as P. Christian's *La morale merveilleuse* (1844), but the German outline style left little or no overt mark on French design. An exception to this is Edmond de Beaumont's design for 'Vivre loin de ses amours' in the third volume of the engraved song-book, *Chants et chansons populaires* (three volumes, 1843), but such examples are very rare.

In any case, the French themselves exhibited a strong Revivalism particularly in this very area of letter forms, the initial. This is much in evidence in Ferdinand Langlé's two

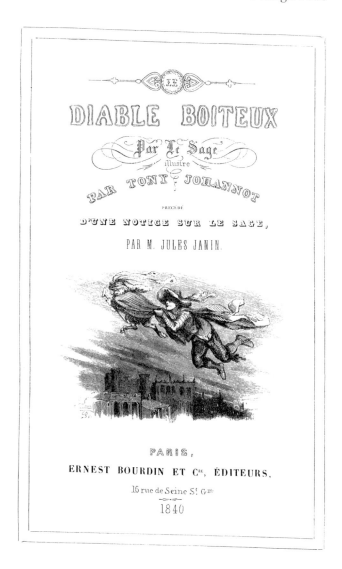

226 The multiplicity of types deployed on the title page of *Le diable boîteux* is typical of the period [BL 1251117]

collections of late mediaeval material, *Les contes du gai savoir* (1828) and *L'historial du jongleur* (1829) [pl. 12], the former illustrated by Monnier and Bonington, the latter with designs by Eugène Lami. Langlé was the friend of both Lami and Monnier and appropriately the paper wrappers of the artists' *Voyage en Angleterre* (1829) should advertise his books. They are described as 'giving a highly accurate notion of the richness of printed books at the end of the fifteenth century', being decorated with 'initial letters, vignettes and fleurons copied from genuine manuscripts'.

Although both of Langlé's books were luxury items, the initials, decorations and wood-engravings coloured and gilded by hand, the same concern to base decoration and letter forms upon authentic examples from the Romanesque period to the late fifteenth century may be seen in books intended for the mass-market [fig. 225]. We have noted it in the borders used by Léon Curmer and it is a characteristic of many of the initial letters used in French Romantic books. This is by contrast with the British practice which more usually adapts or, as in the case of Richard Doyle in *Punch*, parodies both mediaevalism itself and its revivers.

The reason for this more strictly Revivalist spirit in France may well have a great deal to do with the availability there of such works of palaeography as would provide readily available models. Until the mid-1840s, perhaps the only book in Britain was Henry Shaw's *Illuminated Ornaments of the Middle Ages* (1833), while in France there were Count Bastard's *Peintures des manuscrits* (begun in 1832, completed in 1869), Silvestre's *Paléographie universelle* (1841, reprinted in London 1850) and the more practical manuals of Jean Midolle, *Compositions avec écritures anciennes et modernes* (1834–5) and *Traité complet d'écritures en tous genres* (1840).

Initial letters are, however, embellishments to a page of conventional typography: where the Romantic period produced a characteristic style it was in the letter forms used on the title-page. Largely because of the growth of urban society, the increased mechanization and the economic need to reach a mass-market, printed advertising is an especial feature of the early nineteenth century. The battle to catch the public's eye led inevitably to the development of various ranges of decorated display faces which, although primarily intended for printed posters, could and did infiltrate the title-pages of books. Purists will deplore this influence and echo the condemnation of Alphonse de Boisseau of the fashionable bad taste, if not charlatanism, which introduced 'countless founts of giant, pigmy, elongated, condensed, outline, miniature, grotesque, ill-proportioned types' [fig. 226].[10] Indeed, there was a clear temptation to use the title-page rather as a printer's specimen sheet, to which not a few succumbed. Just as the availability of so many methods of graphic reproduction produced illustrated books which are a hotch-potch of steel- and wood-engraving, with the odd lithograph or chromolithograph thrown in, so these new type-faces rub discordant shoulders on the title-page.

Conservatism: Some Uses of Stone and Steel in France

The book is an artefact with a very long history, produced by men who are essentially conservative in outlook. It is, broadly speaking, true to say that once the use of intaglio copper-engraving from the end of the sixteenth century had established its necessity, the *hors-texte* plate became an established feature of the illustrated book, basically unaffected by the possibilities of integration with the text afforded by the revival of wood-engraving in the Romantic period. Indeed, so far from leading automatically to integration with the text, wood-engraving became merely another method of reproducing the *hors-texte* illustration. The established conventions of presenting illustrations in books were to some extent influenced by Romantic concepts of book design, and Romantic integrated illustrations predominated in certain categories of book, but printers and publishers adhered to the old tradition, simply applying new methods of graphic reproduction to an unchanged concept of how particular textual and illustrative material should be presented.

An outstanding example of this can be seen in Baron Taylor's *Voyages pittoresques et romantiques de l'ancienne France* (1820–78) which on every count of approach, content, subject and style of illustration, epitomize the Romantic attitude to the historical monuments of France. Nevertheless, the presentation is completely conventional throughout this long-running series of massive folio volumes of austerely classical type-matter, with their hundreds of *hors-texte* plates. The only concessions to the Romantic style are the occasional tail-piece vignette and the way in which the first page of text, which opens the account of each of the old French provinces, is presented with the type-matter integrated into a full-page lithographic design. This creates the paradox that, being by far the most visually interesting pages in the book, they are generally chosen for reproduction, thus giving a totally erroneous impression of the predominant effect. In fact, Baron Taylor's *magnum opus* is less a monument to Romantic book design than a museum of nineteenth-century technology of graphic reproduction. The topographical and architectural views are printed by lithography, the detailed architectural plans by intaglio engraving, which is also employed to depict archaeological specimens. Lithography is, however, the cornerstone and it is interesting to note how the later volumes as, for example, *La Bourgogne* (1863), adapt to technological advance and include plates which are either printed directly from photo-lithography or from lithographs drawn from photographs.

The aspect of this planographic process most attractive to publishers was that it could provide large plates at a fraction of the cost and infinitely more rapidly than steel- or copper-engraving. Lithography thus became the preferred medium for the large format book of folio or large quarto size. For smaller formats steel-etching or engraving was the preferred method of printing *hors-texte* illustrations although, with the wide choice of processes available, it is dangerous to attempt to be too categorical about this. The French, in particular, used wood-engraving, and often tinted wood-engraving which imitated litho-graphy, in addition to lithography itself as, for example, in *L'Espagne pittoresque* (1848). In the book in question, many of the costume designs which Célestin Nanteuil provided for the Vicomte de Féréal's book are hand-coloured – another common practice.

Similarly, lithography provided a cheap and effective means of reproducing authors'

227 The steel-engraver J. Doherty proves his competence as an artist in his view of Beaugency (Philipon de la Madeleine, *L'Orléanais*, 1845) [BL 10171 h 11]

228 *The Racecourse at Chantilly*: steel-engraving after Eugène Lami (Janin, *L'été à Paris*, 1843) [BL 10172 g 23]

229 *Steeplechasing*:
wood-engraved
chapter-opening
after F.J. Collignon
(Janin, *L'été à
Paris*, 1843)
[BL 10172 g 23]

E rentrais chez moi, lorsque j'entends le facteur de la poste aux lettres qui épelait mon nom avec un sang-froid imperturbable. Ces Français ont l'habitude de donner à tous les noms une désinence française. Vous porteriez un nom tudesque du temps de Frédéric Barberousse, un nom anglo-saxon du temps de *Guillaume le Conquérant*, que le facteur de la poste aux lettres ferait de vous, bel et bien, un habitant de la Chaussée-d'Antin ou du faubourg Saint-Honoré, à votre choix. Au reste, cet humble et très-spirituel employé du Gouverne-

illustrations, and this is a common phenomenon in English travel books of the period. Examples which spring to mind are J. and H. Bullar's *A Winter in the Azores* (1841), H. Keppel's *The Expedition to Borneo of HMS Dido* (1845), and the travel books of Louisa Costello, *Béarn and the Pyrenees* (1844) and *A Tour to and from Venice* and *A Summer among the Bocages* (both 1846). Miss Costello, incidentally, provided the text for an interesting essay in tinted lithography combined with wood-engraving in her *Falls, Lakes and Mountains of North Wales* (1845). Unfortunately her publisher, Longman, produced the book to the format and in a type size normally reserved for children's books, which detract from D.H. McEwan's highly competent landscape designs.

Steel was, nonetheless, the accepted medium for all but the largest topographical books, and its increasing employment on the Continent is a sign of the influence of the English landscape school and of British technological advance. It was used by the Germans, as in *Das malerische und romantische Deutschland* (1836–42), and extensively by the French. A typical example, interesting because it comes from a provincial rather than a Parisian publisher, is G. Touchard-Lafosse's *La Loire historique*, published in five parts as four volumes at Nantes and Tours between 1840 and 1844. The *hors-texte* illustrations were designed by Adolphe Rouargue and E. de la Michellerie and engraved on steel by Emile Rouargue, and there are numerous integrated vignette illustrations and decorated chapter openings. The latter are engraved on wood and are somewhat coarse and heavy by comparison with contemporary Parisian work, doubtless because provincial printers had yet fully to master the art of printing from lowered blocks.

230 Steel-engraved title-page to Victor Hugo's *Notre Dame de Paris* after Adolphe Rouargue. Although his brother Emile was a skilled steel-engraver, this block was executed in London by Finden [BL C61 b 23]

The technique of steel-engraving, too, was very much a British skill and, with the very notable exception of the work of the Rouargue brothers, few French engravings have the finish of British plates – the needle is more in evidence than the burin. This absence of native talent left the way open for outsiders, such as the Englishman Outhwaite and the Irishman Doherty [fig. 227] whose names appear on so many French plates, Outhwaite in particular supplying engravings with all the London high polish.[11] Again, French publishers, like their German confrères, sent designs to London, the best and most typical in terms of subject-matter being the elegant designs supplied by Eugène Lami for Jules Janin's *L'hiver...* and *L'été à Paris* in 1843 [fig. 228].

More surprising, perhaps, is to find that Finden was asked to etch the plates to the illustrated edition of Victor Hugo's *Notre Dame de Paris* which Renduel published in 1836 [fig. 230]. The Johannot brothers, Louis Boulanger, Raffet and Camille Rogier between them provided the eleven *hors-texte* designs for a book which in many ways prefigures the illustrated English novel of the next decade, but it is curious that neither of the Johannots should have etched their own designs, since both were trained metal engravers. In England steel was the medium of the professional illustrator, but in France, where lithography was

231 *Your Money or your Life*: wood-engraved vignette chapter-heading after C.J. Traviès (Sue, *Les mystères de Paris*, 1, 1843) [BL 1458 k 13]

preferred for caricature, topography, portraiture and even historical subjects, their opposite numbers preferred to design for wood-engraving. One exception was Célestin Nanteuil (1813–73), with a series of etched frontispieces and title-pages to half-a-dozen of Victor Hugo's books between 1832 and 1833. Here one must agree with the French critic Georges Duplessis's stricture that Nanteuil's 'lack of experience in the medium is redeemed neither by balanced composition nor by accurate draughtsmanship'.[12] Yet, although clumsy by English standards, the frontispieces anticipate an English convention of placing the leading characters and incidents of the book in decorative compartments, to serve much the same purpose as stills outside a cinema.

Nanteuil was the quintessential French Romantic artist – adopting mediaeval costume and doing battle for his patron and master, Hugo, at the first night of *Hernani* – and his character-playing gives this portion of his book-work an interest which it might not otherwise possess. He was to be one of the most prolific illustrators of Romantic books, for which he provided hundreds of designs for wood-engraving, as well as turning out vast quantities of lithographic music covers. His work is distinguished by a very high level of competence without reaching the heights of some of his rivals.

More interesting as an artist is Charles Emile Jacque (1813–94), whose landscape etchings are of fine quality. Before his apprenticeship to a Parisian map-engraver in 1830, he had visited London and would seem to have maintained his British connections since he, together with Fussell, provided the designs for the wood-engravings in the edition of *A Sentimental Journey* published by John Nichols in 1839 [fig. 46]. Jacque developed into a landscape painter of the school of Barbizon – he was a friend of Millet – and his artistry is shown to best effect in such landscape etchings as he made for Pître-Chevalier's *La Bretagne ancienne et moderne* (1844) or, in different vein, for the second illustrated edition of Hugo's *Notre Dame* of the same year.

232 *Madame Pipelet*: wood-engraving after C.J. Traviès (Sue, *Les mystères de Paris*, 1, 1843) [BL 1458 k 13]

The dearth of etched work and of etchers is a feature of French Romantic art which expressed itself most typically in the lithographic caricature and the wood-engraved illustration. Nor was the original novel really the field for French Romantic book design. The style originated with the aim of providing attractive books for the new mass-market and, not surprisingly, was applied to such safe products as the established classics – Bernardin de Saint Pierre, Cervantes, Defoe, La Fontaine, Lesage, Molière, Sterne or Swift. Illustrated editions of established contemporary novels were published, but illustrations and part-publication on the British pattern does not seem to have been the rule in France.

One exception is Eugène Sue, his best-selling sensational novels *Les mystères de Paris* (1843–4), *Mathilde* (1844–5) and *Le juif errant* (1845), for example, all appearing in parts, heavily illustrated with integrated wood-engraved vignettes and with full-page plates, mostly engraved on wood in *Les mystères de Paris*, but with many etched on steel in the other novels. Célestin Nanteuil bore the main share of the work of illustration, especially in *Mathilde*, but the first volume of *Les mystères de Paris* should be noted for the designs which it contains both of Daumier [figs 192, 193] and of Baudelaire's '*artiste maudit*', the fine caricaturist J.C. Traviès [figs 231, 232]. Sue's novels enjoyed enormous popularity in Britain and, in addition to the recognized translation published by Chapman & Hall and illustrated by electros of the French originals, there were a number of disreputable piracies, including an edition of *The Mysteries of Paris* illustrated by the etchings of Thomas Onwhyn.

The End of the Era

If the Romantic movement can be linked with the upsurge of liberalism in Europe, then 1848 marks its peak, and the failure of revolutionary uprisings in Continental Europe and of the less violent Chartist movement in Britain signal the turn of the political tide. The Romantic book, being the child of those liberal aspirations, suffered the fate of its parent, and from about 1850 entered a slow but steady decline in Britain and France. In Britain, the Great Exhibition of 1851 offers a convenient point from which the new era can be dated; in France, Louis Napoleon's successful *coup d'état* at the end of the same year provides a similar watershed.

Of the French Romantic illustrators, Grandville was already dead – his life had closed in a lunatic asylum in 1847 – and Tony Johannot had died during the course of 1851. Of the survivors, Monnier turned almost exclusively to the theatre, while Daumier, finding the political atmosphere, characterized by his creation the police-informer Ratapol, increasingly uncongenial, concentrated upon his easel painting. Younger men such as Meissonier and Daubigny, having made their reputations as painters, were no longer under financial pressure to accept commissions for book-illustrations from publishers. Others still, and notably Bertall, made the transition from the Romantic to the Imperial age, but the end of the era is most poignantly symbolized by the later career of that fine exemplar of *la vie de bohème*, Gavarni.

In 1848 he found himself an exile in London – but he was there to escape the bailiffs rather than his political opponents. His English friends, Thackeray, George Cruikshank and Albert Smith among them, rallied round to help him. Henry Vizetelly obtained commissions

233 *Buy my sweet Violets*: lithograph after Gavarni ('Les anglais chez eux' in *Œuvres nouvelles*, 1852) [BL KTC 29 b 2]

for him from *The Illustrated London News* and Albert Smith persuaded David Bogue to publish a piece of character-writing, *Gavarni in London* (1849), of which the anodyne quality of the master's illustrations is as surprising to us now as the lack of response to their overtures was to his English friends at the time. The truth would seem to have been that Gavarni was going through a mental crisis which plunged him into the darkest depressions. Matters were made still worse by his London experiences, which were not in the brassy bohemian world of *Gavarni in London*, but in the slums and among the destitute whom he depicted so harrowingly in his *Les anglais chez eux*, the series of lithographs which he published on his return to France in 1852 [fig. 233]. There, following the death of his daughter, he became a virtual recluse in his last years. Something of his mood may be judged from *D'après nature*, an album of lithographs issued in 1858 and inspired by disgust at the sexuality and hedonism which had been the mainspring of his earlier work.

With one of his principal publishers, Hetzel, in exile in Brussels, Gavarni undertook most of the limited number of commissions between 1850 and his death in 1866 for Morisot. They comprised such uninspired illustrations of the literary classics for the school-prize market as those for the translations of *Gulliver's Travels* and of *Robinson Crusoe* which Morisot published in 1863. Earlier, Gavarni had supplied designs for two books by Jules Janin, *Les petits bonheurs* (1856) and *Les symphonies de l'hiver* (1858). They epitomize one aspect of the new world of the Second Empire, the luxury of a *nouveau riche* society expressed in the gloss of steel-engraving. In both books Gavarni, the artist of Bohemia, supplies designs reproduced in steel in a 'book of beauty' style which is its complete antithesis. Both are, however, quite outdone by an earlier essay in this genre, Comte Foelix's *Les joyaux*. Here, Gavarni's designs are engraved in steel by Geoffroy, hand-coloured, framed in lace-paper and mounted on to a leaf of pink paper.

Morisot's most regular steel-engraver was Emile Rouargue, who had already shown himself to be one of the few French craftsmen to match the skill and finish of the London school. This he had demonstrated in Philipon de la Madeleine's *L'Orléanais* (1845), a most attractive book combining good traditional typography with steel-engravings after the designs of a number of artists including Emile's brother Adolphe Rouargue [fig. 234], and delightful Romantic chapter openings engraved on wood [fig. 235]. Earlier, the brothers had played a similar role in Léon Galibert's *L'Algérie ancienne et moderne* (1844), a dull book unredeemed even by its hand-coloured engravings of military uniforms. In fact, Adolphe Rouargue was to become the French Bartlett. In the 1850s, Morisot issued a whole series of

234 *The Château of Blois*: steel-engraving by Rouargue (Philipon de la Madeleine, *L'Orléanais*, 1845) [BL 10171 h 11]

Voyages pittoresques in the Rhineland, the Low Countries, Italy, the Holy Land, Spain and Portugal and Switzerland. Émile engraved the illustration which Adolphe provided for the texts by Paul de Musset, E. Bégin and Edmond Texier.

The popularization of the steel-engraving in France of the Second Empire may almost stand for a symbol of French economic growth, just as its introduction into Britain a generation before expressed the leading position which British industry enjoyed in Europe. Effectively the French – and the Germans, too – developed a new style of engraving which by the 1860s was challenging British dominance of the market, and was even reversing the flow of prints so that they were now imported into Britain from the Continent.[13] The economics of steel-engraving are, however, less important in this context than that the fact of its adoption may be seen as an indicator of social change.

CHAPITRE XI.

DE L'AN 1588 A L'AN 1610.

Guise, voyant la ruine de ses complots, s'efforça de nier toute participation à la révolte, et écrivit une lettre pour protester de sa soumission au roi. Le capitaine Saint-Paul, un de ses affidés, se chargea de remettre cette lettre qu'Henri plaça dans son pourpoint sans daigner y répondre. Le soir, tandis qu'il assistait à vêpres dans la cathédrale, les portes s'ouvrent, et Joyeuse, frère du duc, tué à

235 Wood-engraved chapter-opening after Henri Valentin (Philipon de la Madeleine, *L'Orléanais*, 1845) [BL 10171 h 11]

A Voyage to Brobdingnag.

"I observed a huge creature walking after them in the sea."—*Page 91.*

or hulling. We reefed the fore-sail, and set him, and hauled aft the fore-sheet; the helm was hard a-weather. The ship wore bravely. We belayed the fore down-haul; but the sail was split, and we hauled down the yard, and got the sail into the ship, and unbound all the things clear of it. It was a very fierce storm; the sea broke strange and dangerous. We hauled off upon the lanyards of the whip-staff, and helped the man at the helm. We would not get down our topmast,

89

12

236 Wood-engraving after Thomas Morten (Swift, *Gulliver's Travels*, 1864) [BL 12612 i 13]

237 *Epictetus Dancing*: wood-engraved vignette after Gustave Doré (Rabelais, *Oeuvres*, 1854) [BL 12236 l 2]

Another indicator was the reversion to the older, more classical convention of using wood-engraved vignettes as head- or tail-pieces. An excellent example is provided by the Comte de Chevigné's *Contes rémois* (1858), with Meissonier's exquisite designs [fig. 38]. The Romantic style of the integrated wood-engraved vignette was, nonetheless, retained for the down-market book. This intrusive element of class distinction, noticeably absent from so large a proportion of the books of the Romantic period, may also be found in England, where the persistence of the elements of the Romantic design tend to stamp publications as cheap editions. Cassell, Petter & Galpin provide a good example of such editions with integrated wood-engravings and decorative rule borders in the series published in penny weekly parts between 1863 and 1865 and comprising Shakespeare (H.C. Selous), *The Pilgrim's Progress* and *The Holy War* (Selous and Paolo Priolo), *Gulliver's Travels* (Thomas Morten) [fig. 236], *Robinson Crusoe* (G.H. Thomas), and *The Vicar of Wakefield* (Henry Anelay). The main defect of these editions is the cheaper quality paper, but Morten's is a major work, Selous provides some characteristic designs, and the Shakespeare is in the splendid tradition of Charles Knight.

In France the operations of the publisher J. Bry develop an interesting pattern of the re-use of sets of illustrations designed for up-market books in cheap reprints. As an example, one may take P. Lachambaudie's *Fables* published in 1851 by Michel in royal octavo format, with wood-engraved head- and tail-pieces from the designs of a number of artists, including C.J. Traviès and Célestin Nanteuil. The full-page *hors-texte* illustrations comprise thirteen steel-engravings, among which it should be noted that those designed by Daubigny and Charles Jacque were engraved by the artists themselves. In 1855, Bry produced a cheap edition of the *Fables* in a slightly larger format. He retained twelve of the steels and all the wood-engravings, integrating the latter into a double-column text set within rule borders, and supplementing them with the rather coarse designs of Henri

238 *Panurge despairs*:
wood-engraving
after Gustave Doré
(Rabelais, *Œuvres*,
1854) [BL 1223612]

Valentin. Other authors reprinted in this way by Bry included Alexandre Dumas and Victor Hugo. Bry again employed Valentin to provide additional vignettes when he reprinted Balzac's *La comédie humaine* in this same format, with the designs which had been used as *hors-texte* illustrations in Hetzel's edition integrated into the two-column text. Yet if one criticizes Bry's choice of Valentin as an illustrator, one must in all fairness give him the credit for having discovered the major book-artist of the mid-nineteenth century – and perhaps one of the great masters of the craft – Gustave Doré.

While a schoolboy of fourteen, attending the Lycée Charlemagne in Paris, Doré began contributing caricatures to *Le journal pour rire*. Paul Lacroix ('*le bibliophile Jacob*') took him up when he was nineteen, and commissioned a set of illustrations for his *Romans* (1852). But it was the publisher Bry who gave him his real opportunity with the cheap edition of Rabelais (1854) [figs 237, 238]. The two-column format and the poor quality of the paper on which they were printed did scant justice to the wonderful inventiveness of the designs, but could not disguise the genius of the designer.

500   CONTES DROLATIQUES.   LE DANGIER D'ESTRE TROP COCQUEBIN.   501

gnie de la mère de sa gentille femme. Ores, en l'esperit de ce cocquebin estoyt poulsé comme champignon ung expédient, à sçavoir : d'interroguer ceste bonne dame qu'il tenoyt pour preude. Doncques, se ramentevant les religieux préceptes de son abbé, lequel lui disoyt de s'enquerir en toute chouse ez vieils gens experts de la vie, il cuyda confier son cas à ma dicte dame d'Amboise. Mais, en l'abord, feit, tout pantois et bien coy, aulcunes allées et venues, ne treuvant nul terme pour desgluber son cas, et se taisoyt aussi trez-bien la dame, veu que elle estoyt outraigeusement férue de la cécité, surdité, paralysie voulontaire du sieur de Braguelongne. Et disoyt, à part elle, cheminant aux costés de ce friand à croquer, cocquebin auquel point ne pensoyt, n'imaginant point que ce chat, si bien pourveu de ieune lard, songiast au vieulx :

— Ce Hon ! Hon ! Hon !... à barbe en pieds de mousche ; barbe molle, vieille, grise, ruynée, ahannée ; barbe sans compréhension, sans vergongne, sans nul respect féminin ; barbe qui feint de ne point sentir, ni veoir, ni entendre ; barbe esbarbée, abattue, desbiffée ; barbe esreinée. Que le mal italien me délivre de ce meschant braguard à nez flatry, nez embrené, nez gelé, nez sans religion, nez sec comme table de luth, nez pasle, nez sans ame, nez qui ne ha plus que de l'umbre, nez qui n'y veoit goutte, nez gresillé comme feuilles de vigne, nez que ie hais ! nez vieulx ! nez farcy de vent... nez mort ! Où ay-ie eu la veue de m'attacher à ce nez en truffle, à ce vieil verrouil qui ne cognoist plus sa voye ! le donne ma part au diable de ce vieulx nez sans honneur, de ceste vieille barbe sans suc, de ceste vieille teste grise, de ce visaige de marmouzet,

de ces vieilles guenippes, de ce vieil haillon d'homme, de ce ie ne sçays quoy. Et veulx me fournir d'un ieune espoux qui m'espouse bien... et beaucoup, et tous les iours. Et me...

En ce saige pensier estoyt-elle quand s'ingénia le cocquebin de desbagouler son antienne à ceste femme si asprement chastouillée, laquelle à la prime périphrase print feu en son entendement, comme vieil amadou à l'escopette d'ung souldard. Puis, treuvant saige d'essayer son gendre, se dit en elle-mesme : — Ah ! barbe ieunette, sentant bon... Ah ! ioly nez tout neuf !... Barbe fresche, nez cocquebin, barbe pucelle, nez plein de ioye, barbe printanière, bonne clavette d'amour !

Elle eut à en dire pendant tout le cours du iardin, lequel estoyt ong. Puis, convint avecques le cocquebin que, la nuict venue, il

26

239 *The Sieur de Braguelonge and Madame d'Amboise*: wood-engraved vignettes after Gustave Doré (Balzac, *Contes drolatiques*, 1855) [BL 01255o n 4]

240 Balzac surrounded by
characters from his fictions in
the wood-engraved ending
(after Gustave Doré) to his
Contes drolatiques (1855)
[BL 012550 n 4]

Their effect can be gauged by the number of commissions which now flowed in. Significant, in the light of Doré's subsequent popularity in Britain, are those from two British publishers, James Blackwood and George Bell, which antedate John Cassell's promotion of Doré through the wide dissemination of his work in the firm's cheap part-issues. These earliest commissions were on a modest scale: ten designs reproduced as hand-coloured wood-engravings in W.F. Peacock's *The Adventures of Saint George* (1858) for Blackwood, and others in Shakespeare's *The Tempest* (1860) for Bell & Daldy – an edition featuring the designs of a number of artists, including Myles Birket Foster.

Doré's great series of illustrations to Cervantes, Dante, Milton, Lafontaine and the Bible, to Perrault and to Raspe belong to the new age of book-illustration. The sheer scale of many of Doré's designs mark an epoch in the history of wood-engraving, while the artist's technique of brush-drawing on the wood helped to create the new school of engravers developed in Paris by Sotain and the Belgian Pannemaker. Doré may justly be considered as having had an evolutionary effect upon both the design for and the technique of wood-engraving. Yet attention should not be focussed exclusively upon his mature work, for his youthful designs, firmly rooted in the Romantic tradition, provide the bridge between the book-art of that period and that of mid-Victorian Britain and Second Empire France.

Of the immediate successors to his Rabelais, three books are particularly noteworthy – Balzac's *Contes drolatiques* (1855) [figs 239, 240], and Marie Lafon's *Fierabras* and Taine's *Voyage aux eaux des Pyrénées* (both 1857). The *Contes drolatiques* develop and, if possible, improve upon the grotesque humours of the Rabelais in a way wholly appropriate since Balzac himself is so inspired by the older author that his writing transcends mere pastiche.

241 *Fierabras pursued by Muslims*: wood-engraving after Gustave Doré (Lafon, *Fierabras*, 1857) [BL 11498 g 47]

The book also contains those hints of diablerie, present in the Rabelais, too, and expressed here in gloomy and sinister forests, rushing torrents, tumbling mountains and turreted castles, which find their fullest expansion in *Fierabras* [fig. 241]. Taine's travel book is in complete contrast with the other two, and yet it is as perfect a vehicle for Doré's innate artistic qualities. The caricaturist who, in Balzac's and Marie Lafon's books, allows his extraordinary imaginative powers full play, here bends them to excellent effect in recreating the real Pyrenean landscape and the real people described by Taine [figs 242, 243].

The designs for *Fierabras* were engraved on wood by the Englishman Measom as full-page illustrations, but both in the Balzac and the Taine integrated vignettes predominate. Although published in the post-Romantic era, these books are completely in the Romantic tradition and have a vitality as pronounced as anything published a generation before.

242 *Bridge over the Artigue*:
the real landscape of this
wood-engraving after
Gustave Doré matches
the imaginary of fig. 241
(Taine, *Voyages aux eaux
des Pyrénés*, 1857)
[BL 10173 b 21]

243 *British Tourists*: realistic rather than fantastic wood-engraved vignette after Gustave Doré (Taine, *Voyages aux eaux des Pyrénés*, 1857) [BL 10173 b 21]

They reveal Doré as the last of the Romantic book-illustrators and by no means the least interesting. Indeed, it could plausibly be maintained that this early work is among his best, conceived on a scale suited to the medium of wood-engraving which is degraded from an art to a mechanical method of reproducing his later and monumental designs.

These, moreover, betray the decline of the Romantic book. During the 1850s it gradually ceases to be that intimate conjunction of literature and art in text and image and becomes a mere object – an imposing symbol of newly acquired bourgeois wealth and cultural veneer. In France this is typified by the sheer size of the volumes – Doré's later work is a very good example of this tendency; in England most noticeably by the pains lavished upon the outsides of books and the parallel neglect of internal layout and typography.

An indicator of this trend may well have been provided by the elaboration of the Romantic title-page. The designer would seem to have concentrated all his ingenuity upon what had, after all, developed from a cover to the text. There was a tendency to leave the typography to look after itself. This was satisfactory so long as the traditional values of the old printers survived. Problems occurred in the more commercial atmosphere of the mid-century and can best be observed by a comparison of early and later printings of a sound back-list title such as *The Young Lady's Book*. The original edition, published by Vizetelly, Branston & Co. in 1829, relied for its illustration upon wood-engravings. The text is well printed on good-quality paper and has a touch of Regency elegance about it. By contrast, the 1859 edition for Henry G. Bohn's Illustrated Library has substituted steel-engravings in the 'Book of Beauty' style for many of the original wood-blocks and, although the page-size is slightly larger, the general typographic effect is one of meanness, nor is the somewhat shoddy printing enhanced by the use of chemical paper.

To compensate for the lowering of typographical standards there is an increased use of relief colour-printing from wood-engraving. Edmund Evans is the master of the craft; good work was done both by Kronheim and by William Dickes, while both John Leighton and Benjamin Fawcett deserve mention. Yet, however attractive such work can be – and Edmund Evans produced some very fine colour-printing indeed – the general effect was to degrade wood-engraving from an art to a mechanical process by which a painter's water-colours or oils were reproduced in something approaching their original colours. It ignores the claims of the engraving to exist as an autonomous art-form and betrays a coarseness of sensibility to prefer the more specious attractions of the multicolour process to the natural 'colour' of the black- or white-line wood-engraving.

This was simply part of the trend towards making the illustrated book a cultural object and of neglecting essentials in favour of surface attraction. It culminated in an almost direct relationship between the decline in the standards of typography and the increasing elaboration of the machine-stamped and gilded case binding which covered the book itself.

William Pickering is generally acknowledged to have been the first publisher to have ordered glazed cloth as a binding material in 1821,[14] and by 1825 Archibald Leighton was producing the material commercially. Cloth-bound books continued to be titled by pasting a printed label on the spine until, in 1832, Thomas De La Rue's arming press enabled binders to apply gilt blocking to the covers and gilt titling to the spine. Meanwhile, such inventions as William Burns's rolling press and Philip Watts's stitching machine were mechanizing the manual operations of bookbinding. Nor was mechanization detrimental to the craft since, in the initial stages, binders used the machines as extensions of their manual skills. It can, indeed, be reasonably argued that when many fine binders were simply content to reproduce in morocco or calf the designs of the Renaissance masters, the commercial binders were the pioneers and true representatives of the craft in the nineteenth century.[15]

During the Romantic period proper, that is to say until the late 1840s, the overall effect is relatively modest, in the sense that cover decoration will generally incorporate a centre block reproducing an illustration from the book itself, surrounded by a decorative border, normally stamped in gilt on the upper and in blind on the lower cover. Otherwise the title will often be stamped in the same way within an ornamental framework. Obvious though this is, the style leads to the fullest integration of text and illustration within the external appearance of the book, so that it becomes a completely unified artefact.

This stamped decoration was also enhanced by the use of coloured cloths, for, although the vast majority of books were bound in a uniform shade, attractive effects could be produced by the use of striped and marbled cloths and by printing coloured patterns which imitated the on-lays of a leather binding. Cloths, too, were being produced to imitate, and to imitate successfully, a coarse-grained morocco surface, but, by and large, the introduction of cloth and of the machinery to stamp it were taken as an opportunity to exploit the potential of the new material rather than slavishly to use it as a substitute for the more expensive book-covering.

With the 1850s embossing and gilding, which had previously been applied to leather bindings and particularly to those of the Annuals, now began to be applied ever more widely to cloth-bound books. Splendid examples of the style are to be seen on the anthologies and volumes of poetry which had taken the place of the Annuals both as gift books and as cultural objects. The bindings themselves are virtuoso performances but have less relevance to what they cover than to the pride of possession which they are designed to inculcate. Nor is this cultural-object treatment entirely absent from the text and illustrations. In the latter there is an increase in formality and a steady trend away from the vignette wood-engraving which becomes enclosed by squared, arched and rounded frames.

The sense of formality is heightened by the use of supercalendered papers which impart a hard gloss to the printed page. Comparison, for example, of Burns's editions of *Poems and Pictures* with those of Samson Low (1860) and especially of Cassell, Petter & Galpin (1865) shows how some of the warmth of the wood-engravings can be lost in this way. Yet the book which probably makes the point better than any other is J.G. Lockhart's *Ancient Spanish Ballads*, which was subjected to small but revealing alterations when it was reprinted in 1853 and 1856. Not that these changes are all detrimental. The paper used for the reprint has the higher gloss and the wood-engravings lose some of their warmth in consequence, but the sheet is somewhat larger. This enables Owen Jones to remedy the 'want of unity' of which critics had complained in the original edition by enclosing all the pages within borders, a single rule with fleurons at the corners, or a more elaborate wide double rule enclosing decorations in the same rather heavy style. Greater unity, too, is achieved by omitting the full-page tinted wood-engravings of the first edition.

All these alterations help the overall design of the book, although the slightly wider margins tend to diminish the impact of the arabesque borders. Where the editions of the 1850s seem inferior to those of the 1840s is in a lack of warmth and colour in three specific areas. In the first place, Owen Jones had to reprint the chromolithographic half-titles from new designs which seem poorer and colder than the originals. This is probably due to the employment of a pale blue, to the inclusion of far more white within the area of the design itself and to the lettering becoming more elongated and spiky. In the second place, the borders seem generally more pallid, which may perhaps be due to the ink or to the super-calendered paper. Finally, three-colour printing is virtually eliminated from the book and there are none of those borders printed in two colours which make the early editions so rich and exciting.

This is, however, quite understandable, since *The Times* of 14 December 1841 wrote of the first edition that 'wood-engraving … with … printing in colours … have cost the publisher dear, as we have heard the expense of them estimated at a sum of not much short of £5000 sterling.' Since the first printing of 2,000 copies retailed at two guineas a copy, this was doubtless exaggerated, but it does explain why John Murray could accompany a copy of the book with a note to J.G. Lockhart which reads in part: 'I had hoped to have been able to hold out to you some more substantial result of this publication – but alas when the whole of the 2000 copies of which this edition consists are disposed of at the highest prices which can be put upon them they will not cover the expense, a statement of which I shall some day or other show you.'[16] Doubtless Murray recouped this loss on the second edition of 2,500 copies (1842), but one can well see why he should have been less lavish with the colours in the editions of the 1850s.

This tendency towards formality matches the new spirit of respectability. Thackeray, with perhaps a well-concealed regret, hits the changed atmosphere by remarking, as early as 1854, the change in *Punch* from the mouthpiece of radicalism to that of the middle-classes. The weekly of which he had been a founding-member was no longer 'earning a precarious livelihood by cracking of wild jokes, the singing of ribald songs', but was 'combed, washed, neatly clothed, and perfectly presentable.'[17] This was very far from Thackeray's own days as a journalist and from the bohemian life of literary and artistic London in the Romantic period which he so lovingly recreates in *Pendennis*.

The new age, ushered in by the Great Exhibition of 1851, could well accommodate the older artists of the academically respectable shaded outline school such as H.C. Selous, F.R. Pickersgill, John Tenniel, or John Gilbert whose style had developed in that direction. (John Franklin drops out of the picture after James Burns's conversion to Catholicism and withdrawal from the publication of illustrated secular books, although he continued to receive commissions, the last apparently being for Frederick Warne's *Book of Nursery Tales* [1866].) Indeed, it is unkind to characterize as academically respectable the very much higher standards of draughtsmanship demanded and obtained in the later 1850s onwards. It is apparent in book-illustration and especially in the periodicals. One has, for example, only to look at the very first volume of *Once a Week*[18] and to compare the work of the older illustrators Phiz and John Leech with that of Charles Keene, let alone J.E. Millais, which it contains, to see the difference.

This situation was the direct result of the reforming spirit which characterizes the Romantic period and the efforts of painters like William Dyce and publicists like Samuel Carter Hall to educate public taste and to broaden the scope of art education. Nonetheless, it was hard on the old school of British humorous artists, of whom George Cruikshank was the moving spirit. Cruikshank himself had in 1847 solved his problem of social drinking, which was fast developing into alcoholism, by a conversion to total abstinence as full-blooded as ever his drinking had been. The sad fact was that his style was becoming woefully old-fashioned. This loss of public esteem, coupled with the death of his faithful publisher David Bogue in 1857, meant that although his powers remained undiminished, he received no major commission after completing a splendid set of etchings for R.B. Brough's *Life of Sir John Falstaff* in 1853. The exhibition of his work in 1863 revived his reputation, it is true, but not even the re-issue in the late 1860s by George Bell of a number of his earlier books and the commissions for frontispieces by John Camden Hotten or of designs for wood-engravings for children's books by Mrs Ewing could do much to alleviate the lean years of old age and neglect by the public at large.

Fate was kinder to Cruikshank's protegé, John Leech, whose early death at the age of forty-seven in 1864 removed him from the scene at the height of his popularity as *Punch*'s principal cartoonist and before his old-fashioned style had proved too much even for his loyal following. She was perhaps cruellest to 'the dashing Phiz', whom Dickens so unceremoniously discarded as his illustrator. Admittedly the set of steel-etchings which he had supplied for *A Tale of Two Cities* (1859) is far below his best, but at the root of the matter lies this change both of public taste and of the intellectual make-up of Dickens's readership. Phiz had proved the ideal collaborator when Dickens's readers had been relatively unsophisticated and when the illustrations could be used to reinforce and to extend the texts of the novels. The new generation, as Dickens realized, had no need of an illustrator; they themselves could create the mental images from his writing. Hence Dickens's comparative lack of interest in the illustration of his later novels, whose artists were subjected to none of the detailed instruction and dictatorial criticism which had been the lot of Hablot Knight Browne.

If Dickens proved unkind, Charles Lever remained faithful to the artist who continued to provide steel-etchings for his novels up to and including *Lutterell of Arran* in 1866. Nor is there any falling-off in the quality of Phiz's etched work: on the contrary, the illustrations to Lever's novels contain the most interesting examples in the way in which both his style and technique had developed. The triumph of 'High Art' in the shaded outline school had forced him to refine his own line but, more importantly, Phiz progressed from his 'dark' plates of the late 1840s to a use of 'stopping-out' which enabled him to reproduce the illusion of sunlight with uncanny effect, as in 'The Ferry' (Charles Dickens, *Little Dorrit*, 1857) or 'The Stepping Stones' (Charles Lever, *Davenport Dunn*, 1859).

However, these effects were achieved in a style deriving from the old school of caricature and the style itself had gone out of fashion. Of course, the same is true of the etching, but the style itself is the crucial factor as we can see if we consider one of John Tenniel's very rare excursions into steel. His illustrations for Shirley Brooks's novel *The Gordian Knot* (1860)

244 *It's only Daddy Riddle*: wood-engraving after Phiz (Hablot Knight Browne) (Greenwood, *The True History of a Little Ragamuffin*, 1866) [BL 12621 h 11]

were executed as steel-etchings solely because the book was first serialized in *Bentley's Miscellany*, and the old-established periodical still used the old-fashioned medium. Nevertheless, this very fine set of illustrations matches both in style and quality his designs by J.E. Millais for Anthony Trollope's *Framley Parsonage* being engraved on wood for more or less concurrent serialization in the newly-founded *Cornhill Magazine*.

Wood had ousted steel – Phiz's favourite medium – on economic grounds. The major disadvantage of the steel-etching had always been the slow impression-rate of the special engraving press used to print from the intaglio plates. The problem was so acute that when it came to supplying the monthly etchings for the serial publication of Dickens's best-selling novels, Phiz had been forced to duplicate and even to triplicate his steels so that the large quantities required could be produced in time. The problem became even more acute as higher and higher rates of impression were achieved by the steam-presses introduced as the century progressed, thus forcing an ever more general use of the one method – wood-engraving – which permitted illustrations to be printed in relief and in conjunction with type.

Not that Phiz failed to meet this challenge, nor was the medium new to him, but the sad fact – and this is what has adversely affected his reputation – is that during the 1850s the bulk of his designs for wood-engraving were the poor and sketchy illustrations which he provided for cheap children's books and for a series of reprints of the classic English novelists from George Routledge. In 1866, however, Phiz did produce six designs, engraved by the Dalziels, which demonstrate a recovery of his old mastery. They also show an adaptation of his style to contemporary taste which suggests that had he been given the opportunity he might have gone some way towards regaining his old popularity.

Whether that opportunity would have arisen is a moot point, since the illustrations were for James Greenwood's novel *The True History of a Little Ragamuffin* [fig. 244], which made so little impact as a serial that the publisher, S.O. Beeton, gave up the struggle after twenty-five chapters had appeared. It would therefore seem as if Phiz's reputation was so sunk that a recovery would have been distinctly improbable: it was made impossible by the cruellest stroke of fate. In 1867, during a seaside holiday, Browne caught poliomyeletis. Although the attack initially crippled his entire right side, he struggled heroically to recover the use of his drawing hand and to produce work which is an extraordinary testimony to his courage and artistic skill.

NOTES

1 *Les graveurs du XIXe siècle*, II, 45.
2 Armelhault and Bocher, *Catalogue raisonné*.
3 *Henri Monnier*, 51.
4 Vizetelly, *Glances Back*, I, 315–17.
5 *Joseph Cundall a Victorian Publisher* (1970).
6 Knighted 1875.
7 *See* p. 62.
8 Gigoux, *Causeries*, 34.
9 Linton, *The Masters of Wood-engraving*, 205.
10 *Inscriptions antiques de Lyon* (1854), iv.
11 Blachon, *La gravure sur bois au XIXe siècle*, 240b: born in London, his John James became Jean Jacques in France. Naturalised French (1855).
12 *Gazette des beaux arts* (2nd series), VIII, 534.
13 Hunnisett, *Steel-engraved Book Illustration in England*, 211.
14 Keynes, *William Pickering*, 13ff.
15 Béraldi, *La reliure du XIXe siècle*, III, 173.
16 17 May 1841.
17 Review of John Leech, *Pictures of Life and Character* in *The Quarterly Review*, December 1854.
18 July–December 1861

EPILOGUE

Fashions change slowly, with no convenient cut-off date, yet 1848 was crucial to the history of the Romantic book since it marked a setback to the ideals which inspired so many of its artists and publishers. The failure in Britain of the Chartist movement marked the way in which bourgeois liberalism, having used working-class radicalism to obtain a decisive share of the power from the old landed and moneyed aristocracy, could now abandon its humbler allies. In France, it is true, the Revolution of 1848 ousted Louis-Philippe, only itself to be subverted by General Cavaignac who purged the militant revolutionaries, destroyed the provisional government, drove its leaders into exile and shot down its supporters in the streets. There followed the election of Louis Napoleon as Prince-President, the *coup d'état* of December 1851 and the establishment of the Bonapartist Second Empire. Again, the failure of the revolution in Germany saw pan-Germanism turned from a cultural into a political force which, under Prussian leadership, produced an aggressive German imperialism.

Yet, whatever the wider implications, the immediate result in Britain was the predominance of that middle-class outlook and those bourgeois values which are the characteristics of the mid-Victorian age. The triumph of the liberal, as opposed to radical, ideas induced a degree of complacency among the victors which was not without some justification. They had been able to reform society without shattering its fabric and had succeeded in raising both agriculture and industry from the post-war slump of the 1820s to a degree of prosperity which not only enriched their own class, but which was diffused among the working-class as well. True, there was appalling poverty and industrial squalor, but enormous efforts were being made by individuals and groups of individuals who, having achieved so much in other spheres already, were optimistic of success here, too.

They could also feel that they had raised the moral tone of society and, if we believe with La Rochefoucauld that hypocrisy is the tribute which vice pays to virtue, then the so-called Victorian hypocrisy is a measure of their success in making society at least nominally virtuous. Finally, and deplorably, there is a narrowing of the intellectual horizons and an insularity which is the concomitant of a bourgeois culture bred by successful imperial expansion and British industrial domination across the globe. Checked in the Romantic period by the twilight of the old aristocratic internationalist culture of the eighteenth century, this John Bull arrogance was now the hallmark of the new Philistinism.

If the new age had the solid virtues of maturity, its vices might typify the complacencies and mental rigidities of middle age. By contrast, the Romantic period might well stand for the youth and early manhood of the century. It brings to the lingering flavour of the elegant cynicism and animal brutality of the eighteenth century an engaging moral earnestness, immense high spirits and a sturdy iconoclasm. This, after all, is the epoch immortalized in Henry Murger's *Scènes de la vie de bohème* of which Gavarni catches so exactly the joyous abandon.

But there was a more serious side to the age. There was a concern for the plight of the industrial and rural poor and there was an ardent desire for political emancipation from the shackles of the *ancien régime* re-imposed by the Holy Alliance and by the English Tories after the fall of Napoleon. Political radicalism and a rejection of bourgeois values are apparent in the incisive observation of Henry Monnier, while Honoré Daumier expresses the revolutionary tendencies of the age. Above all, there was the feeling that through education and the raising of the moral standards of society the world could be regenerated.

This is reflected in the commitment of so many publishers on either side of the Channel to raising the cultural level of the working class. However, they aimed to achieve it without condescension, with no abasement of the standards of scholarship nor with any deliberate lowering of the quality of design or printing in books produced for the mass-market. Thus the books of the Romantic period fully merit study not simply as specimens of new techniques of graphic reproduction and printing, but for the way in which new concepts of book design produced work which stands comparison with the fine printing of any age.

APPENDIX I:
WOOD-ENGRAVING IN BRITAIN

When the revival, towards the end of the eighteenth century, of wood-engraving through the refinement by Thomas Bewick of the end-grain technique was taken up at the upper end of the market by fine printers such as William Bulmer and Thomas Bensley, it did not leave the lower end, the chapbook trade which had kept it alive, unaffected. By the 1820s there would seem to have emerged a two-tier structure of fine black- and white-line wood-engraving employed in high-priced luxury books, and a crudely vigorous popular style used in chapbooks and printed ephemera. However, since the same group of craftsmen served both sides of the trade, the effect of Bewick's revival was to lend to the bottom of the market the same high skill in cutting the blocks, however poor the designs actually engraved. The Romantic period sees the creation of a very wide middle range which tried to achieve artistic excellence at moderate cost to the consumer.

That it was able to do so was thanks to the technique of lowering the block, which eliminated the costly process of overlays. Thanks, then, to the pioneering work of Charles Knight in the 1830s and to the rapid expansion of illustrated journalism in the 1840s, the craft of wood-engraving was able to expand its numbers enormously. Thus, if, as we have suggested, the profession of book-illustration was virtually created by illustrated journalism, the same would be true of the craft of wood-engraving.

With the ever-increasing demand for their product and the expanding market for their labour, the numbers employed in the trade grew very rapidly – Knight speaks of there being about a dozen wood-engravers in London in 1813 and about a hundred in 1833, the year after the first appearance of *The Penny Magazine*. Some master engravers were able to accelerate the expansion by themselves providing the capital and the credit for new illustrated periodicals. They met the demand for their product both by increasing the numbers of apprentices and journeymen whom they

employed and by adopting the manufacturing technique of subdividing the work of engraving among their employees. In illustrated journalism, where the pressures of the press deadline were most severe, the process of subdivision was carried to its extreme, as Mason Jackson describes it when applied to the large engraving made from the 1850s onwards by bolting together a number of smaller blocks:

> The drawing on wood being completed, it passes into the hands of the engraver, and the first thing he does is to cut or *set* the lines across all the joins of the block before the different parts are distributed among the various engravers. This is done partly to ensure as far as possible some degree of harmony of colour and texture throughout the subject. When all the parts are separated and placed in the hands of different engravers each man has a sort of *key-note* to guide him in the execution of his portion, and it should be his business to imitate and follow with care the colour and texture of the small pieces of engraving which he finds already done at the edges of his part of the block where it joins the rest of the design…. Though this system of subdividing the engraving effects a great saving of time, it must be admitted that it does not always result in the production of a first-rate work of art as a whole. (*The Pictorial Press*, 321)

A fall in quality is understandable when work must be hurried to meet such deadlines. In book-work, however, where the division of labour related to a single small block, quality was in no way necessarily sacrificed to speed, for there was the master-engraver to act as controller and, where required, to finish the work of his assistants. Whatever the theoretical objections to the system, it must be judged on its actual achievements. Can it honestly be claimed that the blocks engraved by the 'firms' of John Jackson, Ebenezer Landells or Henry Vizetelly, for example, are in any way inferior to those engraved by all but the very best individual craftsman?

There were then, as now, plenty of theoreticians to dispute the evidence of their own eyes. The critic of the *Athenaeum*, for example, in his review of the Mulready-illustrated *Vicar of Wakefield*, wrote that:

Albert Durer and Holbein made their own designs, and by cutting them on the wood themselves, invested them with the utmost expression and feeling, which they, as artists, were capable of conceiving.... A modern designer would laugh if asked to produce a woodcut himself.... Few modern woodcuts have much to do with the draughtsman's designs. The drawing is made at the cheapest rate, and the engraver is left to render it as he pleases. Both draughtsman and engraver are mere manufacturers, neither possessing the slightest *amour propre* of the genuine artist. The first gives the least possible drawing of forms, and the greatest possible quantity of "effect," as it is termed, by means of "washing," or "tinting" with a brush. The latter keeps his establishment of journeymen: Z *rules* in skies, A cuts the face, B the drapery, C the landscape. Some engravers assert that this partnership work is the best; and so reckless are they of all sense of propriety in art, and so thoroughly manufacturing is the spirit that animates them, that cuts are now sent forth unblushingly as the joint production of a firm; and there are such firms both in Paris and in London, though, as we have no wish to annoy individuals, we shall not name them. (No. 759, 21 January 1843, 65–8)

The *Athenaeum* had consistently disparaged wood-engravers and two months earlier, in a letter of 29 November 1843 thanking Henry Cole for a copy of his edition of *Reynard the Fox*, John Thompson could comment:

Touching the criticisms of Wood Engraving, that have recently appeared in the Athenaeum, I cannot help thinking that their general tone is very prejudicial to the Profession and in some details most assuredly unjust, and if the Art is at all worth cultivating, degrading its professors in the eyes of the public, is a bad course, as it will naturally deter young men of talent from persevering in a pursuit from which a very limited profit is, and no reputation will be

obtained. But however as this is a subject we are not likely to agree upon, no more about it, ... (Cole Correspondence, Box 12)

The significance of the last sentence will be appreciated in the light of Cole's views on the employment of women as engravers.

This is, however, a very mild reaction to a review which had treated Thompson himself with insulting condescension and was both prejudiced and historically ill-founded. Far too many critics, and these included the wood-engraver W.J. Linton, constantly contrasted and denigrated in the process the nineteenth-century facsimile engravers with the quite mythical *peintre-graveur* of the late Middle Ages. The basis of this misguided criticism was the belief that Albrecht Dürer and Hans Holbein had themselves cut their own designs on wood. Yet this seems to have been wholly false, the fifteenth- and sixteenth-century *formschneider* performing precisely the same function for these masters as the despised facsimile engraver did for the designer in the nineteenth century.

A.H. Hind has since established that the separate functions of draughtsman and engraver existed from the end of the fifteenth century, and what he has to say with respect to Dürer's wood-engravings is particularly relevant to this issue. Briefly, he attributes differences in quality between certain sets and single woodcuts, not to the one being engraved by the master himself and the other by the *formschneider*, but to the one being engraved, perhaps under Dürer's direct super-vision, from designs drawn on the wood by the artist himself, while the other may have required the engraver to transfer the painter's designs to the block (*An Introduction to a History of the Woodcut*, New York, 1963, 90–92, 375–8, 386–7).

However ill-founded their criteria have been proved to be, the body of opinion of which the *Athenaeum* is representative was of great weight in its day and has continued unfairly to denigrate the achievements of the facsimile engravers. The real point, which not all their defenders have made clear, is that the facsimile engravers were co-oper-ating in the creation of an autonomous genre, the wood-engraved book-illustration. They were not being asked to reproduce a pen-and-ink drawing, but to act as an extension of the artist and with their burins to translate the draughtsman's line into the relief surface which would produce a print. Facsimile wood-engraving should therefore be judged not as a reproductive but as a print-making process, and to compare the resultant print with the pen-and-ink drawing which was its genesis is largely irrelevant.

In the Romantic period, the only way in which the illustrator could communicate directly with his public was through the steel-etching, hence a particular interest must attach to the work of artists in that medium. In so far, however, as steel- and copper-engraving is concerned, Henry Cole, a staunch defender of the facsimile wood-engravers, is perfectly correct in calling it 'a copy of a copy' (*London and Westminster Review*, XXXI, ii, 272). Where an original oil or watercolour painting was to be engraved – and this must have applied particularly to the Annuals and to some topographical books – a scale copy would have had to be made and this in turn would have had to be copied when it was transferred to the metal. Original book-illustrations, although painted or drawn to scale, still had to be transferred. Such illustrations would normally take the form either of pen-and-ink drawings to which the artist added a sepia wash to obtain his 'tints', or else of a watercolour. Tony Johannot, for example, favoured the latter, producing his designs for Gosselin's edition of the Waverley Novels (1826) as watercolours, and providing Furne with a further set of thirty for his illustrations to the 1836 edition of Scott (Marie, *Alfred et Tony Johannot*, 15, 18).

Cole (*London and Westminster Review*, XXXI, ii, 277) rightly emphasizes how much more direct the medium of wood-engraving was, although I would contest the thinking behind his statement that it 'furnishes him [the artist] with a perfect facsimile of his own design' because, as I contend, the so-called facsimile engraver is doing rather more than this. To act as the extension of the artist's hand in making the print implies a high degree of technical engraving skill, draughtsmanship of a considerable order, and a sympathetic intuition into the artist's style and intentions above the mere competence of an artisan. If we would rid our minds of cant and look at these engravings with an unprejudiced eye, I think we should agree that the nineteenth-century facsimile engravers possessed a very large share of these qualities. They may not have been demonstrated in every wood-engraving – the degree of care depended upon the class of work involved – but when John Thompson, for example, was cutting the blocks for William Mulready's illustrations to *The Vicar of Wakefield* in

the early 1840s, or the Dalziels were engraving J.E. Millais's designs for *The Parables of Our Lord* (1864) some twenty years later, they were acting as partners in the joint production of autonomous works of art.

The best engravers possessed all these skills in varying measure; the factory method harnessed the particular skills of less talented individuals. Again, their work should be judged by results: can one point to any glaring inferiority in engravings signed by such 'firms' as Landells, or Jackson, or Bonner, or Orrin Smith or Vizetelly, when compared with the work of most individual engravers? As Cole remarked (*London and Westminster Review*, XXXI, ii, 270), the head of such 'firms' had to 'possess all the talents of an artist to direct skilfully the mechanism of a manufacturer'. The smaller 'firms' of the Romantic period showed that they possessed these qualities, and the highly-regarded work which came from the 'factories' of the 1860s fully justifies Cole's defence of the 'manufacturing' system made some twenty years earlier.

However, the particular interest of the Romantic period resides precisely in this transition from the cottage industry to the full mechanization of engraving, from the freelance with his name on the wood-block to the paid employee. Thus, while the big engravers, the Swains, Dalziels and Evanses probably employed many more individuals in their factories, the earlier period can provide us with many more names of engravers. From it we can see how very much London wood-engraving was still a family affair. Conditions (as John Thompson had observed) were not easy. Freelance earnings probably varied little from the £2 per week at best which was the estimated figure of the *Alexandra Magazine* in 1865. Furthermore, the work was seasonal, and for at least six months of the year earnings could be considerably lower. As a result, the aid of the womenfolk – the sisters and wives of the engravers – was enlisted. Most notable were, of course, Mary Byfield and Mary Ann Williams, sisters respectively of the engravers John Byfield and Samuel and Thomas Williams who are probably the best known, but John Thompson's daughters Eliza, Isabel and Augusta all practised the craft, as did Mary and Elizabeth Clint, cousins of the Byfields, and Jane Hughes, probably sister or widow of William Hughes (1793–1825), to mention only a few.

That women were employed in the trade encouraged those who were concerned with the status and employment of women to try to spread the craft beyond the engravers' immediate family circle. Active among them was Henry Cole. Reference has already been made to his long notice in 1839 in the *London and Westminster Review* of no less than nine books illustrated by wood-engravings, supplemented by sample illustrations from eight of the books reviewed, plus engravings from eleven other similarly illustrated books. Cole had concluded then:

> To that large portion of the educated gentle-women of the middle class, who now earn a subsistence chiefly as governesses, we wish to point out that this art [wood-engraving] is an honourable, elegant, and lucrative employment, easily acquired, and every way becoming their sex and habits. We have already done honour to the exquisite delicacy and elegance of the engravings of Mary Ann Williams; we venture to say that few women of taste, whatever their rank in life, can look on "Le Jardin du Paria au lever de l'Aurore" [from *La Chaumière indienne*] without envying the artist her power of producing a scene so beautiful, and of exciting in thousands the pleasing emotions inseparable from it. Apart from all pecuniary considerations, to be able to do it is an elegant accomplishment, and the study of the principles and details of taste which it implies, is a cultivated and refining process to every mind. All that can be taught of the art may be learnt in a few lessons, and thus an acquirement made, which will afford no slight protection against misfortunes to which, in this commercial country, even the richest are exposed – and means of livelihood obtained, which, without breaking up family assemblies, is at once more happy, more healthy, tasteful and profitable than almost any other of the pursuits at present practised by women. The lady we have named is not alone in the practice of this art: we might name also Eliza Thompson and Mary and Elizabeth Clint, who have furnished excellent engravings for 'Paul et Virginie;' and we have heard of several daughters of profes-sional and mercantile men, not likely to be dependent upon their own exertions for support, who have wisely, by learning this art, acquired both an accomplishment and a profession. The occupations, we also may add, are few indeed to which gentlewomen of this class can more worthily devote themselves, than

to an art which is peculiarly fitted to enhance the enjoyments and refinements of the people, by scattering through all the homes of the land the most beautiful delineations of scenery, of historic incident, and of distinguished persons.

I have quoted Henry Cole at some length to demonstrate his enthusiasm – and his misconcep-tions as to the training required for and the rewards to be obtained from wood-engraving. They were to become apparent at a later stage: for the moment Cole's enthusiasm had full range. He has been called pushing because he got things done – and one of those things is now the Victoria and Albert Museum – and snobbish because, in a snobbish age, he could always obtain the backing of top people. Typical is the conversazione which he organized in 1860 to raise funds for another of his pet projects, the rebuilding of the Female College of Art in Gower Street. The centrepiece of the evening at South Kensington was a display of diamonds the like of which can seldom have been seen before or since, headed as it was by the Koh-i-Noor lent by Her Majesty Queen Victoria, and including other such famous stones as the Hope Diamond.

Thus, when in 1841 he published under his pen-name 'Felix Summerly' *A Handbook for Hampton Court*, he made sure that it came out with 'Embellishments engraved on Wood by Ladies'. In the following year a class was formed as the Metropolitan School of Practical Art, Somerset House, where Miss Annie Waterhouse taught fifteen ladies drawing on wood and the prelimi-naries of engraving for some two to three hours a week. The course proved so successful that in 1853 it was transferred to Marlborough House and, in 1857, to what was to become the Royal College of Art, then in South Kensington. Cole was himself in charge of the school and engaged John Thompson to teach wood-engraving and Miss [Harriet?] Clarke to teach lithography to the ladies.

Such an initiative as Cole had shown was most gratifying to the Feminist movement, and Madam Bodichon's *English Woman's Journal* devoted a long and optimistic article, from which most of the foregoing is derived, to wood-engraving as a career for women in its issue for August 1858. Ironically, this was to appear on the eve of the collapse of Cole's programme, for in 1859 the course at South Kensington was closed.

The reasons for this, and something of the

subsequent history of and prospects for women wood-engravers, are contained in successive issues of April and May 1865 of the *English Woman's Journal*'s successor, the *Alexandra Magazine*. By contrast with the earlier article, their tone is bleakly pessimistic. Classes, it is true, continued to be held at that other of Cole's protegés, the Female College of Art, then in Queen's Square, and they were directed by no less than Mary Ann Williams. Nevertheless, conditions had so changed as to make nonsense of Cole's confident predictions of a generation earlier.

The root of the matter was that the process, already at work when Cole began to support the idea of wood-engraving as an occupation for gentlewomen, by which wood-engraving tended to be concentrated under the factory-system in a limited numbers of 'firms', was completed by the mid-1860s. For most craftsmen it offered, in place of the dubious advantages of independence, the security of regular work and a regular wage. Of course, independent engravers continued to receive commissions on a freelance basis, but it was difficult if not impossible for the unknown freelance to break in – and it was, of course, as freelances that Cole had envisaged his women engravers would work, grossly overestimating, as John Thompson pointed out, the sort of remuneration which they might expect. The *Alexandra Magazine* was therefore being wise after the event in this respect when it reported the anonymous widow of an engraver, who had brought up her family by exercising her husband's craft, as warning aspirants away from what had been ill-paid drudgery.

Furthermore, although masters still commissioned occasional out-work from women, it was from those whose skill they could trust from experience. Here Cole's ill-founded optimism had been of positive disservice: women's training could in no sense compare with the long apprenticeship served by men, and specious claims by some women to an expertise which they did not possess had alienated the masters. The solution, as the writer of the articles in the *Alexandra Magazine* saw it, was to open apprenticeships to women. Master engravers do not seem to have been unsympathetic to the idea, for there was this tradition of women's participation in the craft and the Dalziel brothers, perhaps the largest and certainly one of the best firms operating in the 1860s, had been assisted at the start of the business by their sister Margaret.

One cannot, therefore, jump immediately to the conclusion that it was male chauvinism and Victorian hypocrisy (so-called) which raised an insuperable objection. Contemporary mores dictated the segregation of the sexes: if women were accepted as apprentices they would have to work in rooms separated from the male journeymen and apprentices, and this was simply impractical.

Conditions in the 1860s militated against women working in commercial wood-engraving and their role in the craft now becomes part of the Feminist movement and associated with the Victoria Press. It may therefore seem as if the optimism of Cole and his associates was sadly disappointed in this denial of opportunity and in the fact that few of his pupils actually practised the craft, the majority preferring to use their training as a qualification to teach drawing. Yet it may not be too far-fetched to suggest that the prominent role played by such women engravers as Gwen Raverat, Joan Hassall or Claire Leighton in the inter-war revival of wood-engraving may owe something to Cole's advocacy nearly a century before.

If I have devoted considerable space to this aspect of wood-engraving, it is not simply because it illustrates so well one side of the cottage-industry conditions prevailing in the craft at the beginning of the Romantic period and casts further light on the nineteenth-century Feminist movement, but because the phenomenon was not confined to Britain. In France, where there was the tradition of the family business, and where industrialization of wood-engraving was less pronounced, women exercised the craft throughout the nineteenth century. Charles Thompson's first pupil was a woman, Madame Bougon, and Remi Blachon records the names of nearly fifty women who followed her lead, at least so far as wood-engraving was concerned. Of these, special mention should be made of Adèle and Aglaé Laisné who directed the 'firm' which bore their surname.

So far as foreign engravers are concerned, I have indicated elsewhere that the full development of wood-engraving comes late in Germany and I have mentioned the names of a few of the more prominent engravers. For French engravers and engraving, as I have made clear in my Preface, Remi Blachon's *La gravure sur bois au XIXe siècle* has become the standard work. In Part I he traces the origins and development of end-grain engraving until it was replaced by photogravure at the end of the nineteenth century. Part II provides an enlarged and more detailed dictionary of French engravers and of foreign engravers working in France and the Low Countries. The lists for French engravers are full and comprehensive and they are a most useful and, in some cases, the sole source of information for the foreigners (cf. Henry Brown, 118ff.; 204–5).

In so far as British engravers are concerned, Rodney K. Engen's *Dictionary of Victorian Wood Engravers* (1985) provides a comprehensive and detailed list of most of the individual engravers and all the 'firms' whose employees for the most part remained anonymous. However, some may have emerged from this anonymity when engaged by William Dickes to engrave the wood-blocks for the illustrations to the Abbotsford edition of Sir Walter Scott's Waverley Novels between 1842 and 1847. Their signatures are listed below, together with the dates between which I have recorded them and with notes kindly supplied to me by Mr Ernest Pearce or taken from Percy Roberts's manuscript *Biographical Notes on English Wood-engravers of the Nineteenth Century* (British Museum, Department of Prints and Drawings). They include:

BILL (1846–7); BISHOP (1844); W.C. BLANCHARD (1846; also *Poems and Pictures* 1845–6); BURBIGE (1847); CARTER (1846–7); MARY CLINT (1843–4; also *Paul et Virginie* 1838 and Hall *Ireland* 1841–3); COOPER (1845–6); CRANE (1844–5); G. EVANS (1844–5); FIELD (1843–7: 'pupil of John Thompson' – Roberts); GREENAWAY (1842–6: Kate Greenaway's father, 'best renderer of Harrison Weir's drawings … he died about 1890 at 75 or 76 years of age' – Roberts); MRS JACKSON (1844: perhaps related to John Jackson's family); KECK (1842–7); MALCOLM (1845–7); W.J. MASON (1844); MASON JNR (1843); MASSEY (1845, 1847); NUGENT (1842, 1839–47; also *Arabian Nights* 1839–40, Hall *Ireland* 1841–3, and *Four Gospels* 1847–9); PALMER (1846); PRIOR (1843); MISS PRIOR (1846); RIMBAULT (1842: pupil and assistant to John Jackson; Chatto claimed that he had engraved the bulk of the illustrations to *A Treatise of Wood-engraving*); SCRYMGEOUR (1847); SILVERLOCK (1844–5); WEBB (1847); WEST (1845–7; also Hall *Ireland* 1841–3); YARNOLD (1847)

Other engravers (together with the books in which their signatures occur) include:

J. BAXTER (Gray *Elegy* 1834 and Hunt *The Rhine Book* 1845); BIGGS (*The March of the Intellect* 1830: Ernest Pearce noted him as a frequent engraver of George Cruikshank's work); CHARLOTTE BOND (*Arabian Nights* 1839–40 and Cole *Hampton Court* 1841: Henry Cole's cousin; she married Charles Thurston Thompson); LAURA BOND (Cole *Hampton Court* 1841: Charlotte's sister); ANNIE COWPER (Cole *Hampton Court* 1841: probably the sister of the Charles Cowper who married John Thompson's daughter, Isabel, in 1852); PERCY CRUIKSHANK (Crowquill *Phantasmagoria of Fun* 1843: Isaac Robert Cruikshank's son; Ernest Pearce has noted his work in his uncle George's *Omnibus* 1830); DICKSON (Hall *Ireland* 1841–3); JULIET L. DUDLEY (*Arabian Nights* 1839–40, Cole *Hampton Court* 1841, Hall *Ireland* 1841–3 and *Four Gospels* 1847–9); FELDWICH (*Arabian Nights* 1840); GODFREY (Hall *Ireland* 1841–3); HALE (Cervantes *Don Quichotte* 1837); J. HARRISON (Toepffer *Voyages en zigzag* 1844); C.H. HAYES (*Four Gospels* 1847–9); P. LANGTON (Hall *Pilgrimages to English Shrines* 1850); SERGEANT (Howitt *Visits to Remarkable Places* [2nd series] 1840); ALBERT THOMPSON (Northcote *Fables* [2nd series] 1833: perhaps the J. ALBERT THOMPSON of Molière *Œuvres* 1833, or the A. THOMPSON of Thomson *Seasons* 1842); AUGUSTA THOMPSON (Cole *Hampton Court* 1841: John Thompson's daughter); THWAITES (Thackeray *Mrs Perkins's Ball* 1847: Henry Vizetelly's assistant); WALKER (*Monsieur Mallet* 1830); WALL (*Arabian Nights* 1839–40); SAMUEL WILLIAMS JNR (*Arabian Nights* 1839–40)

APPENDIX II
ENGLISH STEEL-ENGRAVERS AND
DAS MALERISCHE UND ROMANTISCHE DEUTSCHLAND
(1836–42)

Das malerische und romantische Deutschland was issued in parts by the publisher Georg Wigand of Leipzig between 1836 and 1840, but I have been unable to determine precisely when each of the ten resultant volumes was completed. Volume I contains a supplement which was almost certainly completed later than the body of the volume: two supplementary volumes (XI and XII) were issued by Theodor Fischer of Cassel and Leipzig, again in parts, and completed in 1841–2. They stand outside the pattern of Wigand's publishing programme, so that the discussion which follows really concerns these first ten volumes.

They represent a major publishing venture demanding no less than 330 steel-engraved *hors-texte* illustrations, a requirement beyond the capacity of the nascent German trade to supply. As I have noted in the main body of this book, Wigand had direct recourse to the London engraving trade to assist his scheme. This assistance took two forms: the engraving and printing of plates in Britain and their export to Germany; and the emigration of British engravers, stimulated by the opening for the exercise of their craft which the project revealed. The latter was in every respect analogous with the emigration to Paris by British wood-engravers which followed the commissioning of work for *Gil Blas* and for *Paul et Virginie* by French publishers, at about the same time.

While Wigand had obviously planned the import of printed illustrations from London, one must speculate as to whether he envisaged at the outset the scale of participation by British engravers moving to Germany. This, however, is to anticipate, and I would first tabulate the respective shares of the respective engravers, British and German, over the whole twelve volumes, although the supplementaries are relevant only to a study of emigrant British engravers and not to Wigand's plan, something of which emerges if we study the distribution of the engraving as in the table below.

The respective figures are:
1. Volume number
2. Number of illustrations specified for that volume
3. Number of illustrations engraved and printed in Britain
4. Number of illustrations engraved and printed in Germany

Note: The discrepancies between (2) and the sums of (3) and (4) may be due: (i) to the exclusion of anonymous plates; (ii) to the publishers including more or fewer illustrations than specified on the title-page of the volume in question; or (iii) to human error.

I	30	30	3*	(3/–)
II	30	17	14	(–/14)
III	30	–	32	(20/12)
IV	30	22	8	(–/8)
V	30	–	29	(24/5)
VI	60	–	58	(50/8
VII	60	8	51	(28/23)
VIII	60	–	56	(55/1)
IX	30	–	32	(26/6)
X	30	19	6	(–/6)
XI	23	–	23	(14/9)
XII	35	–	35	(21/14)

* Engravings in the Appendix

The figures in parenthesis show the proportions in (4) between:

(a) British emigrant engravers
(b) native German engravers

Note: It was the usual, but not the invariable, German practice for plates to be signed by both engraver and printer. Category (a) comprises only those plates engraved by British craftsmen which bear a German printer's signature as well. I had considered it possible that plates might have been engraved in London and printed and Germany, but the pattern of Samuel Lacey's and J.J. Hinchcliff's work seems to exclude this possibility.

If George Wigand had a deliberate plan for the distribution of engraving work, it is apparent in the first four volumes. Broadly speaking he would have seemed to have envisaged British engravers executing three plates for every one produced by a German craftsman. Thus, to all intents and purposes Volumes I and IV are wholly British, while Volumes II and III are equally divided between the two nations.

To arrive at this proportion I have placed together London and emigrant engravers, since I think that Wigand can hardly have envisaged at the outset the way in which his book was to attract London engravers to establish themselves in Germany. He may well have foreseen that his commission for illustrations to the German painter Karl Ludwig Frommel might bring Henry Winkles back to Germany. Both had previously established an engraving studio in Karlsruhe and had worked together, but the assistance afforded by immigrant craftsmen must have proved a welcome bonus in removing the need to import finished engravings from London, a complication for the tight schedule of serial publication.

The result was that London assistance was only needed, and to a limited extent, in Volume VII, a double volume of 60 engravings which followed immediately upon a single and a double volume wholly engraved in Germany. Similarly, Volume X is the sixth of a sequence of five volumes (nominally containing 240 engravings) of which only eight had been brought in from London. Yet although their location had changed, the British contribution overall to the ten volumes remains substantially as we may suppose Wigand to have first envisaged it. Of the 385 illustrations, 83 were engraved in Germany by German craftsmen, 206 by immigrant British engravers and 96 in London,

giving a proportion of rather more than three to one to the British trade.

In so far as the individual British engravers are concerned, I shall first take the group which, I believe, supplied the illustrations engraved and printed in London. Details of the individuals or firms may be obtained from Basil Hunnisett's *Dictionary of British Steel Engravers* (hereafter abbreviated as *DBSE*) except for those marked with a dagger (†), unknown except for their work here. *DBSE* in some cases shows a cessation of work in the period 1836–46. The exact dates are placed within square brackets after the note of the engraver's contribution to *Das malerische und romantische Deutschland*, for, although the absence of signed work may be quite unconnected with this project, it is just conceivable that these craftsmen may have been moved to emigrate to Germany. The most likely candidates would seem to be R. Dawson and W. Deeble, whom *DBSE* shows as having resumed engraving in England in 1860 and 1851 respectively.

The following are the London engravers:

J. APPLETON: I (2), IV (2) [1841–2]
E. BENJAMIN: I (3), X (1) [1844]
†W. BUCKLE: X (2)
JAMES CARTER: I (5), II (4), IV (2), X (4)
J.J. DAVIS: II (2), X (1) [1840]
R. DAWSON: I (2), IV (2) [1837]
W. DEEBLE: VII (1), I (1) [1838]
W. & E. FINDEN: I (1)
S. FISHER, SON & CO.: IV (1)
G. HOLLIS: IV (2) [1846]
W. KELSALL: II (2) [1837]
J.H. LE KEUX: II (2), IV (2)
J. LEWIS: VII (2) [1837]
A. MACCLATCHIE: X (1) [1834]
†L. NORTON: VII (1)
R. PARR: II (1) [1838]
E. PATTEN: I (1), IV (2) [1836]
T. PHILLIBROWN: I (6)
SANDS: X (1)
W. TAYLOR: VII (2)
VARALL: IV (2)
F.F. WALKER: IV (1)
H. WALLIS: IV (2)
†R. WILLIAMS: IV (2)
J. WOODS: I (2), X (1)

Note: The plates engraved by J.J. Davis and R. Parr are marked as being loaned by the

London publishers Black & Armstrong who specialized in the trade in German books; these illustrations may therefore have been printed in Germany.

While there is no evidence for the presence in Germany of any of these engravers, there are very strong indications that two engravers, J.J. Hinchcliff and Samuel Lacey, did spend some time in Germany, probably in contact with the publisher at Leipzig, before returning to London.

J.J. HINCHCLIFF (1805–75):
DBSE shows a gap in his output for British publishers in the 1830s, and from the evidence of this book it would appear that the time could be accounted for by temporary residence in Germany. Hinchcliff's plates for Volumes I and VI were printed by the Englishe Kunst Anstalt, Leipzig; those for Volumes III and V by F.A. Zehl, Leipzig; while of the plates in Volume VII, three were printed by R.O.O. Binders Kunst Verlag, Leipzig, and two each by F.A. Zehl and by E. Grünewald, Darmstadt. This establishes the pattern typical of the British emigrant, and it should be noted that, with the exception of Volume VII, all Hinchcliff's work is in volumes of which no other plates were engraved in London, for his contribution to Volume I falls in the supplement. Significantly, however, none of his plates for Volume X bears any indication of German printing. The inference must therefore be that he had returned to London some time before the volume was completed in 1840.

This hypothesis is confirmed by *DBSE*'s note of the commissions which Hinchcliff received from British publishers from 1840 onwards and of his position as one of the map-engravers at the Hydrographic Office of the Admiralty.
I (1), III (2), V (2), VI (9), VII (7), X (6)

SAMUEL LACEY (*fl.*1818–57):
Lacey was concerned with Wigand's project both as an artist and as an engraver, supplying two designs for Volume I. The only evidence for a residence in Germany, apart from these designs, is the fact that both the plates which he engraved for Volume III were printed by F.A. Zehl, Leipzig. His stay must, however, have been very brief, since there is no indication of German printing on any other plate and they are all for volumes from which finished prints

would seem to have been imported from London.
I (5), II (4), III (2), VII (1), X (1)

Finally, there remains the very significant group of engravers who were attracted to Germany by the opportunities afforded by this book and who remained there permanently or, at all events, for an appreciable period of time. They comprised:

COOKE:
No initials and not in *DBSE*, but he may be related to W.B. Cooke (1778–1855) who himself emigrated to England from Frankfurt. Our Cooke worked as assistant or partner of the Darmstadt steel-engraver and printer E. Grünewald.
V (8), VI (2), X (4)

J. GRAY:
Not in *DBSE*; an associate, assistant, perhaps, rather than partner of A.H. Payne, with whom he signed a number of plates (see below). His individual work was printed by Payne's Englische Kunst Anstalt, Leipzig, with the exception of the two plates in Volume IX, both of which were printed by F.A. Zehl. Gray also designed one of the illustrations for Volume XI.
IX (2), XI (8), XII (2)

ALBERT HENRY PAYNE:
(1812–1902): According to *DBSE*, he emigrated to Germany and founded the Englische Kunst Anstalt in 1838, settling permanently in Leipzig and being succeeded in his business by his son. On the evidence here, I incline to think that the true date may be slightly earlier.

There is no indication that the four plates which Payne engraved for Volume I were printed in Germany, whereas all the remaining plates – except for those in Volumes XI and XII – special cases, since they do not belong to Wigand's publication – are signed by his own Englische Kunst Anstalt. I therefore infer that these first four plates were engraved and printed in London, that this commission alerted him to the potential market in Germany for an engraver, and that he thereupon set up his business there, his limited contributions to Volumes III and IV being explained by his preoccupation with the move and the establishment of shop and press in Leipzig.

Payne supplied designs for four of the illustrations in Volume XI and four or five in Volume XII.

I (4), III (1), IV (1), VI (31), IX (12), XI (5), XII (8)

PAYNE AND GRAY:

A number of plates was signed jointly by A.H. Payne and J. Gray. All were printed by Payne's Englische Kunst Anstalt with the exception of four of those executed for Volume III. Of these, two were printed by F.A. Zehl and two by the Englische Druckerei. This may, perhaps, serve to confirm that Payne was committed to establishing his business at that time.

III (8), XI (5), XII (8)

H. TYSON:

Not in *DBSE*; two of his plates were 'finished' by A.H. Payne, so Tyson may well have been one of his assistants.

XII (5)

HENRY WINKLES (*fl.*1818–42):

According to *DBSE*, he established a steel-engraving studio in Karlsruhe with the German painter and engraver Karl Ludwig Frommel between about 1824 and 1832. He then returned to Britain, where he worked until about 1836. *DBSE* notes his subsequent return to Germany and the establishment at Leipzig of the firm of Winkles and Lehmann, which *DBSE* dates at around 1843.

The dates of Wigand's publication would seem to indicate that during the period from 1836 to 1843 Winkles was working for it. Since Frommel had been commissioned to supply, *inter alia*, at least half the illustrations for Volume VIII, it is possible that Winkles's return to Germany was actuated by the need to help his friend. In the event, he engraved all the plates for this volume either on his own or with Frommel's assistance. Theirs was, however, simply an engraving studio: all their plates were printed by R.O.O. Binders Kunst Verlag, Leipzig. In addition to his own engraving, Winkles superintended the engraving of two plates in Volume XII.

I (2: both in supplement), III (23), VI (5), VII (20), VIII (24), IX (8)

WINKLES AND FROMMEL:

III (1), VI (3), VII (1), VIII (21)

W.C. WRANKMORE (*fl.*1844):

The absence in *DBSE* of reference to his work for British publishers is a strong indication that Wrankmore was a permanent emigrant to Germany. His three plates were all printed by A.H. Payne's Englische Kunst Anstalt with which he appears to have maintained a connection. In 1842 it printed plates, signed jointly by Payne and Wrankmore, for J.L. Pyrker's *Bilder aus den leben Jesu* (Leipzig, Teubner). It is interesting to note that the relief illustrations for this book were cut by another emigrant British craftsman, the wood-engraver William Nicholls.

III (1), V (2)

Although its publication involved at least six years' work and the engraving of some 450 steel plates, *Das malerische und romantische Deutschland* is a single book. Examination of the distribution of the engraving of its illustrations between British and German craftsmen and their printing in Britain and Germany can only provide a base, albeit substantial, for similar research into the steel-engravings produced in Germany at this time. Whatever the outcome of such investigations, it is not unreasonable to see in Wigand's project the catalyst which provoked an emigration and helped to create a trade which in the latter part of the nineteenth century, ironically, eclipsed that of its parent country, Britain.

APPENDIX III
LONGMAN'S SALES OF ILLUMINATED BOOKS

1. BOOKS BY NOEL HUMPHREYS:

Illuminated Calendar for 1845: 1,000 copies printed and sold

Illuminated Calendar for 1846: 1,000 copies printed; 613 copies (bound and sheet stock) remaindered to Bohn; lost £201.3s.6d.

(Longman's Divide Book IV 221, 223)

The Maxims of Our Lord (1848): 2,000 copies printed of which 1,308 remained unsold in 1851; lost £468

(Longman's Divide Book IV 369)

2. BOOKS BY OWEN JONES

(the figures are incomplete since these books were published on commission and exclude sales made directly by the artist)

The Sermon on the Mount: sales 1844–53; 2,247 copies

Gray's Elegy: sales 1846–54; 775 copies

The Preacher: sales 1848–54; 242 copies

The Song of Solomon: sales 1848–54; 411 copies

(Longman's Commission Books VII 252, 329, 545; VIII 294, 307, 314, 315, 588; IX 284, 285, 290)

Mary Bacon, *Flowers and their Kindred Thoughts*: sales 1847–59; 2,577 copies

(Longman's Commission Books VIII 308, 325; IX 289; X 283 (with letter of 22 October 1859, in which Jones thanks Longman for advice not to reprint and states: 'I am making other use of the stones.')

Mary Bacon, *Fruits from the Garden and the Field*: sales 1849–53; 1,065 copies

(Longman's Commission Books VIII 321; IX 292)

Mary Bacon, *Winged Thoughts*: sales 1850–54; 733 copies

(Longman's Commission Book VIII 296, 342)

3. Although not an illuminated book, sales of *The Poet's Pleasuance* (1847), illustrated with Noel Humphreys's designs for wood-engraving, should be mentioned. Unfortunately the book was a commercial failure. Of the 2,000 copies printed only 432 were sold and just over 1,400 sheets and 100 bound copies were remaindered to Tegg in 1850. In 1864 the blocks, which had cost £356.12s.7d. for the artist's fee, engraving and making electrotypes, were sold to the temperance journal, the *British Workman*, for £65.

(Longman's Divide Book IV, 429)

Courtesy of Reading University Library, where the Longman Archive is deposited.

APPENDIX IV

NOTES ON FRENCH AND GERMAN ILLUSTRATORS

An asterisk beside a name indicates that the artist's work is discussed in the text. See General Index for references.

ADAM, VICTOR (1801–65):
Son of the French history and landscape painter Jean Adam, he was himself primarily a lithographic artist, producing between 7,000 and 8,000 subjects (mainly historical and animal) for the albums. He also illustrated a number of books (including Florian's *Fables*, 1838) generally in conjunction with other artists.

ALOPHE [MARIE ALEXANDRE MENUT, 1812–83]:
French painter and lithographer. A portraitist who worked mainly for the French illustrated press, he designed for a number of the *Physiologies* (1841–3).

BARON, HENRI CHARLES ANTOINE (1817–85):
French painter in oils and watercolours and an occasional lithographer. A pupil of Jean Gigoux, he was a prolific illustrator, working during the Romantic period with Johannot, Français and, particularly often, with Nanteuil. His range included children's books (*Le livre des enfants*, 1836–8), topography (*L'Orléannais*, 1845), and the classics (Tasso, 1841; Rousseau, 1845). A competent illustrator, he later recorded the lighter side of Second Empire life in his watercolours.

BEAUCÉ, VIVANT (1818–76):
French painter and wood-engraver who specialized in decorative design and work in the Russian Imperial porcelain factory at St Petersburg (1858–68). Among the books to which he contributed, his designs for Perrault's *Contes* (1843) should be noted.

BEAUMONT, CHARLES EDMOND DE (1821–88):
French etcher, engraver and genre painter of considerable delicacy. The sources of his inspiration, the French masters of the eighteenth century, are perhaps best exemplified in his

designs for Caxotte's *Le diable amoureux* (1845), but he was equally capable of strong and striking contemporary figure drawing as in Sue's *Les mystères de Paris* (1843–4) or in Lurine and Alhoy's *Les prisons* (1846), some of the chapter-openings of the latter demonstrating his excellent sense of design. He wrote on old weapons, which he collected.

* BENDEMANN, EDUARD JULIUS FRIEDRICH (1811–89):
German portraitist and history painter in oils and fresco. The pupil of the Nazarene painter Wilhelm Schadow (1788–1862), he himself taught at Dresden 1839–55.

* BERTALL [ALBERT D'ARNOUX, 1820–82]:
Draughtsman and caricaturist. A major and underrated French nineteenth-century illustrator.

BOULANGER, LOUIS (1806–67):
French painter and lithographer, the pupil of Léthière and Devéria. A close personal friend of Victor Hugo, he illustrated a small but significant number of books including Hugo's *Notre Dame de Paris* (1836). His illustrations to Hugo are nearly all engraved on steel.

BÜRKNER, HUGO (1818–97):
German draughtsman and wood-engraver. He played a key role in the practice and particularly in the teaching of the craft in Germany.

CHAM [AMÉDÉE DE NOÉ, 1818–79]:
Lithographer and draughtsman. A clerk in the French treasury, he began in 1839 to contribute to Philipon's magazines. A somewhat crude caricaturist and humorous artist, he was popular both personally and artistically in English circles, his style being consonant with the British grotesque school of comic art.

CHARLET, NICOLAS TOUSSAINT (1792–1845):
The pupil of Gros, and the son of one of Napoleon's soldiers, in over 1,000 lithographs

he enthusiastically depicted the military of that period. His speciality was used in such books as Abel Hugo's *Histoire de Napoléon* (1833), Las Cases's *Memorial de Ste-Hélène* (1842) and *Le français peints par eux-mêmes* (1840–42).

COLLIGNON, FRANÇOIS JULES (d.1850):
French landscape painter and engraver. Exhibited in the Salon from 1835. He worked for Léon Curmer (*Paul et Virginie*, 1838; *Le jardin des plantes*, 1842) and may be compared with Daubigny and Français.

CORNELIUS, PETER VON (1783–1867):
German Romantic painter in oils and fresco. Worked with Overbeck and the Nazarenes in Rome 1811–19, returning to Munich where he attempted to revive monumental fresco painting. An important art administrator and teacher.

DAUBIGNY, CHARLES FRANÇOIS (1817–78):
French landscape painter and etcher, the brother-in-law of the artist Trimolet. A prolific illustrator, under the pressures of poverty and the need to support a young family, his work extends from *Les quatre évangiles* (Curmer, 1836) well into the period of the Second Empire. As well as figures it includes landscapes. Daubigny was a very professional illustrator and one of the minority who on occasion etched his own plates.

* DAUMIER, HONORÉ (1808–79):
French draughtsman, lithographer and painter. Political and social satirist.

DAVID, JULES (1808–92):
French watercolourist and lithographer. One of the earlier Romantic illustrators who were strongly influenced by the English school of Thurston, as he shows in his designs for La Fontaine's *Fables* (1837–8).

* DESENNE, ALEXANDRE JOSEPH (1785–1827):
French draughtsman and lithographer. A fine illustrator under the Restauration.

* DEVÉRIA, JACQUES JEAN MARIE ACHILLE (1800–57), and EUGÈNE (1805–65):
French painters, lithographers and book-illustrators. The elder brother, Achille, was more active in the last two roles, Eugène in the first.

EMY, HENRI:
French draughtsman and lithographer of the Romantic period. He specialized in social satire and contributed to *Les français peints par eux-mêmes* (1840–42) and to some ten *Physiologies* (1841–3).

FOREST, EUGÈNE HIPPOLYTE (b. 1806):
French painter and lithographer, he designed for wood-engraved illustration and transferred many of Grandville's designs to the wood.

FRAGONARD, THÉOPHILE (1806–76):
French painter and lithographer who also worked for the Sèvres porcelain factory. Grandson of the draughtsman and painter Jean Honoré Fragonard (1732–1806). His book-illustrations (1837–42) show a nice decorative sense and include somewhat sentimentalized eighteenth-century costume pieces in *Autrefois* (1842).

FRANÇAIS, FRANÇOIS LOUIS (1814–97):
French landscape painter; versatile and highly professional illustrator. On arriving in Paris in 1829 he worked as assistant to the publisher Paulin, subsequently learning wood-engraving, lithography and glass-painting before becoming a pupil of Jean Gigoux. Here he and Meissonier collaborated on the designs for *Gil Blas* (1835) under Gigoux's direction. Français's first commission was for designs for *Paul et Virginie* and his work is to be found in very many books of the period (often in association with Célestin Nanteuil) and comprises landscape as well as figure drawing. Français shows a nice decorative sense in his chapter-openings.

FRÈRE, PIERRE EDOUARD (1819–86):
French painter, lithographer, etcher and draughtsman.

* FÜRICH, JOSEPH VON (1800–76):
Austrian religious painter. The friend of Overbeck.

GAGNIET, J. (the French watercolour painter JACQUES GAGNÉ, 1820–64):
Caricaturist and social satirist of the second rank, his best work appearing in *Les français peints par eux-mêmes* (1840–42) and in some of the *Physiologies* (1841–3).

* GAVARNI [SULPICE GUILLAUME CHEVALIER, 1804–66]:
French draughtsman and lithographer.

GENELLI, BONAVENTURA (1798–1868):
German painter and engraver whose illustrations to Homer (1840) and Dante (1846) are among the most distinguished examples of outline engraving produced under the influence of Flaxman and Carstens. His uncle had been the friend and assistant of Carstens.

GIGOUX, JEAN (1806–94):
French history painter whose designs for *Gil Blas* initiated the *livre romantique*. His history paintings are somewhat flatulent, but he was a fine portraitist. With peasant shrewdness he invested in Parisian house property, which proved eminently profitable when the city was rebuilt during the Second Empire. He lived in considerable style and built up a fine private art collection. His *Causeries sur les artistes de mon temps* (1885) are both entertaining and instructive.

GIRARDET, KARL (1813–71):
French landscape painter, particularly favoured by King Louis-Philippe. Most prominent of a large family of artists, he contributed many landscapes to books, most notably to Toepffer's *Voyages en zigzag* (1844).

* GRANDVILLE [JEAN IGNACE ISIDORE GÉRARD, 1803–47]:
French draughtsman and lithographer.

GUBITZ, FRIEDRICH WILHELM (1786–1870):
German wood-engraver and draughtsman.

* HOSEMANN, THEODOR (1807–75):
German genre painter in oils and watercolours, lithographer and draughtsman; he taught in the Berlin Academy.

* HÜBNER, JULIUS (1806–62):
German history painter, the pupil of Schadow. Married the daughter of the wealthy Berlin banker, Bendemann, who became his patron.

HUET, PAUL (1803–69):
French Romantic landscape painter and friend of Delacroix. He provided designs for *Paul et Virginie* (1838), but I have not encountered his work elsewhere. A Madame L. Huet contributed some rather old-fashioned designs to Saintine's *Picciola* (1843). She may be confused with her contemporary, Mlle Ernestine Huet, who exhibited portraits in pastel 1848–70.

ISABEY, LOUIS GABRIEL EUGÈNE (1804–86):
French landscape painter (much influenced by Bonington) in oils and watercolours, lithographer and draughtsman. Particularly noted for his marine paintings, he contributed land- and seascapes to such books as Janin's *La Bretagne* (1844) or Christian's *L'Afrique français* (1846). His earliest illustrations are probably to be found in *Paul et Virginie* (1838).

JACQUE, CHARLES EMILE (1818–94):
French draughtsman and etcher. A prolific designer for wood-engraving, he is interesting as one of the comparatively few French illustrators to etch their own plates.

JÄGER, GUSTAV (1808–71):
German religious artist of the Nazarene school; a fine portraitist and fresco painter.

JANET-LANGE [ANGE LOUIS JANET, 1815–72]:
Painter, lithographer and draughtsman, influenced by Horace Vernet. He specialized in sporting and military subjects for the illustrated press, but his book-work was more catholic in its social commentary in the *Physiologies* (4 titles, 1841–3), or Lurine *Les prisons* (1846), for example.

* JOHANNOT, ALFRED (1800–37), and TONY (1802–52):
Both brothers trained as metal engravers and turned to draughtsmanship, Tony Johannot becoming perhaps the most celebrated of French Romantic illustrators.

JOSQUIN, ALEXANDRE *(fl. 1846–70)*:
French minor painter who contributed to three of the *Physiologies* (1841–3).

KAULBACH, WILHELM VON (1805–74):
Master of the German classical school; pupil of von Cornelius and an able portraitist; painted frescoes in Munich and for the staircase of the Berlin Museum; Director of the Academy of Fine Arts, Dresden, 1847.

LAMI, EUGÉNE LOUIS (1800–90):
Painter in oils and watercolours and lithographer, and pupil of Gros and Horace Vernet. He enjoyed a great reputation in the 1830s as a battle-painter and was patronized by Louis-Philippe whom he followed into exile in 1848. Enjoyed the patronage of Queen Victoria and of Napoleon III after his return to France in 1852. An occasional illustrator.

LA MICHELLERIE, E. DE LA:
French landscape painter.

LAMPSONIUS, *see* Lorsay

LORENTZ, ALCIDE JOSEPH (b. 1812):
French history painter, draughtsman and caricaturist. A prolific illustrator, some of his best work is to be found in children's books.

LORSAY, LOUIS ALEXANDRE EUSTACHE (b. 1822):
French portrait painter and draughtsman. Minor illustrator, his contributions to J. Bry's cheap edition of Balzac (1851–2) being signed 'Lampsonius'.

LYSER, JOHANN PETER [J.P. BURMEISTER, 1804–70]:
German engraver, journalist, critic and miscellaneous writer. A clever caricaturist with a strongly marked personal style, his best and most characteristic designs are probably to be found in his illustrations to a series of Low German folk-stories, *De Swinegel als Wettrenner* (1853), *De dree Jungfern* (1855) and *De Geschicht von de olle Frou Beerboomsch* (1862).

MARKL, LOUIS (b. 1807):
French lithographer, engraver, draughtsman and caricaturist. A most competent professional illustrator active from the late 1830s, who contributed, *inter alia*, to Balzac (*Le peau de chagrin*, 1838; *La comédie humaine*, 1842–55), to the 1846 editions of Dumas's *Les trois mousequetaires* and *Vingt ans après*, and to a number of the *Physiologies* (1841–3).

MARVY, LOUIS (1815–50):
French engraver, etcher and draughtsman; mainly concerned in reproducing the work of others, his own abilities are apparent in his etchings for Perrault *Contes* (1843). He sought temporary political asylum in England in 1848 where Thackeray, who had met him and become his friend in 1841, wrote the introduction to and helped secure publication of *Sketches after English Landscape Painters* [1850] reproduced in colour by Marvy's special process of etching. After Marvy's early death, Thackeray supported his widow who had been left virtually destitute.

MAURISSET, THEODORE (*fl.* 1834–59):
French wood-engraver, lithographer, caricaturist and draughtsman. His work is to be found in a number of the *Physiologies*, often in association with that of Trimolet.

* MEISSONIER, JEAN LOUIS ERNEST (1815–91):
French genre and military painter.

MENZEL, ADOLF (1815–1905):
The master of German naturalism. His book-illustration is limited in the Romantic period to his masterpiece, of Kugler's *Geschichte Friedrichs des Grossen* (1840), a few frontispieces (mainly lithographic) and a rather disappointing set of designs for Chamisso's *Peter Schlemihl* (1839).

* MONNIER, HENRY (1799–1877):
French lithographer and draughtsman, writer, critic and actor.

NANTEUIL, CÉLESTIN FRANÇOIS (1813–73):
French history painter, lithographer and engraver. One of the most prolific illustrators of the Romantic period during which he was a quintessentially Romantic figure, he closed his career as Director of the École des beaux-arts at Dijon and a chevalier of the Légion d'Honneur (1868).

* NEUREUTHER, EUGEN (1806–82):
German landscape and history painter and engraver whose outline style was influenced by Peter von Cornelius.

NISLE, JULIUS (b. 1812):
German modeller and engraver.

OER, BARON THEOBALD REINHOLD VON (1807–85):
German history and genre painter, and etcher.

OSTERWALD, GEORG (1803–84):
German painter and engraver. His contribution to *Lieder und Bilder* (III, 1846) shows his decorative abilities. In Gellert's *Sämmtliche Fabeln* (1838) there is a nice sense of the grotesque amply confirmed by his contribution to Musaeus's *Volksmärchen* (1842).

OVERBECK, FRIEDERICH (1789–1869):
Painter in oils and fresco, engraver and draughtsman. In 1816 he founded with Franz Pforr the Guild of Saint Luke, from which developed the Nazarene school, so influential upon European painting. His own status as a religious painter is demonstrated by the widespread reproduction of his paintings in liturgical and biblical publishing both in Britain and France, as well as in Germany.

PENGUILLY L'HARIDON, OCTAVE DE (1811–72):
Artillery officer and keeper of the artillery museum at Paris, for which he compiled a cata-

logue in 1862. An amateur whose high standards
of draughtsmanship are particularly in evidence
when the subjects were the people and history
of his native Britanny – his illustrations to
Janin's *La Bretagne* (1845) are outstanding in
what is typographically a very dull book. A good
and undervalued illustrator.

* PLUDDEMANN, HERMANN FREIHOLD
(1809–68):
    German history painter in oils and fresco,
    draughtsman and engraver; pupil of Schadow.

* POCCI, COUNT FRANZ VON (1807–76):
    German writer and amateur draughtsman and
    lithographer.

RAFFET, DENIS AUGUSTE MARIE (1804–60):
    French porcelain painter who learned litho-
    graphy from the military artist Charlet. Like his
    master, he continued to propagate the
    Napoleonic legend through lithographic prints
    and albums and the occasional illustration for
    book publishers.

RAMBERG, JOHANN HEINRICH (1763–1840):
    Hanoverian history, genre and portrait painter,
    engraver, watercolourist and caricaturist; came
    to London as a young man; pupil of Reynolds
    and Bartolozzi; appointed court painter,
    Hanover, 1834.

REINICK, ROBERT (1805–52):
    German painter, lithographer and writer for
    children. A friend of Alfred Rethel, who had
    studied history painting under Wilhelm
    Schadow at Dusseldorf, he was by no means a
    prolific book-illustrator, his earliest essay in the
    genre being 50 lithographic plates after
    Rowlandson for a German translation of
    Combe's *Doctor Syntax* in 1822.

* RETHEL, ALFRED (1816–59):
    German painter, lithographer and engraver.
    His paintings were on a monumental scale
    and include the (unfinished) frescoes in the
    Town Hall, Aachen. He became insane in
    1853.

* RETZSCH, MORITZ (1779–1859):
    German painter best known for his outline
    engravings on literary themes.

* RICHTER, LUDWIG (1803–84):
    German landscape and genre painter, lithog-
    rapher and draughtsman, and an enormously
    prolific illustrator.

ROGIER, CAMILLE (1805–70):
    French painter, lithographer and engraver who
    exhibited at the Salon 1833–48.

ROUARGUE, ADOLPHE (b. 1810):
    French marine and landscape painter in water-
    colours, lithographer and engraver. A prolific
    illustrator of topographical books, in which his
    watercolours were reproduced from steels
    engraved by his brother, the draughtsman and
    engraver, Emile Rouargue (1795–1865).

RUHL, LUDWIG SIGISMUND (1794–1887):
    German engraver, draughtsman and writer;
    associated with the Nazarenes in Rome;
    German secular mediaeval life, rather than
    religion, inspired his art.

SCHNOOR VON CARELSFELD, JULIUS
(1794–1872):
    German painter in oils and fresco of the
    Nazarene school, he was patronized by King
    Ludwig of Bavaria, for whom he executed the
    Nibelungen frescoes at Munich. His major
    book-illustration is the dull but worthy outline
    designs for the German Bible of 1850.

SCHRÖDTER, ADOLF (1805–75):
    German genre painter, lithographer and
    engraver, noted for his humorous designs.

SCHWIND, MORITZ VON (1804–71):
    Austrian painter and lithographer, who made
    his debut as an illustrator by working for the
    publishers of prints and almanacks. His work is
    characterized by enormous verve, humour and
    Viennese gaiety. He was himself a man of great
    personal charm.

SÉGUIN, GÉRARD (b. 1805):
    French painter and draughtsman, the pupil of
    Langlois. He was active as an illustrator during
    the Romantic period, with a specific tendency
    towards religious books – for example Léon
    Curmer's editions of the *Livre d'heures* (1837),
    Imitation de Jésus (1839) and *Saints évangiles* (1843)
    – and continued to work into the 1860s.

SONDERLAND, JOHANN BAPTIST (1805–78):
    German genre painter, draughtsman and
    engraver. His *Designs and Border Illustrations to
    Poems by Goethe* (1841) demonstrate his
    decorative style, while his sense of the grotesque
    may be found in his contributions to *Lieder und
    Bilder* and in his illustrations to such collections
    of folklore as those of Hauff.

* SPECKTER, OTTO (1808–71):
German lithographer, draughtsman and engraver.

STAAL, PIERRE GUSTAVE EUGÈNE (1817–82):
Lithographer, draughtsman and engraver, who abandoned the sale of haberdashery to enter Delaroche's studio. A competent designer for wood-engraving whose work stands up well in the distinguished company of Daumier and Traviès in Sue's *Les mystères de Paris* (1843–4).

STEINHEIL, LOUIS CHARLES AUGUSTE (1814–85):
French history and flower painter, a pupil of the École des beaux-arts and brother-in-law of Meissonier. As a struggling young artist he formed a trio with Daubigny and Trimolet which pooled its mutual resources. His commission to supply designs for *Paul et Virginie* (1838) was particularly welcome, but success with his painting meant that the books which he illustrated are somewhat limited in number. They include Hugo's *Notre Dame de Paris* (1844). Steinheil also practised as a glass-painter.

* STEINLE, EDUARD JAKOB VON (1810–86):
Austrian religious painter who came under Nazarene influence during his stay in Rome (*c.*1828–34). He designed for wood- and steel-engraving in books and collaborated with Schwind and Pocci.

STILKE, FRAU ERMINE (1804–69):
wife of the German history painter Herman Anton Stilke (1803–60), she herself practised flower painting and drawing and was principal of a private art school for women in Berlin.

STRÄHUBER, ALEXANDER (1814–82):
German religious painter and lithographer. His major work of book-illustration was undertaken in collaboration with his former fellow-student, Julius Schnorr von Carelsfeld, for the German Bible of 1850.

TOEPFFER, RODOLPHE (1799–1846):
Swiss novelist and art-critic with more than an amateur talent as a caricaturist. This he displays in *Voyages en zigzag* (1844), and in such precursors of the comic strip as *Les amours de Monsieur Vieux-Bois, Monsieur Crépin*, etc.

TRAVIÈS, JOSEPH LOUIS (1804–59):
French lithographer and draughtsman, Baudelaire's '*artiste maudit*'. He produced work to stand beside that of Daumier when both were employed by Philipon on *La caricature*. Traviès, whose life was embittered by poverty and misfortune, is one of the keenest observers of the social scene and one of the best illustrators of the volumes of character writing which were so typical a product of the Romantic period.

TRIMOLET, JOSEPH LOUIS (1812–48):
French lithographer, draughtsman and engraver. Orphaned at the age of nine, he was apprenticed to a wood-engraver and subsequently practised the craft before entering the studio of David d'Angers. By 1831 his lithographs and etchings were appearing in *La pléiade* and he began designing for wood-engraving. The incisive style which he applied to his observations of the social scene (*Les physiologies*: various titles, 1841–3) clearly owes a great deal to Daumier and Baudelaire ('Quelques caricaturistes français') also detects the influence of George Cruikshank. The bohemian friend and companion of Meissonier, Steinheil and Daubigny, Trimolet was married to a sister of the last-named.

VALENTIN, HENRI (1820–55):
French draughtsman and illustrator of the second rank.

VERNET, HORACE (1789–1863):
French military painter and lithographer. Son of the painter Carle Vernet (1758–1836), he helped to create the Napoleonic legend and ended his career as court painter to Napoleon III. His masterpiece is L'Ardèche's *Histoire de l'empereur Napoléon* (1839), and similar use of his speciality may be found in such books as *Napoléon en Egypte* and Las Cases's *Mémorial de Ste Helène* (both 1842).

VERNIER, CHARLES:
French draughtsman whose work is to be found in *Les physiologies* (1841–3).

WATTIER, CHARLES ÉMILE (1800–68):
French painter and lithographer. As an early devotee of the eighteenth century, he was the precursor of so many sentimentalized costume pieces typified by his own contribution to *Autrefois ou le bon vieux temps* (1842).

APPENDIX V
GLOSSARY OF TECHNICAL TERMS

biting-in: *see* **steel-engraving and etching**.

black-line engraving: in black-line wood-engraving the burin removes all the surface of the block except the lines of the artist's design; in **white-line engraving**, the surface of the block prints as a black background, while the burin removes the lines of the design which appear white in the impression. Blocks engraved with a combination of both methods achieved engravings of great strength and delicacy, the predominantly white-line engraving having a density of black which allowed it to match the brilliance of the modern faces used in fine printing at the end of the eighteenth century.

cliché (Fr): general term applied to **poly-**, **electro-** and **stereotypes**.

colour: variation in the intensity of the black ink in wood-engraving achieved by the use of **overlays** or by **lowering the block**.

electrotypes: Professor von Jacobi of St Petersburg, Thomas Spencer of Liverpool, C.J. Jordan of London and Joseph Adams of New York all simultaneously and independently (*c*.1839) propounded the theory from which developed the trade process described by Mason Jackson (*The Pictorial Press*, 324–5):
When the block is finished … it is … delivered to the electrotyper, who first takes a mould of the block in wax, which mould is then covered with a thin coating of blacklead, that being a good conductor of electricity. The mould is then suspended by a brass rod in a large bath filled with a solution of sulphate of copper in sulphuric acid. A strong current of electricity, obtained from a dynamo-electric machine close at hand, is conducted to the wax mould in the bath and also to a sheet of copper which is placed near the mould. The electricity decomposes the copper and deposits it in small particles on the mould, on which a thin coating of copper is gradually formed, producing an exact facsimile of the original engraved block. This copper reproduction of the woodcut is filled in at the back with metal, mounted on wood, and is then ready for the printer.

lowering the block: shaving the surface of the engraved wood-block to vary the pressure of the platen or impression-cylinder when soft packed with a blanket or similar material to vary the intensity of the black ink and thus give the wood-engraving colour. It was a process used by Bewick and introduced by his pupils to the London trade.

make-ready: the preparation of and fine adjustment to a press before printing can begin.

overlays: varied the thicknesses of the hard-packing of the **tympan** to achieve the same effects as **lowering the block** by producing extra pressure on those areas of a wood-block which needed to be printed blacker than the rest to give the wood-engraving **colour**. While overlays were employed for the hand-press, for the flat-bed machine-press **underlays** remained for the duration of hot-metal printing. They employed paper cut-outs inserted between the plate (stereo-, poly- or electrotype) and the block on which it was mounted to produce the same effects as overlays.

paper sizes: approximate measurements (untrimmed sheet sizes); these will vary from country to country in the period.
crown: 16½ x 21"
demy: 17½ x 22"
medium: 19 x 24"
royal: 20 x 24"
large royal: 21 x 27"

perfecting machine: *see* figs 3, 4.

planographic process: printing an image from a flat surface (as opposed to the relief process of printing from moveable type and woodcuts and wood-engravings, or of the intaglio process of copper- and steel-engravings and etchings). The portion of the flat surface on to which the image is to be transferred is sensitized so as to attract ink and the rest of the surface (to remain blank) treated so as to repel ink. Senefelder (who invented the process) used stones as his printing surface (hence lithography) with grease to attract and water to repel ink.

platen: the plate in the **platen press** which impressed the paper upon the type to obtain an impression.

platen press: *see* fig. 2.

polytypage: a process invented *c.*1795 to make **polytypes**, copies of illustrations and ornaments obtained by dabbing wood-blocks into fluid metal to obtain moulds from which these casts were made. Commonly called 'dabs'.

steel-engraving and etching: these processes used on steel the same methods which had been applied to copper to obtain an intaglio impression of a design. This was first transferred to the waxed surface of the metal plate and a needle used to pierce this waxed ground, following the lines of the transfer. The design was then bitten-in by subjecting the plate to an acid bath. Since the density of the black in the finished print was determined by the depth of the etching, each area was stopped-out with a varnish once that depth had been reached to prevent further corrosion by the acid. This would complete an etched plate, but the finer detail of the steel-engraving was achieved by using a burin on the metal.

stereotypes: following experiments during the eighteenth century with various materials, *c.*1803 Earl Stanhope invented the first generally practical method of making moulds of plaster of Paris to take casts of type-matter and relief blocks. This process was superseded by using papier maché (first employed at Lyon in 1829). Both processes overcame the problem, constant during the whole period of printing from moveable types, of texts which were constantly reprinted (Bibles and reference books, for

example). By stereotyping the standing type, they could then be printed from plates and the types, used in their original setting, distributed for further use. Seldom used for ornament and illustration for which **polytypes** were the more practical alternative.

stopping-out: *see* **steel-engraving and etching**.

supercalendered: paper given a high gloss by passing through a hot-press.

tipping-in: inserting a leaf, or pair of leaves, between the gatherings in a bound book.

tympan: two frames on a printing press interposed between the **platen** and the sheet to be printed and either hard-packed (with paper etc.) or soft-packed (with a blanket etc.).

underlays: *see* **overlays**.

white-line engraving: *see* **black-line engraving**.

SELECT BIBLIOGRAPHY

Adeline, J., *L.-H. Brevière* (Rouen, 1876)

Adhémar, J., and Seguin, J.-P., *Le livre romantique* (Paris, 1968)

Altick, R.D., *The English Common Reader* (Chicago, 1957; 2nd edn, Columbus, Ohio, 1990)

Armenhalt, J., and Bocher, E., *Gavarni: Catalogue raisonné* (Paris, 1873)

Audin, Marius, *Le livre* (2nd edn, Paris, 1924)

Audin, Maurice, *Histoire de l'imprimerie* (Paris, 1972)

Ball, D., *Victorian Publishers' Bindings* (London, 1985)

Bechtel, E. de T., *Freedom of the Press* (New York, 1952)

Bénézit, E.C., *Dictionnaire des peintres, sculpteurs, dessinateurs et graveurs* (new edn, 14 vols, Paris, 1999)

Béraldi, H., *Les graveurs du XIXe siècle* (12 vols, Paris, 1885–92)

—— *La relieure du XIXe siècle* (4 pts, Paris, 1895–7)

Bewick, T., *A Memoir ... written by himself* (edited by Iain Bain, London, 1975)

Blachon, R., *La gravure sur bois au XIXe siècle* (Paris, 2001)

Bouvy, E., *Daumier* (Paris, 1933)

Bridson, G. and Wakeman, G., *Printmaking and Picture Printing; Bibliographic Guide to Artistic and Industrial Techniques in Britain 1750–1900* (Oxford, 1984)

Brun, R. *Le livre français* (Paris, 1969)

Bryant, M., and Heneage, S. *Dictionary of British Cartoonists and Caricaturists 1730–1980* (London, 1994)

Buchanan-Brown, J., *The Book Illustrations of George Cruikshank* (Newton Abbot, 1980)

—— *The Illustrations of William Makepeace Thackeray* (Newton Abbot, 1979)

—— *Phiz! the Book Illustrations of Hablot Knight Browne* (Newton Abbot, 1978)

Carter, J.W. and Pollard, H.G., *The Firm of Charles Otley* (London and New York, 1948)

—— *Publishers' Cloth 1820–1900* (London and New York, 1935)

Carteret, L., *Le trésor du bibliophile romantique et moderne* (4 vols, Paris, 1924–8)

Chambers, C.E.S., *A List of Works containing Illustrations by John Leech* (Edinburgh, 1892)

Champfleury, *Henry Monnier* (new edn, Paris, 1889)

—— *Les vignettes romantiques* (Paris, 1883)

Chatto, W.A., *A Third Preface to 'A Treatise on Wood Engraving'* (London, 1839)

Chatto, W.A. Jackson, J., and Bohn, H., *A Treatise on Wood Engraving* (2nd edn, London, 1861; reprinted with bibliographical notes and index, Detroit, 1969)

Clair, C., *A Chronology of Printing* (London, 1969)

Cope, C.H., *The Reminiscences of Charles West Cope RA* (London, 1891)

Cruse, A.A., *The Victorians and their Books* (London, 1935)

Curwen, H., *A History of Booksellers* (London, 1873)

Dalziel, G. and E., *The Brothers Dalziel* (London, 1901)

Day, K. (editor), *Book Typography 1815–1965* (London, 1966)

de Maré, E., *Victorian Wood-block Illustrations* (1980)

Didot, A. Firmin-, *Essai ... sur la gravure sur bois* (Paris, 1863)

Eliot, S., *Some Patterns and Trends in British Publishing 1800–1919* (London, 1994)

Ellis, S.M., *William Harrison Ainsworth and his Friends* (2 vols, London, 1911)

Engen, R.K., *Dictionary of Victorian Wood Engravers* (Cambridge and Teaneck, NJ, 1985)

—— *Sir John Tenniel* (London, 1991)

Estignard, A., *Jean Gigoux* (Besançon, 1895)

Evans, E., *Reminiscences* (edited with introduction by Ruari McLean, Oxford, 1967)

Faxon, F.W., *Literary Annuals and Gift Books* (London, 1912; reprinted with introductory essays by E. Jamieson and I. Bain, Pinner, 1973)

Fielding, T.H., *The Art of Engraving* (London, 1841)

Gaulthier, M., *Achille et Eugène Dévria* (Paris, 1925)
Gettmann, R.A., *A Victorian Publisher* [Richard Bentley] (Cambridge, 1960)
Gigoux, J., *Causeries sur les artistes de mon temps* (Paris, 1885)
Goncourt, E., and J. de, *Gavarni* (2nd edn, Paris, 1879)
Gray, N., *Nineteenth Century Ornamental Types* (London, 1938)
Gros, A., *François-Louis Français* (Paris, 1902)
Guiffrey, J.J., *L'œuvre de Charles Jacque* (Paris, 1866)[e]
Gusman, P., *La gravure sur bois en France au XIXe siècle* (Paris, 1929)

Hall, S.C., *Retrospect of a long Life* (2 vols, London, 1883)
Hambourg, D., *Richard Doyle* (London, 1948)
Hannebutt-Benz, E.-M., *Studien im Deutscher Holtzstich im 19-Jahrhunderte* (Frankfurt, 1984)
Harvey, J. R., *Victorian Novelists and their Illustrators* (London, 1970)
Heath, J., *The Heath Family of Engravers 1779–1878* (2 vols, Aldershot, 1993; vol. 3, York, 1999)
Herrmann, L., *Turner Prints* (Oxford, 1990)
Hilton, T., *The Pre-Raphaelites* (London, 1970)
Hind, A.M., *An Introduction to a History of Woodcut* (2 vols, London and New York, 1935)
Houfe, S., *A Dictionary of British Book Illustrators and Caricaturists* (Woodbridge, Suffolk, 1978; revised edn, 1996)
Hunnisett, B., *A Dictionary of British Steel Engravers* (London, 1980)
—— *Steel-engraved Book Illustration in England* (London, 1980)
Hurlimann, B., *Three Centuries of Children's Books* (Oxford, 1967)

Irwin, J., *John Flaxman 1755–1826* (London, 1979)

Jackson, M., *The Pictorial Press* (London, 1885; reprinted New York, 1969)
Jamieson, E., *English Embossed Bindings* (1972)

Keynes, Sir G., *William Pickering* (London, 1924)
Knight, C., *Passages of a Working Life* (3 vols, London, 1863–65)

Leipnik, F.L., *A History of French Etching* (London, 1924)

Lemoisne, P.A., *Gavarni* (Paris, 1924)
—— *Eugène Lami* (Paris, 1902)
Lewis, C.T.C., *George Baxter the Picture Printer* (London, 1924)
Lhomme, F., *Charlet* (Paris, 1892)
—— *Raffet* (Paris, 1885)
Linton, W.J., *The Masters of Wood-engraving* (London, 1889)
—— *Memories* (London, 1895; reprinted, New York, 1970)

McLean, R., *Victorian Book Design* (London, 1972)
—— *Victorian Publishers' Bookbindings* (London, 1974)
—— *Victorian Publishers' Bookbindings in Paper* (London, 1983)
—— *Joseph Cundall: A Victorian Publisher* (2nd edn, Pinner, 1976)
Maas, J., *Victorian Painting* (London, 1969)
Man, F.H., *Artists' Lithographs* (London, 1970)
Marash, J.G., *Henry Monnier* (London, 1951)
Marie, A., *Le peintre et poète Louis Boulanger* (Paris, 1925)
—— *Alfred et Tony Johannot* (Paris, 1925)
—— *Célestin Nanteuil* (Paris, 1924)
Melcher, E., *The Life and Times of Henry Monnier* (Cambridge, Mass., 1950)
Moran, J., *Printing Presses* (London, 1973)
Muir, P.H., *Victorian Illustrated Books* (New York, 1971; revised edn, 1989)
Mumby, F.A., *The House of Routledge* (London, 1934)

Nowell-Smith, S., *The House of Cassell* (London, 1958)

Parmenie, A., and Bonnier de la Chapelle, C., *Histoire d'un éditeur* [Hertzel] (Paris, 1953)
Patten, R.L., *Charles Dickens and his Publishers* (Oxford, 1978)
—— *George Cruikshank* (2 vols, Cambridge, 1994–6)
Plant, M., *The English Book Trade* (London, 1939)
Prawer, S. (editor), *The Romantic Period in Germany* (London, 1970)
Pye, J., *The Patronage of British Art* (London, 1845)

Raczynski, Count A., *Histoire de l'art moderne en Allemagne* (3 vols, Paris, 1836–41)
Ray, G.N., *The Illustrator and the Book in England 1790 to 1914* (New York and London, 1976)
—— *The Art of the French Book* (New York, 1982)

Renonciat, A., *La vie et l'œuvre de J-J Grandville* (Paris, 1985)

Robson-Scott, W.D., *The Literary Background of the Gothic Revival in Germany* (Oxford, 1965)

Rümann, A., *Das illustrierte Büch des XIX Jahrhunderts* (Leipzig, 1930)

—— *Die illustrierten deutschen Bücher des XIX Jahrhunderts* (Stuttgart, 1926)

Sadleir, M., *The Evolution of Publishers' Binding Styles* (London and New York, 1930)

Sarzano, F., *Sir John Tenniel* (London, 1948)

Tattersfield, N., *John Bewick: Engraver on Wood 1760–1795* (London, 2001)

Thackeray, W.M., *The Letters and Private Papers* (edited by Gordon N. Ray, 4 vols, London, 1945–6)

—— *The Parish Sketch Book* (2 vols, London, 1840)

Thieme, U., and Beckker, F., *Allgemeine Lexicon der bildenden Künstler* (37 vols, Leipzig, 1907–47; revised edn in progress)

Tillotson, K., *The Novels of the Eighteen-forties* (Oxford, 1954)

Turner-Berry, W., and Pole, H.E., *Annals of Printing* (London, 1966)

Twyman, M., *Early Lithographed Books* (London, 1990)

—— *Lithography 1800–50* (London, 1970)

—— *Printing 1770–1970* (London, 1970; 2nd edn, 1998)

Updike, D.B., *Printing Types* (Cambridge, Mass., 1922; 2nd edn Cambridge, Mass., and Oxford, 1937)

Vaughan, W., *German Romantic Painting* (London, 1980)

—— *German Romanticism and English Art* (New Haven and London, 1979)

—— *Romantic Art* (London, 1978)

Vizetelly, H., *Glances Back through Seventy Years* (2 vols, London, 1893)

Waddleton, N., *Chronology of Colour-printed Books* (5th edn, York, 1993; supplements, 5 vols, York, 1956–2001)

Wakeman, G., *Guide to Nineteenth Century Colour Printers* (Loughborough, 1975)

—— *Nineteenth Century Illustration* (Loughborough, 1970)

—— *The Production of Nineteenth Century Colour Illustrations* (Loughborough, 1976)

—— *Victorian Book Illustration* (Wymondham, 1968)

Watts, A.A., *Alaric Watts* (2 vols, London, 1884)

Waugh, A., *A Hundred Years of Publishing* [Chapman & Hall] (London, 1930)

Wood, C., *The Dictionary of Victorian Painters* (2nd edn, London, 1978)

TITLE INDEX OF BOOKS CITED IN TEXT

Note: See General Index for journals, periodicals, annuals and series (e.g. Family Library, The). References to illustrations printed in **bold type**.